VOICES FOR A CULTURE OF PEACE

Voices *for* a Culture *of* Peace

Compendium of the
SGI-USA Culture of Peace
Distinguished Speakers Series

VOLUME 1

Culture of Peace Press

Published by Culture of Peace Press, an imprint of the SGI-USA
606 Wilshire Blvd, Santa Monica, CA 90401

© 2010 SGI-USA

Book design by Valerie Brewster, Scribe Typography

Printed in the United States of America

10 9 8 7 6 5 4 3 2 1

LIBRARY OF CONGRESS CATALOGING-IN-PUBLICATION DATA

Voices for a culture of peace: compendium of the SGI-USA Culture of Peace
distinguished speakers series.

    v. <1-> ; cm.

Includes bibliographical references and index.

ISBN 978-0-9844050-0-8 (alk. paper)

1. Peace. 2. Peace-building. 3. Peace—Religious aspects—Buddhism. I. Soka Gakkai
International-USA. II. Title.

JZ5538.V65 2010

303.6'6—dc22

                                         2009054135

Contents

Foreword

To Be the Voice of the Voiceless

For centuries, in songs of war, voices of the few have induced the many into confrontation to win battles—for who, for what?—often at the price of their lives. Millions and millions of human beings killed or suffering in a nonstop sequence of conflicts; in the history books, the peoples are invisible. In the scenarios of human societies, with some exceptions, the citizens (including artists, writers, educators, philosophers) do not appear. Only the powerful.

"If you wish for peace, prepare for war," says an ancient and perverse proverb. And—for the benefit of the arms producers and suppliers—people made what they were prepared for: war. "Peace" on the lips—paix, paz, shalom, salam, mira—and war (as swords, guns…) in the hands. Submitting, resigned, the world's citizens were unable, forbidden, to express themselves. Silence. Throughout centuries: fear. And silence. In 1995, I wrote: "Voice / that could have been a remedy/ because of fear /was nothing, was silence."

Now, today's crisis—economic, financial, environmental, democratic, ethical—presents the right moment for radical changes. Aware of the situation on a planetary scale, of the disparities, of the deep gap between the haves and the have-nots, the commitment and involvement of millions and millions of people can make the dream a reality: a transition from a culture of force, imposition and violence to a culture of dialogue, understanding and conciliation.

Crisis, opportunity. It is now more urgent than ever to tirelessly promote a global culture of hope and peace. President John F. Kennedy said in June 1963, "No problem of human destiny is beyond human beings."[1] Peace within oneself. Peace around us. Education for all throughout life fosters attitudes of solidarity, of respect and the practice of human rights and values. Voices to attain and sustain intercultural coexistence and mutual understanding. Education to promote, in the clear words of the preamble of UNESCO's constitution, the "intellectual and moral solidarity of mankind."

Memory of the past and memory of the future! Reality must be understood in depth in order to transform it. Not only the visible news, but the whole picture. As Bernard Lown said, "Only those who see the invisible can do the impossible."[2] Yes, the media play a vital role that must not only be descriptive (retrospective, to explain what happened) but also prospective (to write what they believe should happen). We are living in "times of doubts and renouncements in which noise drowns words," as Miquel Martí i Pol so eloquently wrote.

To be different, infinitely different, is our greatest wealth. To work together will be our greatest strength. Why do we remain silent? At times, because we do not want to speak or do not know how, but also because we look around us for answers that can only be found within ourselves. May we all use our voices, rather than force, to defend our points of view. All ideas are worthy of being heard, but all ideas become defiled in the hands of violence.

The voice we owe.

The voice we owe forever, so no one can ever say: "I have already spoken out enough."

The voice to remember the great creators of our time, the great artists, architects, philosophers and scientists who are forgotten in the "star" events of our daily lives.

The voice to remember that governments have responsibilities that cannot be privatized, and families have responsibilities that cannot be transferred to the schools.

The voice to remember the origin of the resources we enjoy, which too often come from countries that we exploit without fulfilling our promises to them and without promoting their endogenous development.

Indispensable to overcoming the present crisis is a return, as in 1945, to a multilateral system guided by universal ethical values, to prevent the present impunity by the most powerful of transgressions on a supranational scale that regulate world governance.

Is another world possible? Yes, it is if we respect and promote diversity and creative capacity. Yes, if together we seek new roads for the future until we find them or invent them. Yes, if we do not place group loyalties above our conscience—because sooner or later we will pay the price for that indignity and submission.

Now, after the "rescue" of the financial institutions, is the moment to rescue the people!

Another world is possible if the global economy and the management of the great social, environmental and cultural challenges are guided by steadfast values and not by the market; if we reinforce international institutions, first among them the United Nations; and if we have adequate codes of conduct, security councils and punitive mechanisms.

Another world is possible if we have faith in the human condition: creative, unpredictable, immeasurable. If we believe in humanity and its capacity to discern, to overcome the obstacles that those who wish to dominate put in our way.

Now is the right moment, with the leadership of President Barack Obama and all that his election represents, to join our efforts in the transition from an economy of war ($3 billion is spent per day, when more than 60 thousand persons die of hunger) to an economy of global development (investment in food and water production, sustainable energy, environment, shelter...). We have the knowledge, the diagnosis and, frequently, the treatment. It is up to the people, from the bottom up, to put into practice the inspiring and farsighted beginning of the United Nations Charter: "We the peoples of the United Nations determined to save succeeding generations from the scourge of war...."

It is now time for action.

It is time for genuine democracy through non-presential participation (text messaging, Internet...).

It is time once more to place universal democratic principles, based on equal human dignity, at the very core of everyday behavior.

It is time to awaken and not to be indifferent spectators or passive receivers any longer.

It is time to join our voices in a peace-building clamor worldwide.

It is time to be sharing, of otherness, of brotherhood.

It is time to envision brighter horizons for the young generation.

It is time for *all* to plant a seed, to march a step, to raise their voice.

Thousands of voices, millions of voices, billions of voices expressing firmly that the era of domination and warfare is over.

Voices for a Culture of Peace This book has an immense triggering effect and can promote an in-depth shift toward peace building. From now on, if you wish peace, contribute to it with your personal effort.

Voices and action for a culture of peace!

Federico Mayor
Director-General, UNESCO, 1987–1999
March 2009

1. "Our problems are manmade—therefore, they may be solved by man. And man can be as big as he wants. No problem of human destiny is beyond human beings." John F. Kennedy, speech at American University's Spring Commencement, Washington, D.C., June 10, 1963. 35th president of the United States, 1961–1963 (1917–1963)

2. Dr. Bernard Lown, co-founder of International Physicians for the Prevention of Nuclear War, in his conclusion to *Prescription for Survival* (San Francisco, Calif.: Berrett-Koehler Publishers, 2008).

Preface

The Soka Gakkai International-USA launched the Culture of Peace Distinguished Speakers Series in June of 2007 as part of its larger commitment to help build a culture of peace. Our focus for these lectures as been on one or more of the action areas defined in the 1999 United Nations Declaration and Programme of Action on a Culture of Peace, namely: (1) Fostering a culture of peace through education, (2) Promoting sustainable economic and social development, (3) Promoting respect for all human rights, (4) Ensuring equality between women and men, (5) Fostering democratic participation, (6) Advancing understanding, tolerance and solidarity, (7) Supporting participatory communication and the free flow of information and knowledge and (8) Promoting international peace and security.

We are very grateful for the generous participation of well-qualified peace experts from a variety of fields as speakers along with the growing interest the program is attracting from the general public. This book is another significant milestone for the program, the first of what we hope will be a series of volumes bringing these speakers' insights and practical wisdom for individual peace building to an even larger audience.

Our hope in creating this speakers series is to stimulate a wider dialogue about building a culture of peace. For this reason, speakers have been invited from a broad range of backgrounds and areas of expertise, demonstrating through their diverse perspectives how universally a culture of peace is valued and sought, and how many diverse yet interwoven elements there are in the tapestry of peace work. While promoting this "marketplace" of ideas and dialogue toward building a culture of peace, the SGI-USA does not necessarily endorse all the ideas or views expressed by each speaker in this series. We simply hope they awaken the peace builder within each person who hears or reads them; to realize that a true culture of peace requires the active engagement of all citizens, all organizations and all institutions.

On behalf of the SGI-USA, I want to express particular appreciation to former United Nations Under-Secretary-General Anwarul K. Chowdhury for his encouragement to initiate this forum for community engagement and for his continued guidance and support. Further, we are indebted to the president of the Soka Gakkai International, Daisaku Ikeda, for his decades of leadership and his example as an individual working to fulfill humankind's shared desire for a global culture of peace.

Ian McIlraith
Director
SGI-USA Peace and Community Relations

Introduction

I n June of 2007, I completed an eventful decade of service as under-secretary-general and high representative of the United Nations as well as ambassador and permanent representative of Bangladesh to the world body. It is with deep humility that I reflect on having the privilege of being an inspired champion of the global movement for a culture of peace and having the honor of working together with many women and men of peace to promote this noble initiative. I still cherish very proudly the extraordinary opportunity I had to chair the nine-month-long negotiations that led to the adoption by the UN General Assembly in September 1999 of the landmark Declaration and Programme of Action on a Culture of Peace. My proposal, along with scores of other countries the previous year, led to the declaration by the United Nations of the International Decade for a Culture of Peace and Non-violence for the Children of the World (2001–2010).

I strongly believe that the flourishing of the culture of peace will generate the mindset that is an essential prerequisite for humanity's transition from force to reason, from conflict and violence to dialogue and peace. In order to prevent our violence-filled past century from repeating itself, the values of non-violence, tolerance, democracy and respect for diversity will have to be inculcated in every woman and man — children and adults alike. The culture of peace will provide the basic foundation to support a stable, progressing and prospering world. In short, it will give rise to a world that is finally at peace with itself.

As former secretary-general of the United Nations and Nobel Peace Prize laureate Kofi Annan said: "Over the years we have come to realize that it is not enough to send peacekeeping forces to separate warring parties. It is not enough to engage in peace-building efforts after societies have been ravaged by conflict. It is not enough to conduct preventive diplomacy. All of this is essential work, but we want enduring results. We need, in short, a culture of peace."

It is with immense pleasure that I express my appreciation to the Soka Gakkai International-USA for its contributions to the promotion of the culture of peace in several creative ways, thereby doing its best to strengthen the global movement.

In particular, the SGI-USA has opened several Culture of Peace Resource Centers in major cities throughout the United States, including Honolulu, Santa Monica, Chicago, New York, Washington D.C. and San Francisco. The subsequent launching of the Culture of Peace Distinguished Speakers Series from each of these locations has given rise to a growing network of civil society activists emboldened through regular contact with some of the world's most articulate proponents of the culture of peace.

It is my hope that this book, the first in a series of compilations, will share a diverse sample of voices from this lecture series with the broader audience to be found in homes, schools and communities beyond the walls of the resource centers.

I am convinced that with the active support and promotion by individuals, organizations and institutions around the world, the lofty objectives of the culture of peace can be woven into the very lives of each and every individual comprising our global community.

In our conflict- and violence-ridden world, promoting the culture of peace is an urgent task that requires the committed engagement of all the people of the world wherever they are and whatever they do.

THE CULTURE OF PEACE — NOW AND ALWAYS!

Ambassador Anwarul K. Chowdhury
Under-Secretary-General and High Representative of the
    United Nations (2002–2007)
November 2009

Creating a Culture of Peace

Distinguished Speakers Series Inaugural Lecture

Ambassador Anwarul K. Chowdhury

During his tenure as the permanent representative of Bangladesh to the United Nations, Ambassador Anwarul K. Chowdhury undertook a pioneering initiative on the culture of peace and chaired the nine-month-long negotiations that resulted in the adoption by the UN General Assembly in September 1999 of the landmark Declaration and Programme of Action on a Culture of Peace. His proposal, supported by a good number of countries the previous year, led to the declaration by the United Nations of the International Decade for the Culture of Peace and Non-violence for the Children of the World (2001–2010). As undersecretary-general and High Representative of the United Nations, he endeavored to build the culture of peace within the least developed and most vulnerable countries, many of which remain conflict-ridden. In his inaugural lecture, Ambassador Chowdhury emphasizes his conviction that "the young people are and should be the core of the global movement for the culture of peace." Underscoring the first of the eight action areas articulated by the 1999 United Nations Programme of Action, "Fostering a culture of peace through

1

education," he points out that students "want to reach out to people, they want to know about other parts of the world, their religions, their societies, their countries," and that we need to work now to foster that rather than let prejudice creep in. He also issues a call to action: "Worldwide, globally, there are many groups; some big, mostly small, even individuals working diligently for building the culture of peace. I believe that if we can create a network to connect all these dots, dots representing hundreds of such organizations, hundreds of individuals, we can empower them in a big way and enhance the global movement for the culture of peace."

Ambassador Chowdhury is the recipient of the U Thant Peace Award and the UNESCO Gandhi Gold Medal for Culture of Peace as well as an honorary doctorate from Soka University of Japan.

This is a special honor for me to be invited to be the first speaker in the Distinguished Speakers Series on the culture of peace, particularly because this series is intended to carry forward the message of peace through generations. I believe the culture of peace transcends boundaries. It transcends differences in age, and it transcends differences in culture. It is the most universal thing that we can have.

I am very proud that the SGI-USA has thought of this lecture series. I believe this initiative will become a very important landmark in the history of the SGI-USA ushering in a memorable series of events. I can tell you that the initiative that you have taken today with this type of lecture series will go far beyond just being a number of lectures. It will transform individuals—it will transform all of us individually and collectively. This lecture series will be making that contribution not only in this city but also in the other parts of the international community.

I thank all of you individually—all of you who have come to this lecture—because you have made the beginning of your own contribution to a global movement for the culture of peace.

I worked for a decade for the United Nations and as an ambassador for Bangladesh, but this mention of the decade has a different significance for me. It was on July 31, 1997, that I wrote to the secretary-general of the United Nations, at that time Kofi Annan, as the Bangladesh ambassador, asking him to circulate my request for a separate agenda item on the culture of peace for the plenary sessions of the United Nations General Assembly. Since then, it has been nearly ten years, just fifteen days short. That very letter has mushroomed in a big way to this global movement for the culture of peace.

The subject matter under the euphemism "Toward a Culture of Peace" was debated for a number of years before it became a separate agenda item of the UN General Assembly in 1997. The secretary-general was asked to present a draft program of action, which, after long negotiations for nine months, was adopted in September 1999. Earlier in 1997, the General Assembly adopted another resolution declaring the year 2000, the millennium year, as the International Year for the Culture of Peace. The next year, the United Nations adopted a very significant and promising resolution to declare the years 2001 to 2010 as the International Decade for the Culture of Peace and Non-violence for the Children of the World. I believe that during these last ten years, from July 1997 to this day, the international community has reached a point where we can surely call it a global movement for the culture of peace.

For that, all of you deserve a big "thank you" as well!

My heartfelt, sincere thanks to the SGI in particular for giving this special profile to the movement for the culture of peace. I think humanity and the world as a whole owe you a great deal in championing this cause. So, thank you very much! As I am one of the citizens of the world, I believe I can thank you on behalf of the rest of humanity.

Peace is integral to human existence—in everything we do, in everything we say and in every thought we have, there is a place for peace.

Absence of peace makes our challenges, our struggles, much more difficult. I believe that is why it is very important that we keep our focus on
creating the culture of peace in our lives.

Sometimes we see peace as the opposite of war. That is not at all what
the culture of peace would mean. Absence of war or absence of violence
is not peace. It may bring cessation of hostilities, but it is obviously not
peace in its totality—for sure it is not sustainable peace. That is why I
believe that the culture of peace is essential in our lives for many reasons.
I will come to that a little bit later, but the most important thing to realize is that the absence of peace takes away the opportunities that we need
to better ourselves, to prepare ourselves, to empower ourselves to face the
challenges of the world. Absence of peace takes away that opportunity and
that is why peace is essential in our lives.

I have, for many years, and for the last five years with a specific UN
responsibility, spoken up for the most vulnerable countries of the world—
the impoverished, the poorest and the weakest countries of the world.
Advocating for these countries, I found that absence of peace or recur-
ring conflicts cost them so much, particularly in terms of their human
development prospects. I will just tell you that in the year 2000, the cost
of conflict was measured by the Carnegie Foundation to be $200 billion
for the poorest countries of the world. That cost in the year 2000 was ten
times more than the official development assistance that these countries
received at that time. What a waste! That is why I strongly believe that
peace and development are two sides of the same coin. One is meaning-
less without the other; one cannot be achieved without the other.

When we talk of peace being integral to human existence, we also
have to bear in mind that, as the UNESCO Constitution pronounced, it
is in the minds of men we have to build the defenses of peace, because it
is in the minds of men that the seeds of war germinate. That is a crucially
important thing that we need to keep in mind.

The quest for peace is as old as human history. The prehistoric cave
man was also looking for peace, and we are here today talking about
peace, trying to see how best to achieve an enduring culture of peace. I
say that it is the longest human endeavor or quest going on, but it runs
alongside many of the things that we do on a daily basis.

Do not isolate peace as something separate. It is part of our very existence. Anything that we do or say or how we interact with one another

is very important. We should know how to relate to one another without being angry, without being violent, without being disrespectful, without neglect, without prejudice. Once we are able to do that, we are able to take the next step forward in advancing the global movement for the culture of peace. Start with yourself!

We need to do that, but at the same time, I must say that we are lucky that we have a global body, an international institution, a universal organization—the United Nations—that is dedicated to the cause of peace. The United Nations is working to bring development as the other side of the peace efforts in the world.

The contribution of the United Nations sometimes is also seen as something that is universally applicable. It is as if a big organization is moving in to create something called "peace." However, remember, that the work of the United Nations is also to empower people to talk about peace. We at the United Nations devise, arrange or work with people to empower individuals, and that is very important. Therefore, while there are efforts to bring peace in a conflict situation, we must also try to empower people.

This empowerment comes from participation, particularly from democratic participation. I think that is why one of the eight areas of the Programme of Action on the Culture of Peace is democratic participation. This is very important in the lives of people, in the lives of nations, that there should be a participatory democracy encouraging an environment to create the culture of peace. I would like to emphasize that dimension of our efforts to build the culture of peace.

In this context, I should mention—and this is a message to the organizers here—that September 21 every year is observed as the International Day of Peace. The United Nations observes it every year, and I would like you—in your own ways, in your communities, in your workplace, in your schools, in your neighborhood activities—to please observe September 21 as the International Day of Peace. Try to do something to talk about the culture of peace, to do something that contributes to it. That will generate interest, and the impact can be enormous. I am requesting that all of you go to the United Nations and other peace websites and find out about the International Day of Peace. I am honored to inform you that, earlier this month, I was designated to be the honorary chair of the International Day of Peace NGO Committee.

I would like to tell the United Nations that the International Day of Peace is not just a UN resolution, or a little message here or there, or a token celebration. That is not the type of International Day of Peace that we are thinking of. I am going to create some benchmarks for the United Nations, for its secretary-general and others to report how many times the senior officials of the UN spoke about the culture of peace in their statements and speeches; how many times they involved young people in promoting the culture of peace; how many times the special representatives of the secretary-general articulated the culture of peace in the undertaking of their responsibilities. We have to create such benchmarks to ensure that there is accountability. We talk about the accountability of other peoples, other nations, but we need to make the United Nations also accountable for peace. This will be our role during the International Decade for the Culture of Peace. You know, we are reaching 2010, the final year of the Decade, very fast. What have we done to promote—globally and nationally—the culture of peace?

I am very happy that this Culture of Peace Distinguished Speakers Series is being launched here today as we are nearing the end of the Decade. I hope it will help others to know that, yes, through this evening's launch we are making our best efforts to contribute to the Decade. So again, my tribute to the SGI for starting this initiative.

We need to build up a momentum so that by the time we reach 2010, there is a global awareness about what we need to do to build the culture of peace. Again, for that I come back to you repeatedly to see what we can do to promote an effective observance of the International Decade for the Culture of Peace and Non-violence for the Children of the World that will leave its mark in the communities and nations of the world.

I keep saying that the young people are and should be the core of this global movement for the culture of peace. The reason I say this is because I have seen time and again that the young people who are in schools, colleges and universities have the most open minds. They want to reach out to other people, they want to know about other parts of the world, their religions, their societies, their countries. But the pressures of their subsequent professional careers create a situation that brings in the prejudices, that brings in the indifferences, that brings in the intolerance of other people.

Why does this have to happen, when as young people you have the broadest of minds? You are all embracing, but when you get into your professional life, when you get into your adult family life, somehow these prejudices creep in. That question bothers me all the time. That is why I believe it is necessary that we build the culture of peace in the minds of young people, so that when they grow up, it will stay with them always, whatever their profession will be, whatever their way of life will be. We have to empower them in a manner that it stays with them. It should not be a transient thing with them. That is why I believe that this initiative that the SGI has taken to get young people motivated is very important. I am impressed by the logo of this lecture series showing exuberant, empowered young people. That is what they should be.

When speaking about the culture of peace, I often mention an incident during my visit to Kosovo in 2000. As you know, the two communities there—the Albanians and the Serbs—had been antagonistic to each other for decades, and they reached a very bloody point in 1997, 1998 and 1999. This was immediately after the United Nations- and NATO-imposed peace came into existence. In April 2000, I led the UN Security Council's first-ever delegation to Kosovo. On the first day, we visited a school where the young children from both communities were turning a garbage dump into a garden. They were clearing the garbage and planting trees and were doing so like friends, just like members of the same family.

Then we went to meet with the elders in the city hall to talk about the peace process. Very soon, the elders started blaming one another. The blame game nearly started a verbal fight. I told them to calm down, saying: "I just saw your children playing as friends. They have no animosity for each other. They are just friends. Let them grow up as friends. Why are you bringing the past bitterness, animosity into their lives? It is your responsibility as adults to see to it that it doesn't happen. If we as adults have failed, we should not let the shadow of that failure creep into the lives of the young people, into our children."

We need to encourage the young people to be themselves, to build their own character, their own personality, which is full of understanding, full of tolerance and full of respect for diversity. I believe that to be very important, and we need to convey that to the young people. This is the minimum we can do as adults. We should do everything to empower them, and I feel that such empowerment is going to stay with them for life. That is the significance of the culture of peace. That is its essence. It is the process of changing each one of us so that we become the agents of peace. It is not something temporary like resolving a conflict in one area or between communities without transforming and empowering people to sustain peace.

Think of the audience—all of you—in this room. If we transform ourselves, we will have five hundred people empowered with the message of the culture of peace. Start changing yourself; that is the most important thing we need to keep in mind.

This empowerment is so wonderfully visible in [SGI] President Daisaku Ikeda himself. When I speak with him, I feel that he exudes peace. His message is so touching. On August 31 [2006], I had the pleasure of commencing a dialogue with him. I must say that I have never seen a man who is so innocent in his curiosity. He asked me about things that I have not been asked by anybody. It was so refreshing, so liberating! That part of our dialogue was written down, and I gave it to my children, telling them: "If you want to know your father, read this. It is insightful." I gave that to my sister, too, saying that she should also read it.

I believe we have a lot to learn from President Ikeda. A very strong message from him is to never give up in your efforts for peace, because you know working for peace or building the culture of peace, whether individually or in your community or in your groups, can be frustrating and disappointing sometimes. You may find that you are the sole voice for peace. You may find yourself asking: "What is happening in this world? Why am I the only person talking about the culture of peace?" For good causes, this has happened to many people. The world's greatest thinkers, prophets, all have gone through this process. When you talk about something that shakes the existing system, you may not have many passengers with you, but don't be disappointed. It will come to you. It is going to happen.

This distinguished speakers series focusing on the culture of peace has tremendous potential. To the organizers, my request is that the culture of peace, of course, is the goal, but you should think about a variety of topics for the series—issues that have implications for sustainable peace—issues covered by the eight areas as identified in the UN Programme of Action.

Each of these topics is like a pearl—put together each of these pearls and they will turn into a necklace, a very nice necklace strung together. That will be the necklace of the culture of peace. You should also think about the diversity of speakers. Men and women of course, but the most important thing is bringing in young people. Young people! Listen to them! See what they have to share with us. It is very important. Of course, I believe you are thinking of putting the lectures together in publications to share with others so that those become a recorded history of people talking about the culture of peace. I think this is worthwhile.

Let me end by sharing my dream.

Worldwide, globally, there are many groups, some big, mostly small, even individuals working diligently to build the culture of peace. I believe that if we can create a network to connect all of these dots, dots representing hundreds of such organizations, hundreds of individuals, that way we would empower them and enhance the global movement for the culture of peace. A small group in Afghanistan or a group in Angola or a group in Albania will know that they are not alone. They will know that they have hundreds of other groups worldwide who are working for the culture of peace. They would not feel isolated any more. That is the empowerment that I would like to bring in. This is my dream—to create a global network, a global alliance of organizations, groups and individuals joining in the global movement for the culture of peace. Then, we can add others to the network, like schools, institutions and professional bodies. When you connect these dots, we will have a wonderful image for the culture of peace. This is something that I dream of, but I need to give this dream a real shape. So I am on the drawing board, and I am thinking about how to create this network. I know that I have all of your best wishes and all of your support in the realization of my dream. That is my wish and my hope.

Question and Answers

AUDIENCE MEMBER 1: I have a question about what you described as "connecting the dots." We talk a lot about a critical mass. To me, the culture of peace is a unifying goal, a wonderful new paradigm that, if enough people transform and buy into, could change the way this world works and transform violence to peace. Part of the problem seems not only in convincing people who don't support peace but uniting people who do. Sometimes we fail to recognize that we are partners because of our language differences or because we have different views or different orientations on how to unite the many groups who have their own mission for peace. Do you have any thoughts about that?

AMBASSADOR CHOWDHURY: As I keep saying, the critical mass is the individual. It is the most important thing. Peace within can only bring peace outside. That is very relevant. Empower yourself first with the message of peace that you believe. When you are empowered like that, you will never feel disappointed, you will never feel discouraged. But you have a point because I believe that the most important thing cannot be simply stated that the critical mass is the important part.

I have seen that many people have started on an individual basis in a very low-key way. These days, in this technological age, you can share many things without individually reaching out. The computers are there, the Internet is there. You can not only read, you can share, you can develop many things without the physical connection that we needed in earlier days. The physical connection, however, I never undervalue, because that has its own significance.

It is valuable to start at the low-key level, if you feel there are no people with you. I can tell you that, very soon, you will find many, because in each of us that human quest for peace is there. It is manifested in a different way in each individual. You have to strike the right chord to persuade a person to join you in your endeavor for peace. I think that is very natural, but start by talking with your colleagues, talking with your friends, talking with your family members. I think that is the best way to start. I have seen that. If I can get one additional fellow traveler with me, I believe I have contributed in a big way. That is what we need to do. With that simple thinking, you will get results that you could never dream of.

Don't get discouraged. Keep focused. Start with the people you can reach out to first, and then you will find that that needed critical mass is growing.

AUDIENCE MEMBER 2: I've been living in New York for seven years, and my dream is to work for the United Nations. I was encouraged and moved by your speeches and have started to think about how to make my desire to contribute to world peace a reality. It seems that I have to work for the United Nations to make this happen. [How has your experience been, and what practical steps can I take as a woman?]

AMBASSADOR CHOWDHURY: As I mentioned earlier, each one of us can contribute to the creation of a culture of peace wherever we are, whatever we're doing. As a young woman, you have more reason to be proud, promoting a culture of peace in an efficient way.

In 2000, Resolution 13-25 of the Security Council was passed, focusing on women's role in peace and security. When I proposed it, it was met with concern by the other fourteen members, but I insisted because up until then women were only mentioned as marginal contributors to the peace process. The resolution, which passed in October 2000, mentions women as integral contributors to conflict resolution, the peace process and building post-conflict structures.

For example, in Burundi, after President Nelson Mandela was part of the peace process, he noticed that things took off in a positive direction when women were involved in the peace negotiations. Women think of how their children and grandchildren can live. Men think about power or what they can gain for themselves by this peace process. It is not always true of all women or all men, but it has been seen to happen. You should be proud as a young woman that women are such integral contributors to peace.

Start on a small scale, because if you start very big and you don't succeed, you will feel discouraged. Start with yourself and with some people who have similar thinking, making it bigger in a geometric progression—two more people must each bring two. But we have to start with the individuals.

AUDIENCE MEMBER 3: I would like to seek, from Mrs. Chowdhury, your wisdom on the role of a woman supporting a man who is so active in contributing to world peace, and what is your message to young women who are future mothers?

MRS. CHOWDHURY: I think my husband has already said it. I am a housewife who is 100 percent supportive of my husband. As a mother and
friend, I say that you must follow a culture of peace.

AMBASSADOR CHOWDHURY: I think my wife is too modest. Actually, she
is encouraging, compassionate and has a deep empathy for other people. She encourages me every day. She is a human being with tremendous compassion for other human beings.

This is a rare thing. Sometimes, I tell her that she is too compassionate. She is very affected by any misery or suffering she witnesses
around her and has encouraged me to do much more, particularly in
the past five years, in my country of Bangladesh, to contribute to the
reduction of misery.

In a small way, we achieved a little bit. We have been able to speak
for the "voiceless countries." Difficulties should never prevent us from
doing more.

AUDIENCE MEMBER 4: I know that you took a stance when Pakistan was
still West and East Pakistan, and now East Pakistan is Bangladesh. I
would like to hear from you about the experience.

AMBASSADOR CHOWDHURY: That was one of the proudest moments of
my life, to contribute to the creation of Bangladesh, my homeland. It
sowed the seeds of what I'm doing now.

Oppression, discrimination, intolerance, exploitation—all were
being perpetrated on the people of Bangladesh. "Bangla" is the name
of the language, and "desh" means country, so "Bangladesh" means
"the country where Bangla is spoken."

At that time, there was a majority whose voice was not heard. In
1952, I was a student. In 1971, I became a diplomat in India. There was
a Pakistani military crackdown to suppress the people by force. Bengali people are generally very softhearted, but when faced with oppres-
sive military crackdown, they revolted. The people were compared to
the soil: mud is very soft, but when sun strikes the soil, it becomes very
hard and turns into rock.

I was in India at that time. Hundreds of thousands of Bengalis were
being killed, and I could not serve a government that perpetrated this

kind of massacre on my own people. People were fleeing Bangladesh into India and [because of that], I could hear [their experiences]. Many members of my family were wounded or killed.

We all decided to revolt against the Pakistani government and serve the Bengali cause. We physically took over a building, turning a Pakistani Mission into the Bengali Mission. We flew that flag as our flag of independence. We started to contact the Pakistani embassies and told Bengali diplomats to join us.

That started [a movement] to gain global support. On the ground, [Bengalis were] fighting the Pakistani forces. In March 1971, there was a military crackdown. In April, we declared allegiance to Bangladesh. Each room [in the mission] was a different [ministry]. I had to give up my own office. I worked under a mango tree with a little desk for seven months.

My parents were in East Pakistan, but they were being pressured by the Pakistani government. My mother was being pressured [to tell where I was, and so they] moved from one place to another.

I was branded a traitor by the Pakistani government and given life sentences in prison. [*To his wife,*] Thank you for [sticking with me]. That was wonderful.

In December 1971, Bangladesh was liberated and [we took] all the files of the government-in-exile.

AUDIENCE MEMBER 5: Today is the fiftieth anniversary of President Ikeda's release from prison on trumped-up charges. He, too, was pressured about his mentor. At a Victory Over Violence activity in a Brooklyn school, a high school senior shared a story about his friend who [was killed next to him]. Is there a way to secure one's own security—of our own life or the lives of loved ones [while we engage in a battle for the greater good]?

AMBASSADOR CHOWDHURY: We should abolish war as a way to achieve an objective. It should not be considered one of our options. The way I see coming decades, challenges will be faced, but [we will not be] engaging in daily violence.

You raise a good question. There is no single answer. Each of us will have to answer that for ourselves. I am very happy that many of you are [involved] in Victory Over Violence. That's what we have to tell each other—that violence doesn't get us anywhere. This word *revenge* should be deleted from our dictionary. Revenge perpetuates animosity, violence. I am wondering how to get people to come out of the stranglehold of violence "because my parents, the parents of my parents, my tribe suffered."

I have another story, about Bosnia, which was told by a friend who was working there at the time. After the peace process took place, some Muslims were telling their original stories. One man said, "Every day, I tell my son about the hatred that we have gone through," instilling hatred in the next generation. Even if one person has this in him, it's dangerous. That's why we should also talk to adults [about creating a culture of peace].

AUDIENCE MEMBER 6: As a young person, what were your inspirations, examples [in life and] in literature?

AMBASSADOR CHOWDHURY: I get this question often. Again, I keep asking myself the same question. Instead of asking what inspires me, I ask what shaped my mind. There are three things: my parents, the physical nature of my country, and the opportunity that I had to read. I read extensively. I still do. I read anything in print. My wife sometimes takes the paper [away from me].

We have to be creative, to have the desire to read. It made me develop compassion and feeling for people. [I found encouraging] the stories of people who faced challenges and came out triumphant; President Ikeda is one of them. I find that people facing tremendous obstacles aim to come out—this determination [of theirs] motivates me again and again.

I try to learn from everyone, young and old, it doesn't matter. I feel wonderful learning from people.

AUDIENCE MEMBER 7: I tried to start a peace committee in my school, [but I have no one to support me]. What do you do when you're the only one?

AMBASSADOR CHOWDHURY: The best ally in a school atmosphere is a teacher. You have to find either a teacher in your class or another class. [When you share your idea, the right teacher will definitely support you.]

At the culture of peace exhibit at the United Nations in 2004, on opening day, eighty teachers came. We told them, "Bring your students," and they started bringing them, [even ones so young, they couldn't understand the exhibit]. The older students were told to take care of the younger ones [as docents; there were twenty-five or so of them]. Later on, we decorated them with Peace Ambassador awards.

Start small, like a ten-minute video on peace. You can call the United Nations and let them know what you are trying to accomplish, and they will send you material.

Yesterday, I was talking to a rap group that sings about peace. If that's a way of reaching people who will otherwise not listen to you, we should do that. If teachers are not responding, then write to me.

July 17, 2007
New York

Building Peace in Divided Cities

Scott Bollens

Professor, Department of Urban and Regional Planning, School of Social Ecology, and Drew, Chase and Erin Warmington Chair, Social Ecology of Peace and International Cooperation, University of California, Irvine

Dr. Bollens has conducted a thorough examination of urban planning techniques and tactics in a number of conflict-ridden cities. Since 1994, he's interviewed more than 220 urban professionals in Jerusalem, Belfast, Johannesburg, Nicosia and Sarajevo about the role of city building in the midst of nationalistic ethnic conflict. In April 2002, Dr. Bollens presented his findings in a paper titled "Practical Strategies of Urban Peace-Building" at a seminar in Mostar, Bosnia-Herzegovina. The seminar brought together experts on urban cooperation in politically and ethnically contested areas. In his studies of city-planning practices that either serve the ways of war or the paths of peace, Dr. Bollens sees ramifications for America. Worldwide urban studies have shown him that planners in the United States have much to learn when accommodating the American melting pot.

His studies support several of the eight action areas identified by the United Nations Programme of Action on a Culture of Peace. Perhaps his work brings the greatest focus to the third: Promoting sustainable economic and social development. As he says, "Each peace process has its own terrain and its own mountain range, and their sequencing differs. That means, don't try formulas, and don't try models of how peace works.... There may be no logical, predictable sequence at all.... One thing I have found, however, is that if root issues are not addressed in peace processes,... the original causes of conflict will remain and will be joined by new grievances that are sometimes sparked by the very peace process that is trying to move a society forward."

May peace be with each of you today, a freedom from our common and personal struggles. May you have the freedom of that peace with you.

My talk is about peace building and reconstruction in Israel, Palestine, Bosnia, South Africa, Northern Ireland and Spain, with a focus on how urban governance and urban policy can contribute to conflict management.

These are my two main topics. First, urban management and what it can do for intergroup identity conflict. I have studied areas where there is nationalistic conflict, where groups have their own identities, and they are fighting and doing terrible things to each other in pursuit of their nationalistic goals. My second main issue is urban policy amid political transitions. This we can refer to as *democratization* or any sort of transition where we are moving from one political regime to another. I am not a full advocate of democratization, but democratization is one of these political transitions that I look at, as well as the role of urbanization.

These are the cities I have studied. There are eight of them, and I break them into two bunches here because the first set I studied back in

1994 and 1995: Jerusalem, Belfast, Johannesburg—that was during the transition out of apartheid—and Nicosia, Cyprus.

The second group I studied more recently in 2003 and 2004: Barcelona, looking at the transition they had from the Franco regime in the 1970s and also at the nationalistic conflict there between Catalonia and Spanish nationalists; the Basque Country, which many of you are going to be familiar with because political violence is still a fact there; and then Sarajevo and Mostar, two cities in Bosnia and Herzegovina, one of the countries created out of the destroyed, former Yugoslavia.

I propose to you that urban conflict and cities can be put on a scale, defined by the degree that active inter-group conflict over root political issues has been effectively addressed through inclusive institutional and constitutional means.

STABILITY / NORMALCY

Barcelona (Spain)

Johannesburg (South Africa)

MOVEMENT TOWARD PEACE

Basque Country (Spain)

Sarajevo (Bosnia-Herzegovina)

Belfast (Northern Ireland)

SUSPENDED VIOLENCE

Nicosia (Cyprus)

Mostar (Bosnia-Herzegovina)

ACTIVE CONFLICT

Jerusalem (Israel/Palestine)

At the bottom are cities in active conflict. When we move up, we see a situation where cities and societies have suspended violence, but that is about all that is happening. It is like an alcoholic who has stopped drinking but has done nothing to deal with the root issues that are causing the drinking. Violence has stopped, but that is it. It's a dry drunk, if you will. As we go further up the list, we see some movement and advancement toward peace, and at the top, something many would label *stability* or *normalization*.

For the cities I have studied, I have put Jerusalem at the bottom with active conflict, then two situations, Nicosia and Mostar, which are just stuck. Violence has been suspended or exhausted, but they are in a state of concussion, if you will. They really have not moved forward, both the cities and the societies within which the cities exist. In Belfast, I see some movement toward peace. Sarajevo has some movement toward peace, basically because the war was so terrifying. The war is now over, so there is some gradual incremental movement toward peace. I also put the Basque Country moving toward peace with normalized urbanization in a way and strong and innovative city leadership, but at the same time political violence still dictates some of the vocabulary. On the top, one clear case of stability is Barcelona.

You might ask what Johannesburg, South Africa, is doing near the top of the scale of stability and normalization. This brings up a very difficult point. Johannesburg, South Africa, has rampant criminality. It has rampant levels of crime, and yet it has addressed the root issues of that conflict, of apartheid. Now we have a majority and democratic regime in South Africa. What this shows is the extreme concussion and trauma that exist from decades of state oppression. The signing of a peace agreement and the institution of a new regime is one thing, but there are generations of people who have been oppressed and subordinated in those decades. There is almost a backlash now from many black South Africans because of the massive amount of economic inequalities and disparities in South Africa. What this means is that Johannesburg, if you go back to the alcoholic parallel, in a way is a recovering alcoholic. Johannesburg is in twelve-step sessions. They are dealing with the root issues that caused them such pain, and that is black subordination and black disempowerment. All of that has been addressed, but it also shows that once you get to a degree of peace, it is going to hurt like hell still, because there are legacies built up over years and decades of this oppression that still have this effect and will have this effect over decades, even with peace at hand. Peace is not only hard, it hurts.

For Jerusalem, the Israeli wall, the separation wall that is being built today and has been built for the last five years separating the West Bank from Israel proper, is causing huge, damaging, unilateral effects on the Jerusalem urban landscape. It is not only separating the two sides by a wall, but the Israeli government is using the wall as a way to further de facto annex land into Israel proper. There are very difficult and long-term consequences from the building of a wall that separates one side from the other. When one builds a wall, the only thing one learns about the other side of the wall are stereotypes. There is no fresh water coming into the reservoir anymore. Stereotypes build, the animosity builds and the stories of hatred build when a wall separates two sides.

There is also a wall in Nicosia, Cypress. It has been our only walled, divided city since Berlin unified. Now that Berlin is no longer divided, this is the only wall we have now in the world, with the exception of Jerusalem now emerging. Nicosia has been walled and divided into two since 1974. The United Nations is there as a buffer to keep the two sides, the Turkish and the Greek Cypriots, away from each other.

In Mostar, Bosnia and Herzegovina, the three sides—excuse my very simple labels here—are Serbs, Croatians and Bosnian Muslims. In this city, the most dastardly fighting was actually between the Croatians and the Bosnian Muslims. These two sides destroyed massive amounts of this city in the Herzegovina part of the Bosnian state. Today, both sides exist. They are roughly in parity in terms of demography—both the Muslims and the Croatians are roughly about 50 percent of the population—and they are living in a destroyed city. So how does one reconstitute a city like this? This is one of the most difficult cases, because not only is it de facto divided, it was destroyed physically.

In Belfast, Northern Ireland, there are sixteen dividing walls. Unlike Nicosia and formerly Berlin, the city is not separated into two, but separated by more than sixteen different "peace walls" to keep the sides away from each other; again, using very simple terms, keeping Protestants and Catholics away from each other, separating those neighborhoods. These exist today.

Here is another example of how difficult peace building is. On the one hand, we have great success in Northern Ireland today with a major peace agreement, the Good Friday Agreement in 1998, and a major agreement now where two extremists are in a power-sharing government together. Therefore, there is great success here. But look at the city. The city today still exists this way. What do you tell a Catholic kid or a Protestant kid about why these walls are here? What does this mean? This is an example where you cannot forget the urban and local part to the story. You can sign a diplomatic peace agreement and you can have famous handshakes on a lawn, but if you are not tending to the ground up, the bottom-up stuff where people live, work, love and do everything, you're not addressing the main part of people's existence. You need that bottom-up peace building, along with the top-down peacemaking.

Sarajevo, Bosnia, is the saddest city I have ever been in my life. This city was surrounded for four-and-a-half years by artillery and gunmen, and 1,600 citizens of this city were killed. Many children were killed. People were killed burying their own relatives because the cemeteries were exposed to the gunners up on the hills. This is a very emotional place. This is also a very uplifting story in a way. Where once there was a playground, now there is a cemetery, because the [official cemetery] was away from where those gunners, shooters and artillery fighters could shoot at them. One gentleman I spoke with talked about taking his grandchild with him to a playground and now look what it is. Anything that spoke of Bosnian culture was a target of the Bosnian Serb and Serbian armies. For four years, the parliament building west of the historic center was bombarded constantly. It remains that way today as a symbol of the bombarded concept of multiculturalism.

What is very uplifting about Sarajevo is that people can make a difference. We hear a lot about political leaders who use the ethnic card very negatively; use it for hatred. That's how they get in office, and that is how they stay in office. In Sarajevo there is an example of a man who doesn't believe in doing that. He was the military commander for the regiments that stayed in the city, defending the city from this onslaught. Most of the arms and gunnery were fired by Bosnian Serbs upon the Bosnian Muslim population and Serb and Croatian populations of the city. The Bosnian Serbs are the aggressors here. The most amazing thing about this man who stood up for multiculturalism and defended the ideal of coexistence is that ethnically he is a Bosnian Serb. It just shows you that you don't have to line up ethnically all the time, and that there are true leaders. This is a true leader as opposed to other so-called leaders who take the easy path of hatred and ethnic separation. His main concern is how do we not teach children war. It is one thing for adults to be fighting these wars, but what do we tell our children about why they shouldn't do the same thing? How do we not pass on to the generations the hatred that has exercised itself in some of these circumstances?

The Basque Country for decades has been famous for Basque

separatism, extremism, violence and for the ETA paramilitary, which still exists today. The city of Bilbao, once a beat-up industrial city, was given a lot of power since the end of the Franco regime and has used those urban powers to reformulate and revitalize itself. The Guggenheim Museum was scouting around for a site in Europe, and when they first were presented with Bilbao as the possibility, they just laughed because they thought: "*What* is Bilbao? Where is *Bilbao*? Isn't it an old industrial city with major political problems?"

Through some amazing, innovative leadership and entrepreneurialism, not only did the Guggenheim Museum, designed by Frank Gehry, locate in Bilbao, but there has been a tremendously large physical revitalization of that city. A lot of people, me included, actually think this is an example that if you revitalize a city enough with new housing and new services, you actually can, over time—and this is the important part—get people on the side of moderate leadership. They don't cling to the extremist message as much anymore. Over time, they think, "This government is doing good things; maybe we don't need that outright independence for which Basque extremists have been fighting for decades." It leads potentially to a moderation of that extremist message, and it starts to alienate people from the extremist message. That, of course, can be good, but it can also be dangerous when extremists feel alienated.

I flew over Johannesburg, South Africa, in a helicopter in 1995. I talked about the economic disparities before. Within one kilometer of white Johannesburg is Alexandria Township. In the black townships in the city of Johannesburg, there is no housing. There are lean-to shelters. Literally, they are falling down the hillside in a place that no one would ever build, close to a stream. Open toilets. No sanitation. No water. It had absolutely only the most rudimentary services, especially during apartheid.

Then after apartheid, the question became what to do with this? A lot of people think that the easy thing is to get rid of all this. That is easy to say, but it is very difficult because it costs a lot of money. These are the places where people live, so a lot of black South Africans live here. A lot of people think what you do is go in and service these areas, so that they have some minimal quality of life. If you try more drastic relocation efforts, it is going to cost a lot of money, which South Africa does not have because it is being watched very closely by neo-liberal international monetary regimes, such as the World Bank and the International Monetary Fund.

In Barcelona, during the repression under Franco, the city suffered tremendously. Barcelona was the source of Catalonian nationalism. The last thing that Franco ever wanted was any sort of regionalist nationalism. He was a strong believer in authoritarian Spanish centralism. If you have been to Barcelona, you know the story of this over the last twenty-five or thirty years. It has grown into a cosmopolitan, absolutely exciting, internationally connected city, fully expressive of Catalonian nationalism, not of Spanish nationalism. Its regional roots have blossomed since Franco. My point about this is that, along with that Catalonian nationalism, there still is Spanish nationalism, and it is a society that a lot of people believe is really a society of coexisting healthy societies. You can be a Spaniard there or you can be a Catalonian or you can be both. There are various reasons people ascribe to this. You can have two nationalistic groups that are for the most part not only getting along, but the society as a whole is blossoming.

At this point, I think I will stop and just say a few words about the culture of peace, and I want to say some words about what I have found about peace. Some of these words are mine, and some of these words are from other people.

Somebody once described the peace process as not like climbing a mountain but like climbing a mountain range. The successful conquest of each new peak requires different skills and guides. You can be climbing up the mountaintop, and all of a sudden you may feel like you are falling off and that the peace process has halted or regressed. It does not necessarily mean that peace is not developing, but another set of skills and another set of impulses are needed to carry forth and motivate the peace process even further.

Each peace process has its own terrain and its own mountain range, and their sequencing differs. That means, don't try formulas, and don't try models of how peace works. There are unexpected peaks, and there may be no logical, predictable sequence at all. Sometimes there are not even any clear boundaries between phases of peace building. One thing I have found, however, is that if root issues are not addressed in peace processes, the protracted conflict will turn into a protracted peace process. The

original causes of conflict will remain and will be joined by new grievances that are sometimes sparked by the very peace process that is trying to move a society forward. The protracted peace processes are very
susceptible to disruption by extremists who are able to dictate the vocabulary. In many cases, you hear moderate leaders say they will never talk to
extremists because of who they are, yet ironically, at the same time, it is
these extremists and militarists who will very often determine the movement of a society along a peace continuum. They have tremendous power
to halt peace processes, to interrupt, to disrupt them if moderate leadership does not stand up. Therefore, in a sense, there is almost a codepen-
dence on extremists.

Peace hurts. Being comfortable within a frame of hatred is often easier. John Paul Lederach talks about this as generational, identity-based
anger. It's constructed through a combination of historical events, a deep
sense of threat to identity and direct experiences of sustained exclusion. Increasing understanding, tolerance and solidarity (UN action 6)
becomes a hard road to travel, indeed, when "the other" is your obstruc-
tive enemy.

Conflict is, among other things, the process of building and sustain-
ing different perceptions and interpretations of reality. With peace comes
the challenge of dealing with your burned-in sense of injustice in some
constructive way. Burned-in sense of injustice; I have thought about this
challenge and what I would do in such circumstances. If someone in the
past had killed my father or my grandfather because they were from a certain ethnicity or race, I am pretty sure the first thing I would tell my children is who those people were and to never trust them again. That's who
I am as a human being. Could I confront the children of the assailant in
a way other than revenge and friction? I am not sure, but I think every
one of us as people and every one of us as members of society have that
incredible, seemingly impossible challenge to not pass on that burned-in
sense of injustice.

So, when does peace happen? One scholar says it happens when
there are "hurting stalemates." This scholar uses this phrase to describe
when societies tire of conflict and try some peaceful alternative. I think
it can also describe the challenges of peacemaking and its fits and starts
that we see. Peace is not a friendly embrace and mutual trust. It is not a

sentimental happy ending or brotherly love but rather a clenched-teeth compromise. It does not happen overnight; it develops incrementally and experimentally. At times, we don't even know whether it is indeed peace. It certainly doesn't feel like the peace of which we always dreamed. There is no overt violence on the one hand, and that is great. Look at the example of Belfast. But it doesn't feel like that full-fledged peace that we always thought was going to happen.

Amos Oz, who is an Israeli writer, had a wonderful interview with Jim Lehrer back in 2002. He talks about the tragedy of a clash between right and right, between two very powerful and very convincing claims. When one is in a conflict, nobody is going to say they are wrong. I wouldn't. Oz talked about two potential endings to conflict—a Shakespearean and a Chekhovian ending. The Shakespearean ending is the resolving of tragedy with a stage littered with dead bodies and the just are right and the other side is wrong. This is not what I have found in these conflicts. A Chekhovian ending, in contrast, results in a situation where everyone is disappointed, disillusioned, embittered, heartbroken, but they are alive and they learn to unhappily coexist and contain each side's burned-in sense of injustice.

Peace in these places has taught me about time. I was a typical American going into this research, and I thought it might take maybe a few more years at the outset to solve some of these conflicts. When one is immersed in these things and thinks about them a lot, one adopts a much longer time horizon about how peace develops. Rather than three years, one talks about maybe "my lifetime" or maybe "my children's lifetime." Peace unfolds very slowly and is always susceptible to disruption. Yet this longer time horizon does not feel to me like resignation or pessimism. It feels like realism; it feels like a reality that accommodates the utter complexity and the meaningfulness of these conflicts.

Questions and Answers

AUDIENCE MEMBER 1: That was a wonderful lecture. I don't know if this is something you can answer. It is not touched upon. I tend to think of peace in a way that eventually down the road there will be a solution. From your research, are there enough resources for the entire population in the world? It may not be your specialty, but what is your answer to that? Is it a distribution problem of food and resources or not enough resources?

DR. BOLLENS: In my opinion, are there enough resources for all the people in the world? By God, yes, but it is a distribution and allocation problem. It is the utter disproportionality of how massive amounts of resources are used by advanced countries such as our own—the way things are distributed and allocated that makes it so the resources are not enough to go to many parts of the world.

AUDIENCE MEMBER 1: Therefore, ultimately, the problem is the distribution of wealth and money?

DR. BOLLENS: The distribution of wealth and the distribution of consumption across countries.

AUDIENCE MEMBER 2: So you believe it is resources, and you think that the wrong people are in charge of some of the resources that are donated to other countries?

DR. BOLLENS: The question is do I think that the wrong people are in control of the resources that are distributed?

AUDIENCE MEMBER 2: Somehow, they manage to wrest control of the donated supplies.

DR. BOLLENS: That's the other part of the story. The humanitarian aid, the other forms of aid and resources that are distributed to other countries are very often captured by the elite, captured by the political elite, and not distributed to lower rungs of each of those societies. Therefore, that's the other part of it. Often, authoritarian and strong-armed leaders use those resources as power, as ways to get power and hold onto power.

AUDIENCE MEMBER 3: Extremists tend to be very small segments of a population, yet, like you said, they tend to dictate the vocabulary of what is going on. What is the best way to actually deal with these fundamentalists and extremists? Because, as you said, they are going to say, "I will be heard."

DR. BOLLENS: That is true. There are two parts to the question or two illustrations of the answer. One is my own research, and the other one, of course, is the world we live in today with the Islamic extremists. In terms of the cities I have lived in and I have researched, the genuine leadership, in my opinion, is that which holds to the middle. It's so easy for leaders to use the ethnic card as a way to capture constituencies and hold onto them. If you are a leader in a genuine sense, you express the commonality of all humankind and don't go for those easy answers. No matter what the extremists do, you hold fundamentally to your own beliefs about a common humanity.

In the face of extremism, a country such as ours should hold firm to our fundamental qualities of openness and tolerance embedded within our constitution. If you need to deal with extremists, even to get rid of them, you have to do that. I think many people and many Americans, if they were to look back at September 11, 2001, and at the last six years, and if they could roll back the clock, I think they would want a different strategy, a different tactic and a different approach. That is not being light on extremism at all. That is a whole other issue about how you deal with extremism.

AUDIENCE MEMBER 4: You have done a wonderful job of teaching me a little more. How do you choose your countries to focus on? Currently Darfur, Somalia and some of the other African countries are in conflict and are destroying one another.

DR. BOLLENS: Thank you for that question. I am an urbanist, so I study cities. I am fascinated with cities that contain two or more identifiable groups that really are separate from each other psychologically. I was attracted to Jerusalem initially. Jerusalem is, in my opinion, the great puzzle of humankind. Some people say that God created Jerusalem because, if we can find peace in Jerusalem, the whole world will be at peace because it is such a quagmire.

I was attracted to study Belfast for the same reason. I get excited looking at extreme examples of division within cities and then how people deal with day-to-day life. How do they cope with that? How do day-to-day policymakers deal with that? That is what got me interested in that and then in issues of political transition. Johannesburg with its

historic path away from apartheid was too good to pass up as an area
of study in 1995.

It is the same with Spain—a transition from Franco and a transition
in the Basque country, hopefully away from violence, and also the
transition in Bosnia away from war. I focus on urban and transitional
uncertainty. The next logical place would be Beirut for me. Other
African cities that are hosting competing groups and leading very
explosive urban situations would also be very, very relevant.

AUDIENCE MEMBER 5: Your lecture represents not just a view; it intro-
duces us to a mission, a mission that is part religion, I think, and part
science, and they intertwine together. I want to say something that I
am addressing to the speaker but saying to all of us, and that has to do
with vocabulary. I think what has been suggested will, if adopted by
many of us, be a new fundamentalism. It will be the fundamental way,
quite different from the other ways of looking at the problem. *Fundamentalism, extremism* and *radicalism* are labels, which one attaches
normally. I am not suggesting the speaker does this, but I am only saying we fall into these vocabularies. These are words we attach to people we don't like.

Before Mandela was freed from prison in South Africa, what
would have been regarded as fundamentally sound was the constitution. That meant that Mandela should have stayed in prison because
he advocated the use of force *if necessary,* not *if possible.* Like Gandhi, he had a fundamental view, a radical view. Therefore, *extremism,
fundamentalism* and *radicalism,* these are all words that I would like to
attach to myself when I am at my best, and I advise that we not make
them synonyms for people we dislike.

DR. BOLLENS: Thank you very much for that comment. That was wonderful. I will leave it as taken.

AUDIENCE MEMBER 6: I don't know if you can generalize this, but in
your studies, what are some of the first basic steps that a city can take
to create that culture of peace?

DR. BOLLENS: I will answer in a general way, because it is probably most
meaningful that way. Let's say there are two groups in the city. The

city leadership has to be cognizant and aware that there are distinct group identity needs for a majority in control and a minority that has been subordinated. Through the delivery of urban services, through the governance of an urban system, those identity needs and aspirations have to be accommodated. In these cities of division, you cannot impose an assimilative model on all citizens where everyone will be treated the same.

The majority in control has to think through a new lens of coexistent viability. It is important for this minority group to feel they are viable, respected and productive members of that urban society for the city and the society to blossom and to be healthy. Anything short of that or any messages that the minority feels that their identity is threatened or not respected is going to exacerbate the problem. It is not necessarily going to lead to violence, but it is certainly going to add to the social and psychological separation of those two groups in the city and then we are in a situation where we are getting into a downward slope.

I answered your question generally, but there is a whole set of implications this has for how a majority city government would view a minority with respect and viability. Group identity is an important attribute to acknowledge in cities of multiple cultures; its preservation is connected to the UN Programme of Action on a Culture of Peace (#6): Advancing understanding, tolerance and solidarity.

AUDIENCE MEMBER 7: What would you recommend for average citizens of Los Angeles to do to go toward a culture of peace? What small things could average people do?

DR. BOLLENS: What could an average citizen in Los Angeles do to promote a culture of peace? I guess, spend a day and walk the entire length of Wilshire Boulevard, because you will see in Wilshire Boulevard the gradations—the socioeconomic and ethnic gradations—that this city is. Through that exposure, it will enlighten most of us that there are all sorts of different people here and all sorts of urban ecosystems and subsystems of incredible culture and incredible creativity.

Maybe the next time we then look at the newspaper and it's talking about black violence in South Central, it will be easier to detach from that and say: "That's the media, that's what it does. That's what it reports on." But you know that there is a much more complex reality. Certainly, there are problems, but the reality out there is much richer, much more complex and much more worthy of our attention as people, but also as city leaders.

It's one thing to mouth the word *multiculturalism* and do multicultural festivals, but it is another thing to get out there and be exposed to it and feel what multicultural richness is.

AUDIENCE MEMBER 8: Do you think there was some kind of apathy from the world community in Rwanda, Tutsis versus Hutus? If so, why? Because there was no intervention, no help for a hundred days, 800,000 people plus, who knows? What are your thoughts about the whole Rwanda, Tutsi versus Hutu?

DR. BOLLENS: I am going to sidestep that question in a way. I agree with you. I think there was not enough attention on the Rwanda massacre. I am not going to sidestep your question completely, because I am going to apply it to another case.

I think the American and international lack of attention to what happened in Bosnia and Sarajevo for four years is a crime. This is still today a moderate Muslim population in Bosnia that was left on its own for most of those four years. One last final massacre of a shopping area in Sarajevo finally got the world to send in the arms to battle back the Bosnian Serbs. We waited far, far too long, and I don't understand that. Especially in today's world, where we talk about developing moderate Muslim societies and democracy in Islamic societies. Here was a great opportunity, and yet we left them out to dry.

To this day, they remain a moderate Muslim society—a moderate Muslim European society—and they are struggling. What do we hear? We hear about how it is a platform for extremists, but that's just a small part of what is happening. It is still a very moderate Muslim society that has gone through a wrenching transition that is democratic at this point but still very vulnerable. It needs a tremendous amount of attention. However, of course, our attention has moved elsewhere.

AUDIENCE MEMBER 9: I understand that we have a problem in this world, and you pointed it out. I was feeling a little depressed, but I think that maybe we should start with the environment here in this country. We have problems, too. We've got gangbangers, we've got black-on-black crimes, we've got white-on-white crimes, we've got drugs, we've got corrupt cops, corrupt politicians, prisons, you know? The way that I feel I can change things is by changing my environment. I brought my friend here for the first time, so maybe I am planting a seed in him, the seed of the Buddha. You plant it in somebody else and just pass the torch on. That's the way I feel. I have to start with my environment and maybe we can step together, unite together and stop the war, wouldn't you agree?

DR. BOLLENS: I would agree. You're saying by changing your environment, you are really changing yourself, right? It starts within you, very consistent with Buddhist tenets. I fully agree, and I think people only get to that point of wanting to re-examine their own motivations and be open enough to change out of extreme trauma and extreme pain. I think that is what changes us. You talk about the gangbangers and all that stuff. I know people who have battled alcoholism and drug addiction, and they come to a wall—they are going to die from it, or they are going to change. At that point, they see that they are not going to stop drinking if they get a new job or if they get married or blah, blah, blah. They are going to change only when they change within themselves. It's the tenets of the twelve-step program that talks about a higher power, a spiritual essence, because we can't do it ourselves. I don't think we can change by ourselves. Maybe you can. I have had a hard time changing myself without a lot of help, so I think that is what happens. I find Buddhism the most psychological religion we have, because it talks about the inside. We start from what is on the inside, and then how we then experience life. The hard work of fostering a culture of peace through education (UN action area #1), respecting human rights for all (UN action area #3), and advancing our understanding, tolerance and solidarity (UN action area #6) must start from within ourselves.

Now your task is hard, young man, right? Your challenges are numerous, so I wish you well, and I wish your visitor peace himself.

AUDIENCE MEMBER 10: You said that there is evidence that when you have resources in a divided city, that it becomes more moderate. Can you tell me what the examples are?

DR. BOLLENS: Great question. I implied or said earlier that if you bring resources into a city and spread them around, a city can become more moderate, populations can become more moderate. It is an excellent question. There are many who feel that, in these cities that I study of nationalistic conflict, if you can spread the resources fully—good housing, good community facilities and good services—that over time the nationalistic conflict can abate. But there is a big debate about whether material improvement can really help things in a divided context because it doesn't get at the underlying issues. You can be a Catholic family in Belfast and all of a sudden find yourself in a better house and more community facilities, but if the pain from the past is still there and you still do not feel that you are fully empowered within a local governance, whether it's the city or Northern Ireland, the spreading of those material resources still is not going to solve that problem. You are still going to ache with that pain.

I think the Bilbao example shows us that material improvement can give us at least a chance. It can hold the violence, the conflict and the anxiety in abeyance, not so that it is going to go away, but in a way that may enlighten the political leadership and general public. It will buy that leadership some time to do the things it has to do in terms of the coexistent policies of accommodation, of restructuring local governance, of distributing services in a way that reinforces that coexistent viability.

The spreading of material resources is important, I think. Certainly, poverty exacerbates tensions, but it is not the full story when there are group identity needs that are still felt today.

Closing remarks

This topic and this research have changed me fundamentally as a person. I am a fundamentally different person. I have talked to more than 220 different people in eight different cities, and to talk to each of those people was absolutely a delight. Beyond my own personal change, I have so much more confidence and openness about other people and how good other people are. It's unbelievable how good other people are.

The bad part to this, of course, is the political leaders and what I referred to as the games that they play, the ethnic games. The utter good-ness of people stands out in my mind. I remember talking to Israelis and Palestinians. They would talk about each other as brothers who have gone the wrong route, but they knew and respected each other as brothers. I don't know whether that is compassion or not, but it is empathy for one another.

When people get into peace-building forums and negotiations, and I have been part of a couple of these, they experience the other in pro-found ways. I have been in a Northern Ireland discussion, and I have been in an Israeli-Palestinian discussion. It is unbelievable when the two sides start to talk to each other. One commonality is what I just expressed and that is that they know each other so well. They know all each other's games. The other thing that is common to it all is that they are so tired of it. They are so exhausted from going through the same thing over and over again with violence and conflict. You can see these people reach out. They feel incredibly vulnerable. They are scared, but they know that the old way does not work. It is amazing to see these people in these forums reach out on this. It does happen. Israelis and Palestinians do talk to each other in a progressive way. The Catholics and Protestants, even before the peace advances, were talking to each other in this way, because they saw the common personhood and common humanity, and they also saw the absolute futility of continually going through that same violent downward cycle over and over again.

In a lot of the slide shows that I present, I leave with slides of chil-dren, because the one thing that gets these people to the peace negotiat-ing tables is when they talk about their children and their grandchildren. We can screw up our life, but it is another thing when these people start to talk about potentially screwing up children's and grandchildren's lives.

I am more hopeful of the human soul than I ever have been. I have concerns about political leadership and about how the human soul can be distorted, penetrated and taken for a ride by political leadership. I just wish there was some way to have a hermetically sealed barrier between the games political leaders play and the goodness of people's souls.

June 27, 2007
Santa Monica, California

Climate Change and Peace

Richard A. Matthew

*Associate Professor, International and Environmental Politics, Schools
of Social Ecology and Social Science, and Founding Director, Center
for Unconventional Security Affairs, University of California, Irvine*

Dr. Matthew studies the environmental dimensions
of conflict and post-conflict reconstruction and
has done extensive field work in conflict zones in
South Asia and East Africa. In addition to his
positions at UCI, he is also the Senior Fellow for
Security at the International Institute for Sustainable Development in Geneva, a member of the
United Nations Expert Advisory Group on Environment, Conflict and Peacebuilding and a member of
the World Conservation Union's Commission on
Environmental, Economic and Social Policy. Dr.
Matthew has received Certificates of Recognition
for his research and service activities from the U.S.
Congress, the California State Legislature and the
City of Los Angeles. He has written or contributed
to more than 100 publications including five
books. Dr. Matthew's research interest on the
impact of climate change on human security
particularly addresses the second action area of
the 1999 United Nations Programme of Action on a
Culture of Peace: Promoting sustainable economic
and social development.

The Center for Unconventional Security Affairs, which I direct at the University of California, Irvine, in Orange County, has three goals. One of them—and perhaps it is the most important one—is education.

In our country, only 15 percent of Americans have passports. That means, in this nation, which is so powerful, as many as 85 percent of its people have never directly experienced the rest of the world. They have watched world events on television, so they have seen a lot of scary news, but they have not actually been to the places where these events are happening.

Television is not much of a window into the world. But we depend on it, and it is not surprising that we have, as a country, tremendous misperceptions about what is going on in South Asia, Southeast Asia, Africa and the Middle East. We hear a lot about failures and violence and corruption. We do not hear much about innovations, achievements and progress. But these are a key part of every story, every history. When we travel to these faraway places, we see much more of the situation, and we can improve, dramatically improve, our perception of the world around us.

One of the things we do is to try to put American students out in the field. Over the years, we have sent students to Afghanistan, Rwanda, Uganda, Cambodia, India, Israel, Venezuela and many other places around the world. This is exciting, because we strongly believe that if we are going to engage with the rest of the world, and at times lead on world issues, we have to actually experience it and make an effort to understand it.

We also have a number of research programs. Right now, we are doing a large study on microfinance and its potential for combining poverty alleviation with environmental rescue. We are also doing a large study on America's understanding of the world. This is the first nationwide survey combining psychology and political science to explore how Americans look at the world, how they understand it, and what they do in response.

What we are discovering is that some Americans are really afraid of the world. They tend to see it as a threatening and hostile place. But many do not. Many still believe in the world as a basically good place. I have traveled to some fifty countries, and I have spent an enormous amount of time in the Middle East and South Asia, Southeast Asia, East Africa, and South Africa, and these are not scary or threatening places. In my experience, they are indeed basically good places, and we need to trust our instincts and our experiences when it comes to our engagement with them, not be swayed by sensationalist media accounts.

The third thing we do is work with people who can make a difference. We feed them our research—people in the government, at the UN. We also work with a coalition business leaders and philanthropists in Orange County—the Coalition Advocating Human Security. We try to encourage these people, who have enjoyed the prosperity and opportunities of America, to do something, to extend opportunity and dignity to other people outside the world with which they are familiar. We have discovered that a lot of people want to do these things, but they do not always know how to do them, so we are involved in raising awareness, creating opportunities, encouraging people to act and demonstrating that an individual has so much capability in this country to do things. In fact, in many ways, individuals are freer than government officials or elected politicians who feel they have to play certain roles or take certain positions.

A motivated individual with some passion can do amazing things. Each year, the Center for Unconventional Security Affairs gives out what we call the Human Security Award to an individual, an ordinary person, who has done something truly amazing. Last year (2006), we honored Roméo Dellaire. I have gotten to know him a little bit. He arrived in Rwanda as the UN Force Commander in 1994 before the genocide, thinking that this was going to be somewhat of a vacation for him. The Arusha Peace Accord was signed. He was going to kick back and enjoy his life. Then he saw the genocide starting to take shape, and he devoted every minute of the next three months to trying to stop it and to convince the world that it needed to act. His story demonstrates the courage an individual can find in himself or herself and the things that they can suddenly do that they never expected to do. He is truly a remarkable person. He saved thousands of lives.

Those are the things that we do at our center. Change is not an overnight process, but it is a real process, and we are part of a larger set of efforts across this country, trying to respond to the sense that people have that maybe consumption and the next car and the smaller iPod are not the things that are going to be most fulfilling, that maybe somehow exploring and discovering creativity, spirituality, the capacity to help people are far more important. But they do not often give you easy victories. These are not things you do in 15 minutes, but they are tremendously fulfilling when you start to devote some time to them.

Today, I want to talk about an issue that I have been studying for a very long time, and that is climate change. I think it is an issue that has the potential to do tremendous damage to the world. I want to suggest that our country is, in many ways, part of the problem, and yet there is so much opportunity to take advantage of what we have here and to do some good things.

The argument in a nutshell is that we have spent, since September 11, 2001, probably more than $2 trillion fighting terrorism. All of the millennium development goals together would not cost that much to implement. That is an enormous amount of money, and it is not clear that we have achieved a great deal after six years. It is not clear that this is money well spent.

In fact, I am going to argue that our focus is wrong. And I am not dismissing terrorism. It is horrible and needs to be confronted. But we should be looking much more at things like climate change, which are affecting the entire planet and especially affecting the most vulnerable populations on the planet—the poor.

Everywhere we go, we are already seeing people displaced by flooding, displaced by desertification, vulnerable to new diseases that are not endemic in their communities. People are being forced to radically alter the livelihoods that they may have depended on for years or generations. We are already seeing this happen. We need to do something about it, because right now we have about 380 parts per million of carbon dioxide in the atmosphere. A lot of scientific research suggests that if we get to 400 parts per million of carbon dioxide, we will trigger about a 2-degree change. It will put us into a new terrain, a climate area that humankind has never been in before.

We could stop. There is about a degree of climate change locked into the oceans, which we cannot stop, but we can stop beyond that.

Instead of decreasing the problem, however, we are increasing it at about 1.5 parts per million each year, which gives us about fourteen years before we reach 400 parts per million of carbon dioxide. We do not have the luxury of an enormous amount of time to start changing our lifestyles, our consumption patterns, which is probably the first thing that has to be done.

We have to change our expectations about what we should get out of life here, about the rewards of consumption. If we do not, we may have—no one knows how long for sure—perhaps twenty years, perhaps twenty-seven, before we hit that 2-degree change. There is a lot of justification for acting now.

Climate change itself is creating the types of instability of which we are treating the symptoms. We are so worried about people moving across borders or being engaged in drug trafficking or picking up arms or accepting the use of violence to promote their agendas. We are fighting the symptoms, and we are spending a lot on the symptoms, but we are not getting down to the root drivers of all this. Not for everybody, but for lots of people, it is desperation that drives them. It is that they do not have other opportunities. It is that they are so beaten by a world in which there is massive wealth, and yet in some parts of it, so little that they can access or achieve. A little bit of reallocation, a little bit of rethinking, a little bit of shifting our priorities, then enormously positive things could be happening.

I am not saying that terrorism is not brutal and horrible and does not need to be challenged; of course, it does. It also needs to be put into perspective. In order to obtain the oil and gas that we need (which is also fueling climate change), we have had to put an enormous military presence into the Persian Gulf and Saudi Arabia. By doing this, we are causing a lot of the instability and discontent that we then fight later on. We have got to start moving away from this.

I actually brief the military several times a year on these issues. The military is fully aware of the complexity they are facing abroad and of the fact that they can and should only do so much. Right now, the military is being asked to do way too much. To fight on our behalf and also help in emergencies and train people and build schools and distribute food and water and so on. The military cannot do all this efficiently. It cannot do all this well, and force is not the appropriate tool for much of this work.

We are using the wrong tool to fight a lot of these problems. We need to broaden our tool set. We need to use some of the other skills and capital that we have in this country to address these things. There is an enormous amount of wind energy, solar energy and geothermal energy in the world. The entire world satisfies less than 2 percent of its energy needs with all those forms of energy. We concentrate on fossil fuels, 67 percent of which are in the Middle East, which is already a volatile area and to which we put an enormous military presence so we can maintain some control over what we know is poisoning and destroying our planet. It really does not make any sense.

There is almost no way this can be defended or sustained. In fourteen years, we may say, "Wow, how could we have missed this opportunity?" We need to move toward alternative energy, and we need to rethink our lifestyles. I was reading a survey that said the least happy, the most depressed group of people in our country are people over eighty. Their number one complaint is that they are lonely. The second most unhappy group in our country is people eighteen to twenty-five years old. That is a remarkable thing! They are in this superpower country with tons of opportunity and universities and education, and yet they are remarkably unhappy. This is something we should be concerned about. I think a lot of people, at least in my experience, do not regard higher and higher levels of consumption as a guaranteed route to happiness. In fact, we have seen no correlation between consumption rates beyond what you need to live and happiness. You can get more and more and more and more and it does not make you happier and happier and happier.

In fact, it looks like the people who have the most are not the happiest people in our country. They may be happier than the desperately poor, but they are less happy than people below them economically. So not only are our young people unhappy, but also our richest people are less happy than we might expect. This suggests that maybe there are spiritual dimensions to our personality and artistic ones, and things like friendship and family that we need to cultivate, rather than another car, another gadget, another day at the mall.

Let me say a few words about peace and conflict. These are not easy issues where we can say, "Here is the solution, here is what causes conflict, here is how to achieve peace." There are lots of things going on, and we have to be cognizant of all of these things. We promote trade liberalization as a force of peace. We believe that if economies are interconnected, that reduces the incentive to go to war. It makes sense, and there is a strong empirical basis for that, but we also know that it is not a simple relationship. It is not simply that you force other economies to open up and then everything works out well. The terms on which this opening takes place and the extent to which the informal sector, the area where poor people are forced to exist, the extent to which these things are integrated into this openness, are tremendously important. So is it a good thing? Yes, but it is a mixed thing, and it needs to be attended to carefully.

Ditto democratization. Again, we have lots of evidence that says democracies are peace-loving. They do not go to war with one another. They do not engage in genocide. They do not engage in civil war. Promoting democracy makes sense, but that is not an easy thing to do, and hosting elections is not enough. Hosting elections does not create democracy. Democracy is a condition in which people are somehow participating in crafting the system of rules that apply to them, in which they have real opportunities, in which they are empowered, where they can speak and do things and shape things. Going to a poll is only a very small piece of that. We pin far too many expectations on things that are just the cosmetics of political change.

Severe environmental stress is one of the factors that affect peace and conflict, and my research, which is focused on this, suggests that it is a growing factor. We need to understand environmental change. It is not *all* bad, but an awful lot of it is bad. It is of concern to all of us; it affects the prospects for peace and the probability of violent conflict around the world.

One of the amazing features of our world is that probably the pace of those things that affect peace and conflict—the pace of economic globalization and the pace of democratic change, the pace of technological innovation and diffusion, and the pace of environmental change—are all unprecedented. The world is a huge, complicated and rapidly changing place, and it is easy to be overwhelmed by it. It is hard to know what is encouraging peace and what is undermining it. Are we moving forward or not? It is easy to watch the news for a couple of days and say, "This is too big a challenge."

We have to avoid the myth that this place—peace on planet earth—is just beyond our reach. In fact, the solutions to most of these problems are within our reach, but we can make them look very complicated and difficult. We can make them look impossible, and we can persuade ourselves that we cannot do anything, so we might as well just turn on the TV and veg out for a little while.

I am not going to delve deeply into this, but I will say that our approach in this country to security—to peace—was defined in 1947 in the National Security Act, and that is still the Act that organizes how we understand the rest of the world, the threats it poses and how we organize our defense, our intelligence and military activities. That was sixty years ago! The world is completely different. Even the military itself asks why we are being held hostage by this Act.

In 1947, there were two categories: combat operations, which were 99 percent of what we did, and noncombat operations, which were about 1 percent of what we did. Today, that has changed completely. The military finds itself more and more working at the site of an earthquake or a tsunami or dealing with an infectious outbreak rather than on a traditional battlefield. Now it has great tools for blowing things up—for applying force. But it does not have great tools for building things, for creating things, for bringing hope and dignity. That is not what the military is trained to do, and yet we are asking it to do these things—bring in food and medicine, help people in a crisis, stabilize an area of dire poverty— and then we are giving it old tools to work with. We are saying: "Here is a bunch of tanks and some weapons. Go in and win the hearts and minds of these people." We cannot be doing that.

When the military itself recognizes that it needs to be transformed in a dramatic fashion, surely our civilians who run it, who control it, need to listen. It is unprecedented that we have had generals speaking out time after time, saying that we are misusing force. We are putting our soldiers in situations in which they should not be placed. We are asking them to do things that they should not be asked to do. We need to rethink this. We should be listening to these people. They actually have been outside of our country; they know the complexity of what is happening around the world. Generals have no desire to waste or misuse force. Let's help them out.

And here I want to focus more on the environment. Here is a core insight of a lot of research over the past few years. We have about 13 billion hectares of productive land. That is about a middle calculation. Maybe it is 11 billion and maybe it is 14 billion, but let's call it around 13 billion hectares of land. About 8.8 billion hectares of this land is productive. That gives us all the stuff that we use for everything from construction to food to you-name-it. It is productive land. There is disagreement over how much the other 10 to 100 million species on the planet require. Biologists have calculated somewhere between 12 percent to half of the productive land is stuff we should not even be touching because the rest of the web of life needs it. We should be leaving this part to the 10 to 100 million other species on the planet.

What remains is probably not more than about 4.5 billion hectares. Now we are using much more than this—probably more than the productivity of 12 billion hectares. Even if we were optimistic and only assigned 12 percent to all the other living systems on the planet, the bottom line is that we are using more than what likely exists. We are already using more productive land than is available on the planet's surface. We are overshooting. What does that mean? It means that if a forest takes fifty years to grow, we are using it up in five years. Therefore, we are seeing that productive land is being destroyed. We are losing forest, we are losing fisheries, and we are losing species. We are losing species at somewhere around 10,000 times the natural rate of extinction for species. These things are gone forever. Forest cover is gone forever.

What are we getting more of? We are getting more of desert. We are creating larger and larger swaths of desert, and yet the population is still growing. We know the population of 6.5 billion today is probably going to reach 8 billion, maybe 9 billion, during our lifetimes. The amount of productive land is going down because we are overusing it. This is clearly not a sustainable relationship. Everybody recognizes that we are not using the resources of the planet in a way that can be sustained for very long, maybe fifty years, maybe a hundred years, possibly, but at enormous cost.

We have to do something about this, and climate change is accelerating this process. We have cut down lots of forests ourselves. We have transformed lots of different ecosystems into roads and housing developments, but climate change is accelerating the process. Climate change could, very easily, over the next fifteen to fifty years, destroy most of our coastal cities. We do not know what to do about that. Only the Netherlands is developing a solution to this, because it is used to this problem. We do not know what to do about this. We are losing productive land, we are growing the number of people, and this is an untenable situation that climate change is going to aggravate.

The good news, of course, and I am sure that you are all aware of this, is that it looks like fewer people are dying in war than ever before. There are fewer wars than ever before. Since 1946, the trend has been clearly downward—fewer wars and less lethal wars. Since 1992, there have been fewer civil wars and less lethal civil wars. There are areas that are tremendously violent, and areas that are violent tend to line up very nicely with areas that are most ravaged environmentally, and the areas that are in the front lines of climate change. Those populations are experiencing layers of adversity. They have corrupt or weak governments, they have tremendous poverty, they are vulnerable to infectious disease, they have low rates of literacy, and they are facing flooding and desertification. This is a tremendous burden, and it is one for which we are largely responsible. We have played a major role in creating these conditions. Ironically, they largely have not affected us in ways that have mobilized us to do anything—even though we all saw the damage done by Hurricane Katrina (2005), the sort of event climate change to which science alerts us. Hurricane Katrina has not changed our behavior very aggressively, although it should have.

Climate change is doing a whole lot of things that are now no longer subjects of discussion among researchers. Researchers accept that climate change is happening. There is some disagreement over certain areas, but they are very technical and they do not affect the story we are telling. There is no disagreement over the basic story that I am telling. Everybody agrees that climate change is already displacing people. I was in Bangladesh during the floods four years ago (2003). There were 20 million people displaced—20 million people! It is going to get worse. It is going to magnify disasters.

I write a regular column for a magazine called *Disaster Preparedness*. In that magazine, we look at our readiness for disasters. We no longer think of once-in-a-hundred-year storms, because the evidence suggests that these are now once-in-ten-year storms, or once-in-five-year storms. These things are now going to happen several times during our lifetime. They are going to happen repeatedly. Katrina is not going to be an isolated example of a terrible configuration of events.

It is going to put an enormous strain on food systems, something that we are accelerating by using corn for biofuel as a solution to our energy crisis. Of all the solutions, that is probably the one that is least likely to be successful. It pays a lot of money to our farmers, so politically it is an easy sell. But from every other perspective imaginable, it is a disaster. We are essentially taking food out of the global system, and we know that climate change is going to reduce agricultural productivity in many of the world's 192 countries.

There are about five countries that are expected to be net food exporters over the next twenty years. That means there are going to be more than 180 countries that are going to be net food importers. They will not be able to produce all of their own food. Meanwhile, we are taking food out of production. It does not make a bit of sense, especially since nobody thinks that this is a good way to deal with climate change.

Climate change might also encourage pandemics. Historically, of course, there was almost no flow of species from South to North. There were a couple of species that migrated up into North America from the South, but the flow was mostly the other way. Now, we are actually seeing parasites, pathogens, move up into the North. We now have tropical diseases in Texas and so on. This is going to change our world in a dramatic way.

The basis for what I am saying here is pretty secure. Essentially, we know that there may have been hominids a million years ago or two million years ago, but most of what we know about humankind comes from the last 8,000 to 10,000 years. In terms of climate, this period is what some call a sweet spot. It has been very congenial to humankind and to many other species. We are about to move out of this climate sweet spot because of our own activities. The consequences of that could be tremendously dramatic. Let's look at the evidence.

The temperature is going up. When temperature goes up, water warms up and we have what is called *thermal expansion*, which causes the sea level to rise. It is not the amount of water; it is the temperature of the water. Snow cover is going down. This is undisputed. Everybody agrees. Not everybody agrees exactly how much this will affect things over the course of fifty or a hundred years, but everybody agrees this is a concern.

Not only is it going up, it is going up very quickly. In fact, when the Intergovernmental Panel on Climate Change released its report (in 2007), its six-year synthesis of research, it said, "This is happening much more quickly than we thought." All the things that are going wrong are accelerating now, and it is because of what we call *positive feedbacks*. A good example is when you put an ice cube in a glass of water; it melts faster as it gets smaller, because more of its surface is covered by warm water.

We are discovering that the glaciers are melting faster than we thought. In fact, now people believe that the glaciers that feed the six major river systems in South Asia, the glaciers in the Himalayas, the Hindu Kush, the Karakorum, the premier mountain ranges, could be gone in twenty years. Gone! They have been there for 20,000 years, but they will be gone, and that will be a catastrophe for India, a catastrophe for Pakistan. It will put a lot of pressure on Nepal. Nepal has a lot of water. It will be a catastrophe for these countries that have developed along these freshwater systems.

The monsoon, which is the basis for the agriculture economy and the fishing economy of Bangladesh, is becoming erratic and could reverse. What will these people do if they no longer can predict or have a monsoon season? There will be no fishing industry and no farming industry. We will have tens of millions of people with no jobs. This is not happening over decades or centuries where they can adjust, this is going to happen over years.

These are the twelve warmest years on record and everybody in this room has lived through them. Arctic sea ice has shrunk by 2.7 percent a decade. The permafrost is disappearing, and seasonally frozen ground cover is reducing.

Precipitation is increasing in the wealthy countries and decreasing in the poor countries on the whole. What we are going to see is more rainfall over the oceans and more rainfall in the middle of Australia, up in Canada, up in parts of Russia, up in parts of Europe and parts of our own country, but much less throughout the tropical world.

There will be much less rain for much of Africa and much of Asia and much of Central America and South America. That is a problem. We see these tremendously intense droughts and horrifying heat waves that are now already killing thousands and thousands of people.

Or maybe we do not see them. They often do not get reported on CNN, but they are far more lethal than anything else that is taking place. Drought, disease, malnutrition, these are killing people.

We are having fewer and fewer cold days. The days are getting less and less cold and heat waves are becoming more and more frequent. Cyclones and hurricanes are becoming more and more intense. It looks like there might be some agricultural gains in Australia, Canada and maybe in parts of Europe, in Russia and in Argentina. The rest of the world is going to experience agriculture losses. They are going to be able to produce less. The evidence is very, very powerful.

Basically what scientists are telling us is that what we are experiencing now is already quite unusual, but we are on the threshold of a set of changes that will put us outside of where humankind has ever lived. That is of grave concern because it will put us into an era of severe storms, massive droughts, horrifying heat waves, tremendous flooding. It will be congenial to certain types of microbes and parasites and so on. It will be uncongenial to larger species that do not adapt very quickly.

Why is it happening? This is where people have been confused by arguments that it could be natural. The IPCC report is a consensus report. That means every single word in that report was agreed to by 3,000 scientists representing every single country. The scientists from our country were our most prominent scientists. They were not handpicked by anybody. They are the ones who publish research, and they are the ones whom everybody recognizes as the best—as well as the best in Brazil, the best in Ecuador, the best in Israel, the best in South Africa, the best in Uganda and so on. There was not one person who abstained from that report. They all agree that human activity is the cause of this, and that it is caused by the use of fossil fuels.

The only people we know who disagree with that claim are consultants for some TV networks, and they are getting paid to disagree with this. None of these scientists are paid for their research. They are doing their research as part of their normal jobs.

It looks like this increase [in climate problems] correlates perfectly with the increase in fossil fuel consumption. There is no other way of explaining what is going on. There is nothing that has been missed after about fifty years of research. The research began in the 1950s, accelerated in the 1970s, through the 1990s and into today and has been the work of thousands of people. There is no basis for arguing that human activity is not the cause of these problems. We produce 25 percent of the world's greenhouse gases in our country. We are 3 percent of the world's population, but we produce 25 percent of the greenhouse gases. Our military produces more greenhouse gases than most countries of the world; it produces 2.5 percent itself.

Of course, nobody wants to admit they are wrong. We all have these defense mechanisms, and they have been linked to survival. It is hard to say, "I was wrong." We want to find some way of shading it so that we do not look bad, but we are wrong and we have made a mistake and we need to correct it. Only we can correct it. Only we can reduce this, and that means moving away from fossil fuels. We know exactly what to do. We know it will be inconvenient. We know that it is not always going to be easy for everybody, but we know exactly what to do.

We have 650,000 years of data and we can see what has happened as a result of fossil fuels. We have moved outside of all the measures for greenhouse gases from the past 650,000 years. We have moved the world outside the parameters we might say are natural.

The report concludes that it is a 90 percent probability that it is because of our fossil fuel burning. Scientists can never say 100 percent; they say 90 percent, which is their highest level of confidence that something caused something. If I hit the ground rather than the ceiling when I jump, it is 90 percent likely that it is because of gravity.

If we continue on the trend that we are currently on, we are going to have the largest population of people over age one hundred in history in the next few years in the United States. People are living to be a century. In the span of a single lifetime, we could move the world beyond this 2-degree change.

For twenty thousand years, we have lived within a 1-degree fluctuation. The average global temperature has never moved outside that 1-degree band. We know that, historically, it has moved out as far as 2 degrees. We are on the course for pushing it out to 4 degrees. People say they cannot even model the scale of storms, drought or heat waves that would be associated with a 4-degree temperature change. Already at 2 degrees, they are predicting that our planet will be unlike anything we have ever known. We clearly want to move off this trajectory that we are on. We have enough time to stabilize this, to change things.

We have to do something. If we do not, all of these problems that we are seeing are going to worsen. They will get worse until they reach what scientists call a *tipping point*. The tipping point will be the point at which our models no longer can predict what is going to happen. We do not know what will happen at that point. What scientists suspect is that if we hit a tipping point, life will not be very congenial to most species. The climate will not be congenial to most species.

[Now is the time] to move toward alternative energy, which is available, to reduce consumption of fossil fuels, which we can do, to change our lifestyles a little bit, to change our technologies a little bit and to recover efficiencies. Right now, when you drive your car, 90 percent of that fossil fuel energy is dissipated into the environment. In our most efficient cars, only 10 percent drives your car. The energy transfers will never reach 100 percent, that is impossible. No matter what you do, energy is lost to the atmosphere, but right now 90 percent is lost to the atmosphere. That is tremendously inefficient. We are moving very aggressively and very steeply upwards in terms of fossil fuel consumption.

If we do not change, severe weather events, dramatic changes in microbial activity and disease outbreaks, massive flooding, massive water scarcity, changes in the supply and demand for food and energy, all this combined will cause economic disruptions that economists cannot model. We can model the natural changes somewhat. We do not yet know how to model the social changes as well, so analysts just say "massive disruptions." Is that disruption on a global scale? Nobody knows. Massive food shortages, disease outbreaks, mass population movements and government confusion—these are going to place high demands throughout the world.

If there is a global disease outbreak, what is our plan in this country? If there is an outbreak of bird flu, for example, we will send our military over, because we have no one else to send. We do not have a citizen peace corps that we can send.

That is our only plan, because that is the only organization where we have thousands of people who are prepared to leave the next day to go and do something—and serve. Those are the only people in our country we can send abroad. We send them abroad for an earthquake today, storm, tornado or flood tomorrow, disease outbreak, crime, war. We send these guys, mostly eighteen- to twenty-year-olds, to deal with complicated things they are not always trained to deal with.

What we need, of course, is some sort of citizen peace corps so we can send our talent out there, so we can organize and deploy those who want to deal with these problems and who can understand these problems. We should encourage our youth to join a citizen peace corps, arm them with science knowledge, and pay for their university education when they return. When we send the military, we are using the wrong tool, and a very expensive tool, and we are using it more and more often because the problem is getting worse and worse.

There are going to be a lot of famines in the days ahead. There will be a need to distribute food to help people who are moving, to build shelter, temporary housing and permanent housing. All of these needs are getting more acute. The number is enormous. When 20 million people move as they did in Bangladesh during that summer, that is a lot of people. When desertification starts to move people, they need housing. Think of when the Soviets invaded Afghanistan, about 3.5 million people moved into northern Pakistan. Pakistan had no strategy for dealing with that many people. I have been to several of the refugee camps there. They had no strategy for housing, energy, water, waste management or food supply. They were at a loss. We are going to see more of those situations.

We are already facing large-scale threats, and we are in danger of watching our position, our capacity, our human capital, military capital, financial capital disappear if we do not try to get to the roots of the problem.

The last thing I want to do is show you the parts of the world that are already experiencing water scarcity, all through Central America, Africa, the Middle East, South Asia and that is the part of the world that is in the front lines of climate change. Those are the parts of the world where the situation is going to get intensely worse over the next twenty years.

Unless we invest in solving problems, the problems of the world will get worse. We are showing that we can make smaller and smaller iPods and faster and faster computers, and about 6 billion people of the world do not need those things. They need energy, water, housing, hope and dignity.

We could be using a little bit more of our tremendous capacity to work on these things, and a little bit less to get everybody another different colored iPod or a faster computer. Right now, I watch my students go through a computer every year. Every 15 minutes, they have a new technical gadget. It does not improve their lives; it is just this massive sort of frivolous use of the world's resources and time. We need to find ways to bring some of the sort of bounty that we have enjoyed for two hundred years into the rest of the world. We have a responsibility. It is not just in our interest. We have a moral responsibility. We are a large measure of the cause of this particular problem. We have a responsibility to be a large measure of the solution to this particular problem.

Let me conclude with a few words on a very important text: the 1999 UN Declaration and Programme of Action on a Culture of Peace. It identifies eight action areas. I will read them to you:

1. Fostering a culture of peace through education

2. Promoting sustainable economic and social development

3. Promoting respect for all human rights

4. Ensuring equality between women and men

5. Fostering democratic participation

6. Advancing understanding, tolerance and solidarity

7. Supporting participatory communication and the free flow of information and knowledge

8. Promoting international peace and security

I challenge you all to do something in each one of these areas. Buddhism has an eightfold path to end suffering. Perhaps we can think of this Programme of Action as an eightfold path to restore dignity to politics and bring hope to change.

Questions and Answers

AUDIENCE MEMBER 1: After all that incredible information, I just wanted to hold up this magazine. It is called *The Nation, Surviving the Climate Crisis*. There is an extraordinary amount of hopeful information about how we can change things. These giant windmills that will make energy just from the wind. There are amazing things out there if we have the force; people calling their representatives in Congress saying, "Put more money into this technology, so that we can get our energy in a clean way, so we do not have to be dependent on fossil fuel."

AUDIENCE MEMBER 2: Yes, I have heard all of this many times, for example, when I saw Al Gore's movie (*An Inconvenient Truth*). What I want
to know is what we are going to do when we keep electing a Congress
that does not go there and represent us. In the last election, the message was loud and clear that we wanted this war over, and yet they did
not override the president's veto. What are we going to do when what
we need is a change in Washington? I have never been a very political
person, and I belong to a grassroots organization trying to get a department of peace underneath the president. What I want to know is what
are we going to do when we keep having people in Congress who
obviously must have some idea of what is happening, and they are not
doing anything about it. What can we do?

DR. MATTHEW: we have 300 million people, a democratic system and,
depending on definitions, probably around 5 percent of the population is politically engaged. Essentially 95 percent of the population
sits back and complains. They say: "I do not care. I do not like the
situation in Iraq, but I am not going to do anything. I am going to sit
here and watch TV." I worked in Washington, D.C., for four years.
Congress responds to the people who are there lobbying them. Our
eighteen- to twenty-five-year-olds, they do not vote, and they do not
become involved politically. They have the capacity to reshape this
country dramatically. Politics has become unattractive. People do not
want to participate in it. People do not want to campaign. They do not
want to force or bring up new issues. They sit back, and they are pas-
sively fed by television. We are a democracy. A democracy requires
that we become engaged politically. It requires that we attend meetings, that we make that extra effort, that we send letters, that we do
things. If we don't, of course, nothing is going to change.

You are right. Many, many people in this country disagree with the
government on Iraq, on terrorism, on stem cell research, on Cuba, on
all of these issues. Gay marriage, they disagree with the government's
position, but they don't do anything. I think that one thing we have
to do is get involved. That is the beauty of a democracy—we can say
what we want; we can do what we want.

Today there are some real signs of light. America's youth are exper-
imenting with information technology, and politics will respond to

this. Everyone here can support Internet politics, join discussions, make donations, send email to our people in Congress. We are tired of war, we disagree with torture, we want alternative energy, we want to help alleviate poverty here and abroad, we want to expand the zone of dignity and peace. That is what our country is all about, and we should keep reminding our politicians of this. We are a long way from exhausting all the opportunities our democracy affords for progress and change, for doing what is right instead of what is easy.

AUDIENCE MEMBER 3: First of all, thank you. I think what you are doing is great. It is very encouraging. I just wanted to say that I am a member of the SGI-USA in Orange County, and years ago we took the initiative to start cleaning up a park, because the only dwellers there were drug addicts and the park was very dirty. There is a beautiful lake there, but at that time, the lake was so polluted because of neglect. The birds were dying. We had beautiful swans there, ducks, geese and cranes. They were not coming back to the lake because they were actually floating dead on the water. Some SGI-USA members took the initiative and started raking the dirt from the water and started raking the park and picking up plastic and picking up whatever people threw there. We had our first Earth Day celebration at that park three years ago. Last year, we repeated it. The park is so beautiful now. The birds are coming back. The people are coming back. This year, the people who live in that area are starting to take initiative on their own. We moved out to a different park where we had another Earth Day celebration. I truly believe that if we take a stand and do something ourselves, the government will start listening, but if we don't, then the government will never change.

DR. MATTHEW: I think that is a wonderful story. You know, I have spent my entire life trying to get people to do something. I have never met a single person, not a single person in my life, who has decided, "I am going to help land mine survivors," or "I am going to petition the government to sign this treaty," or "I am going to work on this," who five or ten years later did not look back and say: "I am amazed at what I achieved. This is the best thing that I ever did. I am so glad I did it."

If you decide to do something, the opportunity to have an impact is enormous. If every one of us in this room decided, "I am going to make one little change at the community level, the neighborhood level or a household level," then it adds up. It makes a difference. We can all see some level of transformation; every single person can, with ourselves, with our families, with our neighborhoods, and all the way up to inside the beltway. We cannot simply sit and complain. We actually have to do something. We cannot wait for somebody else to do it. We have to say, "Why not me?" So, congratulations on taking action.

July 21, 2007
Santa Monica, California

We Must Become the Change We Seek

Seven Ways To Build a Culture of Peace

Michael D'Innocenzo

*Professor of History and The Harry H. Wachtel Distinguished Teaching
Professor for the Study of Nonviolent Social Change, Hofstra University*

As the Chair of the Advisory Board of the Center
for Civic Engagement, Michael D'Innocenzo is
working to strengthen democratic values by
encouraging students to actively participate as
knowledgeable citizens in their campus, local,
state, national and global communities. The CCE is
founded on the premises that students who are
engaged in their communities are more satisfied
with their lives and social environment, including
their university experience; that those who learn
about civic engagement while young are likely to
remain engaged, thus strengthening the democratic fabric; that specific activities and skills make
for engaged citizens, and that these activities and
skills can be encouraged and fostered through
sustained deliberative and dialogic programs; and
that students equipped with civic engagement
experiences and skills can more effectively move
from awareness to action.

Professor D'Innocenzo's emphasis on becoming
attentive citizens and seeking reliable knowledge

particularly address the fifth and seventh action
areas of the United Nations Programme of Action on
a Culture of Peace: Fostering democratic participation and supporting participatory communication
and the free flow of information and knowledge.

It's a special pleasure for me to be here as part of the SGI-USA-sponsored Culture of Peace Distinguished Speakers Series, and there are a lot of reasons for that. It was our particular pleasure at Hofstra University to be sponsors with the SGI-USA and with Morehouse College of the Gandhi, King, Ikeda: A Legacy of Building Peace exhibition, which helped us to launch our new Center for Civic Engagement. This has been a great boon for Hofstra, and I am sure we will do a lot of work together as time goes on.

I am delighted to be here and to have made friends with so many wonderful people, developed associations with them as well as the Buddhist humanism that is represented by this organization. I have also been inspired because of the course I taught focusing on Gandhi, King and Dr. Ikeda and by Dr. Ikeda's writings and advocacy for a culture of peace and justice. He truly walks in the path of Gandhi and King. It has been a privilege for us to develop and learn about the depths of those associations, and for me in particular to have read so many of his books.

I also want to celebrate the continuing relationship that we have with the SGI-USA, the projects that we are planning for the future and one particularly that resonates closely with one of Dr. Ikeda's strongest themes, the importance of working for nonproliferation of nuclear weapons and for nuclear disarmament. It's a huge, huge, issue and we are going to share some of the work on that. I know the fiftieth anniversary is coming up this year [2007] of the SGI's commitment to that purpose.

I am also delighted to be here in the context of the United Nation's Decade for a Culture of Peace and Non-violence for the Children of the

World. It is sad to say that a lot of people are not aware that the United Nations has a Decade for a Culture of Peace and Non-violence for the Children of the World. It is also sad to say that the decade spans from 2001 to 2010, so we only have two-and-a-half years left to go. There is a lot [of work] left before us, and I think we have a chance to bring about some more effective change.

Like Dr. Ikeda, I believe that we all have a responsibility to ignite a sense of possibility in people and in nations. Like Dr. Ikeda, I believe in the innate goodness of people and in the feasibility for lasting and significant change. Like Dr. Ikeda, I believe that people can be inspired to imagine and act for the public good, that we can help to create more advocates for *res publica*—for the public life rather than the selfish individual life. Like Dr. Ikeda, I believe that leaders and citizens have a responsibility to create conditions for people to tap their potential in order to make a difference when they join together to work for the common good.

[There is] an old folk song called "Make a Difference." It is a rousing, terrific, spirited song about making a difference, about how people can stand up individually but particularly together to make a difference.

I am inspired by Dr. Ikeda's and the SGI's commitment to these goals and values, and we are certainly not alone. The encouraging news is that more and more people are becoming involved in seeking these kinds of changes—the transformational changes that we are committed to—of non-violence and peace and justice.

I also want to celebrate Richard Harwood, who is the author of a book called *Redeeming Hope* and who has a blog that I recommend to you called The Harwood Public Innovator, Imagine and Act for the Public Good. It certainly speaks to the kind of values that Dr. Ikeda and the SGI represent and represents the ideals for which many of us are striving. I particularly liked the title of Dr. Ikeda's 2006 peace proposal, *The New Era of the People, Forging a Global Network of Robust Individuals.* I like that idea of robust individuals.

My goal tonight is to explore some of the ways to foster robust individuals. I take the title of my talk from Gandhi's great statement and commitment.

Then I remembered that Dr. Ikeda has seven paths himself to a culture of peace and justice [a reference to Dr. Ikeda's book *For the Sake of*

Peace: Seven Paths to Global Harmony, Middleway Press]. Mine are a little different.

I think there are as many ways to foster and engage civic society as there are caring people. I would like to focus mostly on the values and process of trying to build a society of greater peace and justice.

Seven Ways To Build a Culture of Peace and Justice

1. NURTURE ATTENTIVE CITIZENS.

You may think that is self-evident. All of us know of the existence of Attention Deficit Disorder, but not many are aware of Attention Data Deficit Disorder. In fact, there are a lot of people who are not aware of much of what is going on. As my good friend [Harry Chapin]—a force for good, Long Island Cares, world hunger, civil rights and many other things—used to say: "To know is to care. To care is to act. To act is to have the chance to make a difference." It all begins with a sense of awareness, with a sense of raised consciousness, and that can only happen if people are paying attention.

Several years ago, there was a major study published about American government and politics in society. It had the embarrassing title, "A Nation of Spectators." The extent to which people are onlookers in the bleachers, they are not in the activity; they are being acted upon by someone else instead of being a force for change. We need to learn to be better models for our children and one another. It is a citizen's duty, indeed it is a human duty, to be aware of what is happening in politics, society and the world and to be cognizant of how leaders, no matter what their political party is, act in our names.

Harvard University has a website called "The Vanishing Voter" (www .hks.harvard.edu/presspol/research/vanishing_voter/) and one could look at it. They do an analysis about why, with all the political innovation we have had in our country, we have one of the lowest voting participation rates in the world. What I would say here simply is that there are lots of good people who are disengaged, and it is not all their fault. I think the challenge is that there are people who are capable of doing better and doing good. The question becomes how do we get them more engaged?

Positive change will only be feasible when we can foster more attentive civic engagement. That's my first goal.

2. CLARIFY IDENTITY.

This is certainly a big issue for Gandhi, King and Ikeda. All of us have multiple levels of identity. We are male, we are female, we are ethnic, we are religious, we are politically affiliated, our residence, our nationality. I am an Italian-American male who lives in Long Island, in New York, in the United States of America—all of those things are part of my identity.

Martin Luther King emphasized, as Dr. Ikeda does and certainly Gandhi did as well, and I quote Dr. King on this, "Every nation must now develop an overriding loyalty to mankind as a whole." We have got to get beyond this narrowness of identity.

Dr. King expressed that view many times, most strongly in the most important speech he ever gave. Most people think that was the speech he gave in 1963 at the Lincoln Memorial, the "I Have a Dream" speech. That was a great speech, but it was the second most important speech. The most important speech that Dr. King gave was at Riverside Church in New York City on April 4, 1967, when he spoke out against the Vietnam War and urged people everywhere to recognize that we had a shared objective in working against what he called the "triple evils" of racism, poverty and war. He said there is an interrelationship with those things. As I have seen Dr. Ikeda reinforce on many occasions, King and Gandhi have also said that peace is more than an absence of war, that one must make non-violence a way of life. In the spirit of E.M. Forster, we must connect; we must always seek to connect.

King emphasized that all our lives are interconnected, all our lives are related. I am sure many of you know his famous statement, that "Injustice anywhere is a threat to justice everywhere." Wherever Dr. King went, particularly in the South when he was trying to seek civil rights, people would say: "Get out of here. You're a troublemaker; you don't belong here."

He said, "I belong wherever there is injustice, because I am a human being and I must bear witness against injustice and try to do something about it." He also said, "Isn't it ironic that Americans tend to honor their live conformists and their dead troublemakers."

When people told him to stop causing problems, he said, "I love to study American history, and I learned that the greatest lesson of American history is the right to protest for rights." That certainly was a key to much of Dr. King's commitment.

I think this goal of having a larger identity—a global identity connecting us around the world, is the second key objective. I submit to you that one of the perspectives on this comes from the remarkable revolutionary who helped launch the American nation, Tom Paine. Actually, he helped three revolutions. He wrote *Common Sense in America*. Then he went to England, wrote *The Rights of Man*, started a reform rebellion, and then he went to France and he wrote *The Age of Reason*. Then he wrote his motto.

Here is Tom Paine's motto. What a motto! "The world is my country. My mind is my church, and my religion is to do good." It is hard to improve on a motto like that, I think.

3. SEEK RELIABLE KNOWLEDGE.

Even if we have attentive, globally focused people, they need to be able to seek reliable knowledge. Reliable knowledge is critical for people to make informed, personal and public judgment, and it is not an easy matter. Once again, there are critics who dismiss the public. The Greeks had a word—*idios*, or idiot. The word *idios* in Greek referred to people who didn't participate in politics, people who didn't vote and were uninformed about public matters. We have a lot of idiots in America, but they aren't necessarily bad people.

My friend E.J. Dionne has written two wonderful books that capture some of this. The first book is called *Why Americans Hate Politics*. Part of his assessment is that there are a lot of reasons people hate politics and do not want to participate. It is one of the best analyses, along with the Harvard Vanishing Voter Project, identifying how people are detached and not involved.

Now, ten years later, E.J. Dionne has a book of some encouragement with a great title about the American public: *They Only Look Dead*. He doesn't mean it in a condescending way. People's lives get caught up with all kinds of activities, and they get deflected from engagement and particularly from the key aspect of engagement, which Dr. Ikeda describes when he says, "You must always be inquiring, you must always be searching." That is the key to making a democracy work and to making civilization work better: to have reliable knowledge on which one can make informed judgments that can lead to better public policy.

It is not easy, even for attentive, well-intentioned people, because issues are complex, no matter how smart you are. People's lives are busy. This is the part the Harvard Vanishing Voter Project points out. When the issues are complex, people's eyes glaze over sometimes, and they say they can't figure that out.

I have been involved. I have run for Congress. I have been involved politically and a lot of other ways. I actually lost when I ran for Congress, leading some people to raise the question, "Is it better to have run and lost than never to have run at all?" The answer is *yes*.

When I was in politics, one guy who was a real power broker came up to me and said, "D'Innocenzo, you will never succeed in politics, unless you learn to be more boring." His argument was that you don't want to engage people, because they will pay attention, and they won't like what you are doing. Hold the meetings during the daytime when most people are working and can't attend. Don't give out much information. Control the flow of information. A lot of politicians still operate that way; they don't want to engage the public because then the public is likely to pay too close attention.

I think he was paying me an indirect compliment, although I am not sure all my students would agree that I have succeeded in not being boring. Beyond that, it doesn't take much sophistication to be aware of how much manipulation goes on by politicians of many stripes, manipulation of data and opinion in so many ways.

It's amazing how much the media trivializes what is going on. I don't want to read another thing about Paris Hilton or Lindsay Lohan or whoever that other woman is. It makes you ask how much attention [does the media] give to the issues of nuclear disarmament or nuclear proliferation, something that could end our lives or affect the whole world.

The media has become complex in a lot of ways. We are a long way removed from Edward R. Murrow. I will give his conclusion at the end of this talk in a little while. In the age of muckrakers, in the age of investigative journalists who would train the spotlight and hold those in power accountable for their actions and their programs so citizens could evaluate them, too many people in the media today are "buck rakers." They are making a lot of money, and they aren't very involved. There is a whole literature about the failure of the American media. Thomas Fenton's book, appropriately called *Bad News*, argues that 9/11 [Sept. 11, 2001] could have been prevented. However bad the government was, the media should have been more attuned to what was going on and held the government accountable for its failures. The book is an account of the decline of the effectiveness of the American media. That is another whole big issue.

It's actually one of my special areas of study, and I have written a great deal about the evolvement of the American media, including a biography of William Cullen Bryant, who was the editor of the *New York Evening Post*. I still look at the *New York Post* when I can pick up a clean copy on the train or the subway. I certainly wouldn't pay for it, but I do read it.

James Fallows has a book called *Breaking the News: How the Media Undermine American Democracy*. Frank Rich's recent book, listen to the title, [is] *The Greatest Story Ever Sold: The Decline and Fall of Truth from 9/11 to Katrina*. Most Americans are still unaware that *The New York Times* was forced to apologize repeatedly for how badly it covered the issues leading to the war in Iraq in 2002 and 2003. *The New York Times* is as good a newspaper as we have, but it apologized on page 14. Luckily, the public editor—and one of the good things about *The New York Times* is that it has a public editor who gets a two-year, no-fire contract who can be an ombudsman—said: "The readers complained and they were right, and that story should have been on page 1. The finger should have been pointed at [*New York Times* reporter] Judith Miller, who [*New York Times* columnist] Maureen Dowd said was the 'woman of mass destruction.' *The New York Times* finally [let her go]. She now writes for the *Wall Street Journal*."

That is a very complex story, but *The New York Times* would never have done it if it hadn't been for *The Nation* magazine, and especially for the *New York Review of Books* and Michael Massing, who said *The New York Times* had been inept. When [Judith Miller] said she was just reporting what Ahmed Chalabi and others told her, Maureen Dowd responded,

"Investigative reporting is not stenography" (*The New York Times*, Oct. 22, 2005).

Too much of journalism has ended up being stenography. In *The New York Times*, this was a powerful, powerful story that led to a lot of demoralization here and around the world. The question is how can citizens focus on evidence over assertion? Anybody can say anything, but how can we validate it? How can we check it? There is a lot of one-shot journalism; important stories appear once, often not on page 1, and they disappear. However, Barry Bonds is in the newspaper every day, and other trivial things, but we don't have a sustained focus on matters of significance that can affect our lives.

I don't want to go back to Orwell, but he certainly set the stage for this. Orwell established the brilliance of 1984. It was published in 1948. He just flipped the years to make it seem futuristic as a literature of warning. Of course, the book is just brilliant. He establishes the Ministry of Truth, which is really the Ministry of Lies, but if you call it the Ministry of Truth, then people will believe it. That's newspeak; it's the "big lie" technique. You keep saying it over and over again and soon, people say, "Well, you have got a Ministry of Truth, but it is really the Ministry of Lies."

The reason it is the Ministry of Lies is that not only does it use secrecy, which is a big issue in any society, but it has memory holes where it destroys the records so the public does not have access to what is going on. If you can get rid of the past, then you create what is going on. Orwell has that brilliant statement, "Whoever controls the present, controls the past; and whoever controls the past, controls the future." If you control access to the information people get, Orwell says, "Political language is too often designed to make lies sound truthful, murder respectable, and to give the appearance of solidity to pure wind." It is sad to say there is too much of that. There is too much of that around the world, and I think we have that challenge of how we hold leaders accountable for this.

Any leader can be sincere and make a mistake. No one is infallible. But we certainly have a right to expect leaders to recognize and correct errors and not try to manipulate and dissemble information. No party has a monopoly on that. We have seen that happen at different times. The irony, of course, is that when Daniel Ellsberg, who was a big supporter of the war in Iraq, got involved in the Pentagon Papers project, which has another whole interesting aspect, and saw the lying and manipulation that went on about the war in Vietnam by Democratic President Lyndon Johnson, he wanted to release it to show how we got into that quagmire. Nixon tried to prevent it because Nixon was doing the same thing and worse. All the Watergate papers were not about Nixon, they were about Johnson.

Ellsberg risked going to jail for a hundred years, and [his action] led to Nixon's resignation because he stood up and brought that focus to the public. Again, it was overcoming the secrecy and the extent to which things were buried. As J. William Fulbright said in the sixties, it represents the arrogance of power. We are not going to have a better world, no matter what political party people are in, if they are arrogant and live in a bubble, and they think that somehow they are anointed. You know, we have seen that with both parties; certainly, Lyndon Johnson did it in the Vietnam War, and there may be people later who have done it as well, but I don't want to get partisan.

The year 2007 is the fiftieth anniversary of the Southern Christian Leadership Conference, the organization that was established by Martin Luther King Jr. to try to grow out of the Southern religious groups and bring about an effort to get people to pay attention to injustice and how to address the injustice. I want to mention very quickly King's six-stage approach to deal with injustice. I went to the Martin Luther King non-violent training programs in the sixties and I was privileged to be involved, although I had friends who were badly beaten up. One of my friends in Louisiana almost died before they removed his kidney that was split by someone kicking him when he was demonstrating non-violently.

Look at King's approach. I think it is a model for how we seek reliable knowledge in terms of this goal. Those of you who have read Dr. Ikeda, you will see a lot of similarities in that regard as well. First, King says, gather data and evidence, so that any reasonably attentive person can see the merit of the reliable knowledge. It doesn't mean people will accept it, but you make that effort to say, 'I am not just saying this, and I am not engaging in name-calling.' It is like a lawyer building a case so that the evidence will speak so loudly that you don't demonize and personalize. You just point out with the evidence that it is an injustice. Fair-minded people should be able to recognize that.

The second step is always to strive for negotiation to resolve the problems. Again, King never demonized the opposition. He didn't engage in name-calling. He said, in effect: 'Here is the data. We want to meet with you and deal with this.' Some of King's opponents agreed, but they wouldn't do enough. King said that, in such cases, we have to make a judgment. Indeed, Dr. Ikeda emphasizes the importance of gradualism.

There is a lot of debate about how fast we should move. Some of Dr. King's critics said negotiating with the opposition was pointless because they wouldn't move fast enough. King said, if you are not compromising principles and you have reasonable progress, it's important to give people a chance to respond when you present them with the reality.

There is a second benefit in negotiating, and that is if people won't negotiate or won't respond, you then have the high ground. You can say: 'Hey, we reached out. We didn't call you names. We didn't say you were bad people. We are talking about the actions and the injustice and not saying that you are bad people. We are trying to address what happened here.'

The third step for King was to use every lawful means to call attention to the injustice to the larger public. This meant using the First Amendment. The glory of the United States, the First Amendment—the right to assemble peaceably, the right to demonstrate, the freedom of the press and freedom of speech. King first went through all of those steps and, as Gandhi always emphasized, injustice was made visible.

Again, people aren't going to pay attention unless you can bring it onto their radar screen. King understood the importance of the media and trying to get those stories out, again, not in a demonizing way, but saying, 'Look at these things.' The brilliance about King in the "I Have a Dream" speech is, as he said: "I still have a dream. It is a dream deeply rooted in the American dream." He was asking the United States to live up to the Declaration of Independence. That was very powerful, and it is one of the values of getting any group of people to say, 'We have got high standards, we have humane standards.' Once people say something positive and constructive, others say, 'Gee, we would like to help you live up to them.' King was brilliant in taking that approach.

The fourth aspect for King was that if this process still doesn't work, then you have to take a more severe step of civil disobedience. You have to be willing to be arrested, be willing to disrupt society and traffic non-violently, doing it in public and daylight, unlike the Ku Klux Klan, which covered themselves with masks and rode at night so no one knew what they were doing. King's non-violence was public and open, saying, in effect: 'We are willing to be punished for it, because we think we have to bear witness against unjust laws, and certainly Gandhi was a major advocate of that. Even if we pay a price for it, our suffering may shame the people who are doing this or the people who are bystanders and not intervening to do something about it.' That was the non-violence approach.

The fifth factor was related to non-violence, and it goes to the core, I think again, of both Gandhi and Dr. Ikeda, what King called "self-purification." Dr. Ikeda calls it a kind of inner transformation, but this is a huge challenge. How do you prepare people who are going to confront haters—people who want to beat them up, people who want to kill them, people who will deny their humanity—and not hate the haters and not retaliate and have a humane view that you want to, at some point, be able to work things out with them. You practically have to be saint-like, and part of King's brilliance was to inspire people to do that. Not all black activists did that obviously. Stokely Carmichael and some others said, in effect, 'We are mad as hell, man, and we are going to start hitting them back.' One could understand their rage, and that ended up being a tension with Dr. King.

Finally, the sixth step for Dr. King was reconciliation. You don't make society better by vanquishing and defeating an adversary. You try to help [your opponents] come to a realization of their humanity and understand the circumstances in which the bad conduct has occurred. You focus on the actions rather than the people. The people are redeemable if they can see this. The openness to reconciliation was always there.

The fourth factor is next, which I take from E.L. Doctorow, who says we must foster a community of discourse. Certainly, Dr. Ikeda highlights over and over and lives the idea of dialogue. How do you bring people together to exchange views, to expand their horizons and recognitions?

4. FOSTER A COMMUNITY OF DISCOURSE.

Attentive individuals who seek reliable knowledge need to come together in public spaces where they can get beyond their different backgrounds to seek some common ground. Dr. Ikeda writes about this in several of his books about the tradition of American town meetings. These American town meetings sometimes have been overly romanticized, but the ideal of a town meeting is that people come face to face. In these meetings, you have a chance to explore the pros and cons of different issues, why people hold certain views and what their values are. Giving people a chance to air those views helps to clarify what steps you might make in trying to move toward an informed public judgment, and that's a shared endeavor. It is an endeavor that can be done less through debate than through deliberation.

I am very proud of my work with the Kettering Foundation. Since the early 1990s, the foundation has worked on strategies to strengthen democracy. The primary question addressed by its research today is "What does it take to make democracy work as it should?" Their goal is to bring people together in civic engagement, which is not adversarial. To explore very complex issues takes time; it takes people who are willing to talk, and I think that is part of the goal and the second part of number four.

The last thing I would say about the fourth item is Dr. King's response to the Kerner Commission Report shortly before he was killed in 1968, which said, "Our nation is moving toward two societies, one black, one white, separate and unequal." He was so perceptive in so many ways. King said: "Men hate each other because they fear each other. They fear each other because they don't know each other. They don't know each other because they can't communicate with each other. They can't communicate with each other because they are separated from each other." That was a sense of what we need to do to move toward a community of discourse.

5. CULTIVATE PEOPLE OF VIRTUE.

My fifth factor is that communities of discourse work best if we have the involvement of people of virtue. That is a huge issue for all of the great thinkers and for those of us who worked on the Gandhi, King, Ikeda project; all three of those philosophers thought about how to foster virtue. They always thought about the best ways to foster virtue. King, as I mentioned, called it self-purification. Like Gandhi, he said that non-violence is not a tactic to get a goal. Non-violence must be a way of life. It must permeate everything you do.

Dr. Ikeda, in his book *For the Sake of Peace,* has a chapter called "The Path of Self-Mastery." Here he writes in views that Gandhi and King would support 100 percent: "[The greater] self always seeks ways of alleviating the pain and augmenting the happiness of others, here, amid the realities of everyday life" (p. 36). I want to emphasize that [Dr. Ikeda doesn't] say that the big reward is coming in the next life.

I mentioned that because Dr. King, most people don't know, had a lot of problems with a lot of black ministers, whom he referred to as "sky pilots," because he said they are trying to fly people to heaven. He said, "Any black minister who spends more time talking about the big payoff in heaven than addressing the real problems here on earth is being irresponsible." King got kicked out of the black Baptist ministry because he challenged those views. I think Dr. Ikeda pointed to that as well, that it is here and now, not some then and there where you do it. Dr. Ikeda and others loved to cite Socrates, of course, "The unexamined life is not worth living."

6. ENGAGE IN PUBLIC ACTIVISM.

The cultivation of private virtue must entail, then, the responsibility of public activism. You don't achieve glory by yourself, no matter how good you are. I am so struck by the erudition of Dr. Ikeda and the people he cites from so many cultures, combining their perspectives. He cites Ralph Waldo Emerson, who said, "What is man born for but to be a reformer, a renouncer of lies, a restorer of truth and good." How do we move from the sense of personal virtue, from the personal to the social? Theodore Roosevelt, a complex man who won the Nobel Peace Prize and helped to democratize America in many ways, said: "Words without action are intellectual debauchery. One must enter the arena and strive to do the deeds."

What King said at Riverside Church in 1967 is an example of this. Lyndon Johnson had passed the Civil Rights Act, had passed the Voting Rights Act. He did more for civil rights than any president in American history did, and the question for King was what could he do? How far could he go in criticizing this president who had gone through a transformation on race issues?

What he did initially was to send out Coretta, his wife, who was more radical than Martin. When she was in college, she joined the organization that Jane Addams had founded. Jane Addams was the first American woman to win the Nobel Peace Prize, and the organization she founded was the Women's International League for Peace and Freedom, and for that and many other things, she got the Nobel Peace Prize. Most people don't know that Coretta Scott King was a member of WILPF, and she went around speaking out on these issues when Dr. King had to be a little more careful politically.

At Riverside Church, on April 4, 1967, one year to the day before his assassination, Dr. King said: "There comes a time when silence is betrayal. I agree that the hottest places in hell are reserved for those who in a period of moral crisis maintain their neutrality." King apologized for not coming forward sooner and speaking out. It takes acts of courage to bear witness, to speak truth to power, no matter what the power is, but there is a multiplier effect when more people join you in doing it. That's where the associations can build staying power and greater impact. That's why an organization such as the Soka Gakkai International and many others have a chance to bring people together who share values and can have a greater impact by doing that.

7. AVOID BECOMING PRISONERS OF THE PRESENT.

We must take care to avoid becoming prisoners of the present. My friend Howard Zinn, who is now about eighty years old, has been a great activist. Howard Zinn was one of the few white teachers at Spellman College in the early 1960s. He was an advocate of change and a critic of racism. He was a freedom writer. He participated in sit-ins with people of color, and he got fired from Spellman College by the black male president of Spellman College, because maybe white people wouldn't give any more money if Spellman had people causing trouble like that.

In the same way, John Lewis—one of the great freedom writers and civil rights activists—got chilled by the president of his college in Nashville, Tennessee, when he wanted to start an NAACP (National Association for the Advancement of Colored People) chapter with a black presence. [The fear was that] people might think [the college was] too radical.

Howard Zinn got fired at Spellman College, but two years ago when

Beverly Tatum, an African American herself, became the president of Spellman College, she invited Howard Zinn back and gave him an honorary degree. These are examples of avoiding being prisoners of the present, because we get a perspective of what has come before, and we are not just overwhelmed by the bad news or by what seems not to work now.

If you take the larger view, look what has happened. We have made a lot of progress on racism, and there is more to go, but look at what has happened in fifty years. Look at how many strides have been made for women's rights and equality, and the advances in recognizing the inclusion of gay people and people of different sexual orientation. These things were off the radar screen earlier.

Being a prisoner of the present is like having a blackout or as though you just woke up today, and you are only looking at what is in the news without having a sense of what has gone on before.

I just want to say in my big wrap-up that a culture of peace really requires a hall of fame of role models who show what can be done, through not only their individual actions but also their ability to work with organizations and groups. There are a lot of wonderful examples. I already mentioned Jane Addams, William Lloyd Garrison, who were part of the 1 percent of the American population who started speaking out against slavery. It doesn't often happen quickly, but this is an example of how things can build. Susan B. Anthony, who was at it for sixty years. Frederick Douglass, Eleanor Roosevelt, who almost single-handedly brought about the Universal Declaration of Human Rights at the United Nations. There is a book that I like very much called *The Impossible Will Take a Little While* [by Paul Loeb]. If you not only have hope but also have commitment to make these things happen, [they will].

Václav Havel, Nelson Mandela and Jimmy Carter are now part of a group called The Elders. They are going to be roving ombudsmen around the world. They said, in effect: 'We may only be alive for ten more years or so, but no one is going to say we are out for money or power. We are going to try and make the world better.' Therefore, we have the roving Elders, and in a few more years, I might be qualified to be part of that.

Gloria Steinem often emphasized that lasting social change is constructed the way houses are, and that is from the bottom up. That involves not only good leaders but also lots of smart, attentive people who will be engaged. When Martin Luther King received the Nobel Peace Prize (I am writing a study of the impact of the Nobel Peace Prize on King), he gave an acceptance speech in which he talked about the tens of thousands of people of all races and many religions who are committed to making social change. He said: "Every time I take a flight, I am always mindful of the many people who make a successful journey possible—the known pilots and the unknown ground crew.... You honor the ground crew without whose labor and sacrifices the jet flights to freedom could never have left the earth."

Václav Havel refers to the power of the powerless, that numbers matter when you go through those kinds of changes. To act for anyone is to create at least the possibility of changing the world. To act together with others can make the possible more plausible.

I like Robert F. Kennedy's view. Kennedy was one of those people who evolved and emerged in a lot of good ways over time. When he said, "Each time a man [or woman] stands up for an ideal or acts to improve the lot of others or strikes out against injustice, he [or she] sends forth a tiny ripple of hope, and crossing each other from a million different centers of energy and daring, those ripples build a current that can sweep down the mightiest walls of oppression and resistance" (Day of Affirmation address, June 6, 1966, Capetown, South Africa). I think that is a notion of what people can do together.

Stephen Spender looks at it from the other perspective about what the leader can do when he writes: "I think continually of those who were truly great.... / The names of those who in their lives fought for life / Who wore at their hearts the fire's center. / Born of the sun they traveled a short while towards the sun, / And left the vivid air signed with their honor" ("The Truly Great," poem written in 1933).

Theodore Roosevelt—who was born not far from here, I think, on 26th or 28th street (in New York)—frequently said, "This won't be a good country for any of us unless we learn how to make it a better nation for all of us." A century later, we have to update Theodore Roosevelt and say this will not be a good globe for any of us unless we improve it for all of us.

I conclude now with a few lines from a poem that Dr. King very much appreciated by Edwin Markham, when he wrote, "He drew a circle that shut me out—/ Heretic, a rebel, a thing to flout. / But Love and I had the wit to win: We drew a circle that took him in!" ("Outwitted").

Questions and Answers

AUDIENCE MEMBER 1: I am a teacher in Brooklyn, and one of the things that troubles me a lot is the separation between ages, young people and old people. You mentioned that briefly. Could you talk on that just a little bit?

PROFESSOR D'INNOCENZO: This has become my major project now, partly because I am one of the old people, whom I prefer to call the elders, because it is an anthropological term that signifies experience and perhaps wisdom that comes with experience.

I do have a chapter coming out in a book (in 2008). The book is titled *Deliberation and the Work of Higher Education* (Kettering Foundation, 2008). My chapter is called "From Youth Ghettos to Intergenerational Civic Engagement."

In my many years of teaching and community work, what I have discovered is the age segregation that is occurring. *Ghetto* is the word for it, and some of it is unintended. It is a passionate subject of mine. I will give you three examples.

Parents, especially high school parents, are more invested in trying to help their kids and paying huge amounts of money to get them tutors for college and so on. Even in college now, my college and others have set up a division to deal with parents. It used to be that colleges didn't want to have anything to do with parents. To an excess, they wouldn't even give the grades or anything about the students, but *The Chronicle of Higher Education* did an article last year that said now colleges have helicopter parents.

Any of you who have children who went to middle school from elementary school, the phrase *helicopter parents* described parents who, like helicopters, were hovering over the school. The reason for this was that now the kids were going to go to different classrooms, and they had anxiety about it. Helicopter parents have expanded to the high schools and even to the colleges. However, what my study and others have shown is that high school and college students almost never speak with their parents about matters of substance, about what is going on in the country and the world.

We did our surveys with residential students, all of whom have cell phones. I still don't have a cell phone, but someday I will. Almost all of them spoke to one parent every day, sometimes for a minute just to be in touch, sometimes for an hour or two, and in a way it is lovely that children keep in touch with the parents. When we asked them what they talked about, they almost never talked about what it means to be a citizen, what is happening in our country, what is happening in the world, where they read newspapers and so on. That's been true for a lot of youth, because they are doing other things, so they aren't engaged, so that's part of the challenge of engagement. But what about their parents? Where are the parents modeling this stuff?

There is a book called *The Other Parent*. It is already outmoded because it is about television. The point of *The Other Parent* is that with the husband and wife working, the more professional they are, the more exhausting it is. It's easier to put the kids in front of a TV because the parents are exhausted. That book was very disturbing. Now, of course, we are way beyond TV. We are into MySpace and YouTube. The study showed in a disturbing fashion how many people have their own TVs, how many young people have computers where their parents aren't monitoring it, not talking with them, and not even eating together. I don't blame the parents so much, because they are experiencing what sociologists now call "time poverty." Arlie Russell Hochschild referred to it as the "time bind." How many things can you do?

I think the cost is trying to get the kids to succeed but without paying attention to their character. I blame the grandparents. I always blame the grandparents. Hey, the parents are too busy; it is up to you—the elders—to model these kids. Grandparents have been doing more of it. Then, when the children go to college, of course, they are really in a youth ghetto. The only adults they encounter are their professors, and that is not reality for a lot of them.

What we found in our study is that most colleges give students access to something like a hundred TV channels free. I can't tell you how many hours that college students spend watching television. Where is the discipline to stop doing that? We are making efforts to bring people together. It is sad to say our best success has been in bringing very old people together with high school students and college students, primarily because old people are in fact more available to do it. People in their fifties, forties and thirties are so busy. The public library is one of the great public spaces in our society that has trouble attracting people in their thirties, forties and fifties.

The last thing I want to say about that is that I have made efforts to bring together young people and the elders. I write about that. What happens is when I bring young people together, the elders outnumber them, because I bring a class of thirty and there are maybe seventy or a hundred or a hundred and fifty elders, and we have a discussion on current events and perspective.

After it is over, I take the young people aside and ask for their responses. The responses go like this, "Wow! I never saw so many old people in one place." That is the first response. Then they all sit separately. They don't mingle. I let them do that at first so we can have a debriefing. Then they say: "Those old people know a lot, but they don't have anything to do. It's not as if they are going to school or working as we are. Later on, we will be able to know stuff. They do care, you know, but they have got a lot more time to do it." Then they get shamed. I don't shame them, but eventually they say, "Well, gee, maybe we should be doing some more of this."

I was asked a question earlier about whether students go through changes. This experience has literally transformed many young people, who say: "Wow, I think I better register to vote. I think I should become better informed, because there are people who are doing it and I am not being responsible." Those are encouraging signs.

AUDIENCE MEMBER 2: People don't have enough time to spend with others. I see very much with the college-age students, even if they are not in college, but that particular age group, that many of them come to me. I am a doctor and I am seeing them for treatment, and they ask me about going into a certain career. I tell them, "Instead of worrying about what school to go to, why don't you find somebody who is already employed in the field that you want to go to and ask them how they got there." I think the colleges would be better served if they brought in people who were already engaged in their communities in doing certain activities or professions in this case, but anything that could foster this sort of mentor-disciple relationship. Some careers have internships, but I think this goes beyond the formal one-to-one relationship with someone.

PROFESSOR D'INNOCENZO: That is an excellent suggestion. There is some of it but not enough. The role of mentoring can be terrific in that regard of bringing people in to do that. The internships are personal and intensive in terms of the work, so people shy away from it, but I think that can be a very powerful thing in doing it.

What we found is that when [mentoring] does happen, it is very gratifying at both ends. I mean older people like to know that what they have experienced and what they can contribute are acknowledged, recognized and appreciated. Young people become more sensitive and appreciative of the experiences and the travails that other people have gone through. The connectedness can be insightful as young people do projects and try to understand what the life cycle has been of the struggles and what it took to make accomplishments, and even to look at what people consider their failures. One of the things we try to do is to get young people to do studies of grandparents or communities of people as another way of getting at it.

AUDIENCE MEMBER 3: We live with a government that has decided we don't need a constitution, that has decided you can vote how you want but will hijack the election anyway. We live with a government that has decided to do away with the purpose behind the First Amendment. What do you do with this? How do you live with this?

PROFESSOR D'INNOCENZO: I did promise to be nonpartisan today. We do indeed live among the most troubled times in our history, I think, in lots of ways. Whether it is through sincere misguided efforts or mistakes or whether it is through hubris, however one assesses the accountability. There is a book called *Hubris*. It is our version of the arrogance of power about people who felt they knew better than anyone else did and they could impose a better system on the world. In fact, I just reviewed yesterday the book by Cullen Murphy called *Are We Rome?*, which I recommend very strongly to you.

There are many people who have written about such a thing—that we have become an empire. We are a power more than super. It is legitimate to ask about what both parties are doing in that regard. We are spending two-thirds of a trillion dollars for our military each year, not unlike the Roman Empire as it declined. We spend more on our military, as Chalmers Johnson points out, than the whole rest of the world combined.

In *Are We Rome?*, Cullen Murphy cites Eisenhower in his farewell address. Most people remember he referred to the military industrial complex. In his first draft, he actually said, "the military congressional industrial complex," because members of Congress were doling out the earmarks that helped them get reelected. That's why I didn't get elected, because it is hard to beat an incumbent. What people don't remember from that speech by Eisenhower, which went to the heart of building a culture of peace and justice, is that the power of the budget is where you choose what your priorities are. What Cullen Murphy says in *Are We Rome?* is that, like the Roman Empire, when so much of the resources are going into the military, what is left for education? What is left for health care? What is left so the bridges don't collapse in more places than Minneapolis, because the resources have been squandered? Who makes the choices on those things?

Eisenhower said, "Every gun that is made, every warship launched, every rocket fired, signifies in the final sense a theft from those who are hungry and not fed, those who are cold and not clothed" (April 16, 1953). That's pretty radical for a republican president. It is a matter of determining how you establish priorities. I think we all have the responsibility of saying we have to hold people accountable who are making decisions and the policies and look at the alternatives and evaluate what the alternatives are and see whether either is suitable or how much one needs to bring about change in that regard.

I think what Cullen Murphy says is that, like Rome, the other two things that are very powerful are the movement more and more to secrecy and the politics of fear. There are reasons to be concerned about danger, of course. If you scare people, they aren't going to be willing to do anything else. Chapter three of the book *Are We Rome?* is about the privatizing of our society and the demonizing of the government—the government is bad, and private initiative is good.

Hundreds of billions of dollars go to private groups, much of it non-bid, that gets wasted. There is no oversight, and people get rich on it.

August 9, 2007
New York

Educating Against Imperialism

Critical Pedagogy, Social Justice and the Struggle for Peace

Peter McLaren

Professor of Education, University of California Los Angeles School of Education and Information Studies

Dr. Peter McLaren is internationally recognized as one of the leading architects of critical pedagogy worldwide. He is the author, co-author, editor and co-editor of approximately forty books and monographs. Several hundred of his articles, chapters, interviews, reviews, commentaries and columns have appeared in dozens of scholarly journals and professional magazines since the publication of his first book, *Cries From The Corridor,* which was one of the top ten best-selling books in Canada in 1980 (according to *MacLean's Magazine*), initiating a countrywide debate on the status of inner-city schools. Peter McLaren's papers are housed and on permanent exhibit at the Paulo and Nita Freire Center for International Critical Pedagogy, McGill University, Montreal, Canada. Professor McLaren's book *Life in Schools* was named by an international panel of experts as one of the world's twelve most significant books in education. A special Peter McLaren Chair (La Catedra Peter McLaren) has been created at Venezuela's Bolivarian University in

Caracas. And La Fundacion McLaren has been founded by Mexican activists and scholars in Baja California and Sonora, Mexico. Two other books are *Peter McLaren, Education, and the Struggle for Liberation* (edited by Mustafa Eryaman), published by Hampton Press, and *Teaching Peter McLaren* (edited by Marc Pruyn and Luis Huerta Charles), published by Peter Lang Publishers.

Dr. McLaren's comments on the need for critical pedagogy and his emphasis on dialogue particularly support the first action item of the 1999 United Nations Declaration and Programme of Action on a Culture of Peace: Fostering a culture of peace through education. As he says, to cultivate a culture of peace, "It is crucial to approach revolutionary groups, societies or collectives by relying on dialogue and consciousness-raising among all the groups involved."

I was thinking that the theme for my discussion today could reflect some of the work that I have been doing in Latin America, particularly in Venezuela. I have been involved in this research with a friend and colleague, Professor Nathalia Jaramillo. We've been involved with Centro Internacional Miranda in Venezuela (a Chavista think tank of sorts) and we have also been doing some educational work for La Fundacion McLaren in Mexico as well as work in Cuba, South Africa and the Middle East. So perhaps I will have time to discuss some of this work with you today, even if only briefly. In the main, however, expect my discussion to be eclectic.

Since the core theme of today's event is peacemaking, I think it best if I draw heavily on a recent paper that I coauthored with two colleagues, Professor Steve Best, associate professor of humanities at the University of Texas, El Paso, and Tony Nocella, who is doing a doctorate at Syracuse University. Steve's newest book is *Animal Rights and Moral Progress: The Struggle for Human Evolution* (Rowman and Littlefield, 2007). Anthony is a visiting scholar of SUNY Cortland's Center for Ethics, Peace and Social Justice, as well as a teacher at Le Moyne College in sociology and criminology. He is the co-editor with Steve of *Terrorists or Freedom Fighters? Reflections on the Liberation of Animals* (Lantern Books, 2004) and *Igniting a Revolution: Voices in Defense of the Earth* (AK Press, 2006).

So the spine of my talk will be the paper, but there will be plenty of caesurae, or interruptions, where I will engage you extemporaneously.

As all of us know, life is going from bad to worse for those who bear the brunt of exploitation under the merciless sword arm of neoliberal capitalism and the class-racialized inequalities that continue to follow in the brutal wake of colonial history. Decisions driven by a monetary calculus—which is, more than ever, the case with the rich industrial countries at the center of the capitalist system that continue to use the economic surplus of the countries on the periphery to advance their expansionist agenda and consolidate their advantage—will only continue to reproduce the underdevelopment of peripheral capitalist countries while ensuring that the ruling classes at the core amass the vast majority of the world's wealth. Liberals airily blame events on labor's aristocrats and their penchant for greed. But that is a bit like blaming the sinking of a freighter by a submarine on water's hydrogen and oxygen molecules.

For those of us who are fortunate to have some protections by means of our social capital, our daily needs are Lilliputian in comparison to those millions who barely scrape by. State violence and corruption-fueled domestic policies are a common threat to those whose lives have been declared redundant by the aristocrats of labor and the pooh-bahs of commerce who religiously adhere to the unfettered rule of market capitalism, to those who live on the wrong side of the razor-sharp racial divide, to those who suffer most from the destruction of the ecosystem's regenerative capacities, to those who have been tragically forsaken by the political establishment and to those who have joined Marx's reserve army of labor whose "food-free diet" isn't some fashion trend for the children of

the Paris Club. Even today, decades after the so-called victory of capitalism over communism, decades after the election of Pope John Paul II and
decades after the Thatcher/Reagan revolution to abolish the welfare state,
the words *there is no alternative* weigh on the brains of the living like an
unspoken epigram in a horror tale about corporations who rule the world
with cyborg armies of the night.

Clearly, then, the current global political atmosphere is—unques-
tioningly in my mind—steeped in an intense rhetoric about political violence and terrorism. Of course, the ideological excrescence that seeps
out of the fetid fissures of this rhetoric is what is produced when public debate becomes infected with dishonesty and fear and when dialogue
is debarred in the public sphere. Amid this turbulent environment, it is
clear that scholars and practitioners need to get beyond the manufactured
fear and the historical rhetoric, much of it magniloquent and pedaled by
the corporate-state-military-media-complex, or simply what we could call
the "power complex." Instead, we need to seek a deeper understanding
of political groups that defend or deploy the tactics of economic sabo-
tage, which can refer to property destruction or armed struggle in order to
attempt to challenge and change repressive, violent and social structures.

So what I am going to talk to you about today is the importance of
dialoguing with terrorists. We'll reflect upon who gets to name who the
terrorists are and why, and who is able to undertake terrorist activities
under the banner of fighting terrorism and bringing corporate democracy to barbarous enclaves that punctuate the far corners of the world.
And all through this I will stress the importance of creating a true culture of peace by urging, in the spirit of Paulo Freire's concept of dialogue,
that we engage in critically self-reflexive communication with individuals and groups with whom many governments in principle would refuse
to negotiate.

We remain at a political impasse by refusing to dialogue with those
politically branded as terrorists. If we want to eliminate the culture of violence and move toward the culture of peace, we need to co-construct a
space of understanding so that we can see events from the perspective of
the Other, and so that the Other can do the same, and we need to cultivate a willingness to enter into uncomfortable zones of understanding—
precincts of possibility and hope—and self and social introspection.

Such understanding is important to slow down and possibly even reverse the current trend among legislative and policy-making bodies and political leaders who increasingly marginalize, demonize and exclude radical opposition groups from arenas of debate. Radical groups are anathematized as if they are all plague-ridden. Thrilling to the pulse of fighting the bad guys with the white-hot intensity of a supernova, law enforcement agencies and so-called counter-terrorism experts around the world see no alternative to the fierce repression of dissenting groups, or at least choose not to see viable alternatives to these practices, but this approach typically backfires, producing even more resistance in multiplying the very tactics it seeks to eliminate by this short-term political firefighting.

While law enforcement agencies, from their perspective, must address and take action against groups using illegal tactics, they need not always vilify them as terrorists or view their actions as imprecations or maledictions. These groups may be patriots, they may be part of the common parlance, they may advocate just causes or they may be none of these. But—and this is a central point—law enforcement agencies should attempt at the very least to understand the motivations and arguments of people advocating and working toward social change, even radical social change, through violent means. Yes, even violent means. Similarly, Western capitalist states should refrain from a visceral, unreflective and politically motivated demonization of governments or groups opposed to their policies as terrorists if they wish to minimize rather than exacerbate tensions and threats. They can do this by attempting negotiations with dissidents, opponents and enemies before using violence, before waging warfare and before violating human rights.

In addition, citizens and people everywhere should critically consider the complex histories, social conditions and numerous points of view that underlie conflicts rather than blindly accept what their governments and media report as truth. I'm thinking here of the attacks on Venezuela. Personally, I not only support the Chavistas in their Bolivarian Revolution, but I am trying to play whatever part I can—a modest effort, to be sure— in bringing about socialism for the twenty-first century.

The heightened state repression we've experienced in the United States, since the tranquility of our lives was eviscerated on September 11, 2001, has led government and law enforcement agencies to identify a wide range of non-violent U.S. activists as terrorists. Without question, some radical groups, such as the Animal Liberation Front and the Earth Liberation Front, do not compromise or negotiate with ruling state authorities. Nonetheless, it is a hasty and timorous move to equate smashing the windows of a fur store with terrorism and violence, in the same category as flying fully loaded passenger jets into the World Trade Center. Such is the crudeness one finds routinely in the reactions of corporations, the state, mass media and much of the public as well.

Moreover, one must understand that militant resistance inevitably emerges from exploitative and repressive capitalist societies, which make the achievement of genuine democracy and justice difficult, if not impossible. As the saying goes, "No justice, no peace." The so-called war on terrorism is more accurately viewed as a war against those who threaten the interests of transnational corporate domination and the neo-conquest for world empire. This Orwellian phrase has meaning only as a smokescreen for transnational corporations and the transnational capitalist class. They gain control over oil markets and world resources in general, while ruthlessly crushing anyone who dares to oppose the exploitation of animals, of people and of the earth, or anyone who opposes the U.S. global military establishment with its practices of extraordinary rendition, its secret military bases and the 725 bases worldwide listed by the military.

After September 11, 2001, the war on terrorism provided the perfect cover for war on democracy in the form of government, corporate and law enforcement attacks on civil liberties, free speech and domestic dissent of virtually all kinds. Flags waved everywhere, oblivious to the underlying cause of September 11. The Bush administration was militarizing public space, spying on citizens, torturing "enemy noncombatants," gutting freedoms, shredding the Constitution and moving the United States ever closer to tyranny. The state's tactic can only backfire, for if all dissenting groups are branded as terrorists, then none are terrorists, and the true terrorists are those who use physical violence against innocents or noncombatants for political gain. They become harder to identify.

U.S. policy failed in Afghanistan and Iraq, with anti-American hostilities, soldier casualties, public opposition and foreign terrorist threats expanding exponentially. Yet while the nation's ports, railways, subways, airlines and nuclear power plants remain vulnerable to attack, the government nonetheless squanders massive resources to persecute dissenting political groups and so-called domestic terrorist networks. Students, community activists, Quakers, Food Not Bombs, PETA, Greenpeace, professors vocally critical of the Bush administration or supportive of the Cuban revolution or Hugo Chavez's Bolivarian Revolution in Venezuela and even people in vegetarian groups have been surveyed, harassed, prosecuted, arrested, jailed and smeared as violent and demonized as terrorists. Ecosocialists, anarchists, Marxists and greens of all stripes are being characterized as tantamount to terrorists. This is a calculated attempt to capture all anti-capitalist and anti-imperialist groups, all groups critical of patriarchy, racism and homophobia in the net of terrorism and anti-Americanism.

We note that peacemaking is working, as is dialoguing with radicals and militants, a point that many academics, government and law enforcement agencies so easily forget. We wish to show that revolutionaries often—*often*, not *always*—have legitimate goals, needs and demands, which if not addressed and respected can prompt them to commit extreme or even more violent acts. Peacemaking, critical pedagogy (*pedagogy* here is simply another word for education) and conflict studies can provide us with a direction in which we can move closer to our goal of dialoguing for peace.

We argue that conflict transformation is not something we simply adventitiously choose to do when engaging in peacemaking. Rather, it must be broached with everyone in conflict situations, especially if they involve or can lead to violent struggles. So I am going to begin with a brief sketch of the current sociopolitical climate in the United States and show how the Bush administration's policy hinders efforts to negotiate or reduce conflict with individuals in groups that are, by their skewed definitions, radical, violent or terrorist.

Then I will attempt to explain the deception and hypocrisy of the "war on terrorism" and examine the complexity of the whole notion of terrorism as a concept. Finally, Steve Best, Tony Nocella and I advocate a position that we call *revolutionary peacemaking* as a way to communicate and negotiate with dissidents and radicals. This process is impeded, unfortunately, by the dogmatic and politicized use of the terrorist label.

I am going to skip over some of the history that you probably all know, the history of how the war in Iraq and Afghanistan began—remember "If you are not with us, you are against us"? Before the rubble of the World Trade Center had been cleared, the United States took a major step toward becoming a police state, whose enforcers had virtually unlimited powers matched by zero degrees of accountability. No one was spared. Thousands of foreigners were rounded up, jailed and deported without evidence of wrongdoing. Have we forgotten this? Have we forgotten that the FBI organized a domestic spy ring, and tens of thousands of American citizens were spying on their neighbors and sending information to the FBI?

Thousands more abroad were corralled and herded into compounds, such as Guantanamo Bay, where they languished and still languish, many of them in legal limbo. Torture policies were drafted, approved and implemented, as the CIA captured hundreds of enemy combatants. A nifty new label stripped captives of all rights. International treaties like the Geneva Convention were flouted. Laws and agencies that once monitored suspected foreign spies and criminals—for instance, the Foreign Intelligence Surveillance Act—were redeployed for domestic police.

Like a scene out of Orwell's novel 1984, the government built massive surveillance systems to monitor the communications of every citizen as big business fully cooperated with Big Brother. Bush rejected even the most minimum review laws as obstacles to catching terrorists and ordered illegal, warrant-less wiretaps on thousands of U.S. citizen phone calls and e-mail communications, far more than initially realized or admitted. Demonstrators and activists of all kinds became targets of surveillance and persecution, and dissent in many forms was criminalized under the new category, which we now call *domestic terrorism*. The Patriot Act endowed the state with powers such as clandestine searches of one's home or office and access to all records, including student, medical and library research. While demanding open access to citizens, the government also cloaked itself in secrecy by withdrawing presidential papers and historical records from the public domain and restricting citizen use of the Freedom of Information Act.

I recall that during this time I was targeted by a right-wing group and put on the top of a list that came to be known as the "Dirty Thirty List." I was described as UCLA's most dangerous professor. This group offered students $100 to secretly audiotape not only my classes but those of other radical professors. A sum of $50 was offered to students to take notes during our classes.

Although the turn of any century may bring feelings of optimism and hope for a brighter tomorrow, the twenty-first century began as a time of war, as a time of terrorism with violence on a global scale. Social, economic and environmental problems mount to ever higher levels of crisis in response to aggressive capitalist globalization policies, which are devastating the earth, animal species and humans on a global scale. Intense forms of resistance are mounting against the great endorsers of corporate domination, such as the United States and the United Kingdom, as is evident in the anti-globalization movement and indeed in Islamic jihadism as well.

In conditions that foster political dissent in warfare, there is a need for peacemaking with revolutionary groups in order to prevent violence and to establish a cooperative resolution for all disputing parties if and when possible. Many governments believe that mediating and negotiating with radicals who use tactics of violence legitimate and embolden them. Typically, repression of opposition groups exacerbates conflicts more sharply. Mediation is not about winning or losing but rather attempting to reduce conflicts, especially in catastrophic terrorist attacks or where nuclear weapons are involved. Mediation is to reconcile differences and to promote fairness and peace as much as possible.

Sometimes it is possible, and sometimes it isn't. I've been invited to Israel a few times, spent a brief few days in the occupied territories and engaged with Israelis and Palestinians—mostly academics and philosophers. I remember I gave a speech in Haifa during a conference on Israeli citizenship, and a third of the attendees left the hall during my talk when I remarked about the absence of Palestinians at the conference. But the dialogues need to continue. Consider the lamentable fact of Cuba. I was in Cuba recently and did a two-hour interview for television in Havana on U.S. imperialism, neoliberalism and education. It is interesting that Cuba has not posed a threat to the United States since the Soviet Missile Crisis showdown in 1963. Nonetheless, for the past four decades, it has been officially identified as a rogue nation. In this era of global capitalism and vast porous markets, trade and travel embargoes remain firmly in place. Only due to its primal fear of socialism does the United States maintain this irrational and archaic stand. The conflict could easily be resolved if the United States were to abandon its own hostile policies and intractable outlook.

The U.S. administration is now confronting stiffer opposition, thanks to the consciousness-raising work of grassroots organizations and social movements that continue to shed critical light on the lineaments of our geopolitical present.

Recent years have seen the emergence of Latin American attempts at regional integration as a defense against U.S. imperialism, led by Venezuelan President Hugo Chavez. It is interesting working in Venezuela with the Chavistas in their educational programs there.

Professor Nathalia Jaramillo and I were present at a taping of *Alo Presidente*, Chavez's weekly television address to the people of Venezuela, and were sitting next to the great Nicaraguan poet of the revolution Ernesto Cardenal. Responding to President Chavez's efforts to imagine a new relationship of solidarity and anti-imperialist struggle between people of goodwill in the United States and those in Venezuela, Cardenal called President Chavez a prophet who was proclaiming a desire for a mystical union among people from opposing nations based on love:

> Mr. President, you have said some things that are very important and moreover are also prophetic.... When I was a monk, my teacher prophesized that one day the people of the United States and the people of Latin America were going to unite but not with an economic union nor political nor military but a mystic union of love of two peoples (or nations) loving each other. I have now heard this from you, and I want this to be revealed because it is something that hasn't been heard. I have heard it from my teacher and now you have made it a prophecy.
>
> (translated by Nathalia Jaramillo)

This was, for me, a very Freirean moment.

What is needed now are pedagogies that connect the language of students' everyday experiences to the larger struggle for autonomy and social justice carried out by groups in pursuit of genuine democracy and freedom outside of capitalism's law of value, organizations working toward building socialist communities of the future. That is something taught by Bolivarian educators who are struggling to build a socialist future in a country deeply divided by class antagonisms.

I have been very impressed with what I have seen so far in Venezuela. It's called socialism for the twenty-first century. I am a socialist, and I believe that one of the ways we can bring about a culture of peace is to bring about socialism, a socialist alternative to capitalism. I don't think it can be done within the value form of labor under capitalism. I say that as a humanist, and I say that as a Marxist. I don't think it can be done. It certainly can't be done with socialism in one country.

The transnational capitalist class doesn't want to see socialism succeed. It's too threatening, it's too dangerous, and they can't let it succeed. They have to demonize socialism, just like they demonize groups by calling them terrorists.

In general, what are the rules of U.S. foreign policy in dealing with terrorists? First, make no concessions to terrorists and strike no deals. Second, bring terrorists to justice for their crimes. Third, isolate and apply pressure on states that sponsor terrorism to force them to change their behavior. Fourth, bolster the counter-terrorism capabilities of those countries that work with the United States and require assistance.

Do you know how repressive these states can be, especially when the United States helps them become more repressive? People who are being repressed in these countries rightfully acknowledge that the United States is helping to bolster this kind of state repression with funding and with training of police and military. What do you think that does?

Because the United States and other governments will not negotiate with militant groups or enemy states, the peacemaker is not supported and can be seen as a traitor or supporter of revolutionary ideology. The U.S. Patriot Act defines any efforts to assist a terrorist group as itself a terrorist action. In the media, the Bush administration to this day continue to stigmatize critics of the invasion of Iraq or efforts to build a garrison state as traitors and collaborators.

I will tell you how this attempt to demonize people who oppose current policies of a wartime president affects people in a secondary way. I was invited to give a talk in Bogota, Colombia. It was by a relatively progressive group associated with the mayor's office. I came in and gave a talk for a week. People were wonderful, the reception was amazing, and with my very limited Spanish and the help of some good translators, I had some wonderful conversations with folks.

When I returned home, I got an email from the organizers and some professors who were there. They said: "We want to thank you, Peter, for coming to Bogota and spending a week of your time. We didn't want to tell you this when you were with us, but it took us months of negotiating to get you there, because people heard you were associated with the 'Dirty Thirty,' that you were on this right-wing list. People were trying to use that to prevent you from coming to Colombia, but we fought and we won! We are glad, and we would do it all over again if we could, but we can't do it all over again, because some of us have just been fired and have lost our positions."

So the sad, pathetic irony of this is that while I'm sitting drinking a latte on the beautiful UCLA campus, these brave and courageous educators are pounding the pavement in Bogota trying to find work because they made the mistake of inviting me. That's how these efforts to attack and demonize can work. They might or might not affect the person being targeted, but they often can affect the lives of other people.

Because I am Canadian, I thought this rather far-fetched example would be appropriate. This example is admittedly rather extraordinary, but sometimes absurdities can capture elements of truth needed to put current historical events into perspective. What would happen if a Canadian scientist working in a basement laboratory at the University of Toronto, my old alma mater, happened upon a scientific discovery that allowed the Canadian military to develop a super weapon and become the world's most dominant military force? And what if, moreover, this weapon was deployed successfully against the U.S. military in a Canadian offensive designed to occupy the United States until it eliminated its scientific resources so that the United States would be rendered incapable of ever creating a like weapon — in other words, so that Canada could claim the status of being the world's sole superpower. Perhaps they would do this under the pretext of installing in the United States a universal health care plan, the argument being that not having such a plan was the moral equivalent to murdering millions of uninsured civilians. And you know there is some truth in that.

Well, if that were the case, would there be armed U.S. civilian resistance? Surely, there would be. Right-wing reactionary groups along with left-wing militant groups, communitarians and libertarians would fight hand-in-hand to drive out the occupiers, while some admittedly might welcome the occupiers as liberators. The Canadian government would lump all these ideological, divergent resistance fighters into one category as insurgents or terrorists or Al Qaeda. Would that mean that none of these groups had any legitimate claim to attack the occupying Canadian forces?

I am merely trying to make the point that the occupiers have the official means to define who the terrorists are.

Now back to the real world. Following our own hermeneutical counsel, we can try to understand the U.S. position that there is no resolution to the Al Qaeda threat other than the military solution of total extermination of the radical Islamic enemy. The enemy is, of course, far more diverse and widespread than just one group, given the unyielding resolve of jihadists to kill as many U.S. citizens as possible, to overthrow corrupt governments and to oppose draconian *sharia* law throughout the world.

But rather than weaken or destroy groups such as Al Qaeda through the military option, the failure of the United States to recognize the legitimacy of some jihadists' complaints — such as those regarding U.S. imperialism — and to make necessary policy changes, choosing instead to pursue a senseless invasion of Iraq and thus whip up anti-American hatred, exacerbated the terrorist threat to its citizens, destabilized the region and alienated moderate Arabs so that they are more sympathetic now to the radicals.

In a world racked by deep, persistent and ominous conflicts — such as between Israel and Palestine, India and Pakistan, the United States and North Korea and in Iran — it is critical that governments and authorities that want to move toward peace understand the mission of a peacemaker. It is critical that they understand the need for a peacemaker, and it's not going to be Tony Blair. It's imperative that they undertake sincere and authentic diplomacy. President Bush's morality divides the world into those who do evil or do good, and it morphs into this Manichaean politics rooted in dogmatic refusals to deal with the enemy in any way except through silence or violence.

In our post-9/11 world of radicalized Islam and suicide bombing, there is a need, more obvious than ever, for peacemaking with revolutionaries. Global political relations are increasingly volatile and increasingly unstable. Globalization and militarization, as driven by the United States in particular, create poverty and animosity and thereby breed jihadism, anti-imperialism, anti-Americanism and terrorism. Peacemaking with revolutionaries is the work done by agents of social justice, agents of history, who use dialogue, negotiation, education and other forms of praxis that make communication possible in order to resolve conflicts.

How do we get beyond terrorism? We know that the whole lexicon of terrorism is now part of the structural unconsciousness of everyday life for U.S. citizens. To Israel and the U.S. government, for instance, Palestinian organizations are terrorist. The Palestinians and their defenders regard their warriors as freedom fighters opposing a terrorist invasion and occupation of their homeland. How do we begin to develop peacemaking strategies in that context? In the 1980s, the Reagan administration championed the Contras as freedom fighters against the "totalitarian state" of Nicaragua, whereas Nicaraguans revile them as U.S.-sponsored terrorists who killed thousands of innocents to overthrow their elected government. The Contras murdered children and women and purposefully targeted them.

Menachem Begin was a leader of the infamous Irgun group that carried out political assassinations. In 1946, he bombed the British headquarters in the King David Hotel, killing ninety and wounding forty-five, yet he became the prime minister of Israel and won the Nobel Peace Prize in 1978.

Nelson Mandela and the African National Congress used bombs and assassinations in their struggle against apartheid and were reviled as terrorists. Yet, in 1993, Nelson Mandela was awarded the Nobel Peace Prize and became an international hero.

While the distinction between terrorists and freedom fighters can be difficult to discern, often it's palpably clear. It is imperative that we resist corporate, state and mass media definitions in glib conceptual conflations. We need to do this in order to distinguish between freedom fighters, those who defend themselves or others against unprovoked violence and unjust aggression, and so-called terrorists, those individuals, those groups or governments who initiate aggressive acts of violence toward others in an attempt to control, exploit or oppress them. These are issues we need to debate. These are issues we need to discuss. These are issues we need to come to some understanding about, not simply to avoid or refuse to discuss. We have to bring them out into the public square and begin to unpack them, begin to, in a sense, undress them for what they are instead of refusing to dialogue about them.

The Reagan administration organized and funded the Contras, who blew up ports and sought to destroy the economy, who killed tens of thousands of innocent men, women and children with bombs, grenades and bayonets.

We don't discuss these issues. When President Reagan was being put to rest, there was nothing about this in the newspapers, no discussions of the Contras in the Reagan administration, in the public corporate-owned media, which was shameful. I was wondering about this.

I was reading an article recently by John Pilger, the journalist. I love John Pilger. He said:

> I remember Edward Herman's marvelous essay about normalizing the unthinkable. For that's what media cliched language does and is designed to do—it normalizes the unthinkable; of the degradation of war, of severed limbs, of maimed children, all of which I've seen. One of my favorite stories about the Cold War concerns a group of Russian journalists who were touring the United States. On the final day of their visit, they were asked by the host for their impressions. "I have to tell you," said the spokesman, "that we were astonished to find, after reading all the newspapers and watching TV, that all the opinions on all the vital issues were, by and large, the same. To get that result in our country, we imprison people, we tear out their fingernails. Here, you don't have that. What's the secret? How do you do it?"
>
> What is the secret? It's a question now urgently asked of those whose job is to keep the record straight: who in this country have extraordinary constitutional freedom. I refer to journalists, of course, a small group who hold privileged sway over the way we think, even the way we use language.

I have been a journalist for more than 40 years. Although I am based in London, I have worked all over the world, including the United States, and I have reported America's wars. My experience is that what the Russian journalists were referring to is censorship by omission, the product of a parallel world of unspoken truth and public myths and lies: in other words, censorship by journalism, which today has become war by journalism.

For me, this is the most virulent and powerful form of censorship, fuelling an indoctrination that runs deep in western societies, deeper than many journalists themselves understand or will admit to. Its power is such that it can mean the difference between life and death for untold numbers of people in faraway countries, like Iraq.

On August 24 last year, *The New York Times* declared this in an editorial: "If we had known then what we know now, the invasion of Iraq would have been stopped by a popular outcry." What this amazing admission was saying, in effect, is that journalists had betrayed the public by not doing their job and by accepting and amplifying and echoing the lies of Bush and his gang, instead of challenging them and exposing them. What the *Times* didn't say was that had the paper and the rest of the media exposed the lies, up to a million people might be alive today. That's the belief now of a number of senior establishment journalists. Few of them— they've spoken to me about it—few of them will say it in public.

(Published in the International Socialist Review,
November–December 2007)

John Pilger noted that he began to understand how censorship worked in so-called free societies when he reported from totalitarian societies. He wrote:

> During the 1970s, I filmed secretly in Czechoslovakia, then a Stalinist dictatorship. I interviewed members of the dissident group, Charter 77. One of them, the novelist Zdener Urbanek, told me, "We are more fortunate than you in the West, in one respect. We believe nothing of what we read in the newspapers and watch on television, nothing of the official truth. Unlike you,

we have learned to read between the lines of the media. Unlike
you, we know that that real truth is always subversive."

By *subversive,* he meant that truth comes from the ground up, almost
never from the top down. (Vandana Shiva has called this "subjugated
knowledge.")

Pilger went on to say:

> A venerable cliché is that truth is the first casualty in wartime. I
> disagree. Journalism is the first casualty. The first American war
> I reported was Vietnam. I went there from 1966 to the last day.
> When it was all over, the magazine *Encounter* published an article
> by Robert Elegant, another correspondent who covered Vietnam.
> "For the first time in modern history," he wrote, "the outcome of a
> war was determined not on the battlefield but on the printed page
> and, above all, on the television screen." He was accusing journal-
> ists of losing the war by opposing it in their work.

I am going to end my comments with you this evening on a note
about education because, after all, I work in the field of education, and
we have to remember that Malcolm X said, "Education is the passport to
the future." One of my great mentors was one of the persons with whom
I had the opportunity to work for a number of years, both in the United
States and Brazil. His name was Paulo Freire, a great Brazilian educator
who wrote a book called *Pedagogy of the Oppressed.*

Freire was a great admirer of Malcolm X and, of course, I am a great
admirer of Malcolm X. Freire agrees with what Malcolm said and would
emphasize that the approach one takes to education is as important as
the content. Thus, before one ventures off to become educated about
revolutionaries, one must decide on the proper or ideal approach to take
for engaging in research and teaching. And one way to comprehend the
task before us is what we see to be our ontological vocation. For me, that
has always been the class struggle and the struggle for socialism and for
the possibility of building a post-capitalist social universe where human
capacities can flourish, where we can work toward eliminating racism,
homophobia, patriarchy, environmental devastation. Now that struggle
sometimes involves violence. Here let me summarize some points made

by Professor Michael Rivage-Seul in his book *The Emperor's God.*

Religious figures such as Dom Helda Camera and Oscar Romero spoke of a "bloody trinity" of three levels of violence: structural violence or first-level violence or violence of the "father" (social, economic, political and military systems and arrangements codified in law and custom that are responsible for tens of thousands of innocent deaths throughout the world each day); revolutionary violence or second-level violence or violence of the "son" (responses to first-level or structural violence); and reactionary violence or third-level violence or violence of the "evil spirit" (the reply by the state to acts of rebellion against structural or first-level violence). While clearly structural violence prevails in today's imperial regimes and their client states, revolutionary violence is the only violence officially condemned by such states. However, revolutionary violence, the violence condemned by the state, is the only violence that can at least be theoretically justified as, in Rivage-Seul's words, "peasants and workers [seek] to defend their families from aggressions of the rich represented in the first and third levels."

Structural violence in the United States is very rarely addressed by the state, but revolutionary violence, especially post-9/11, is rejected out of hand. On this issue, Rivage-Seul's comments are apposite: "The reality is, however, that violence at this level is the most understandable and even the most justifiable, at least from the viewpoint of American history, Just War theory, and perhaps even in the light of Jesus' own sympathies." While Rivage-Seul agrees that the example of Jesus "challenges Christians to implement the practice of non-violent resistance, both as a matter of practicality and spiritual conviction," it nonetheless "seems inappropriate for First World Christians to insist that Third World resisters adopt strategies and tactics of non-violent resistance in situations where they must actually defend the 'least of the brethren' in contexts shaped by extremely violent structures financed by U.S. tax dollars." In any case, Christians living comfortably in the United States must overcome the impulse to condemn second-level violence while excusing systematic aggression in service to U.S. corporate interests. Perhaps Philip Berryman says it best, and I quote from Rivage-Seul: "I would assert that people who have not actively opposed the violence of the powerful against the poor, at some cost to themselves, have no moral authority to question the violence used by the poor."

Now, having said that, let me return to the question of education.

While there is much talk about labor today and the decline of the labor movement, what is important for educators to keep in mind is the social form that labor takes. In capitalist societies, that social form is human capital. As my colleague in the United Kingdom Glenn Rikowski has argued better than anyone I know, schools are charged with educating a certain form of human capital, with socially producing labor power, and in doing so enhancing specific attributes of labor power that serve the interests of capital. In other words, schools educate the labor-power needs of capital—for capital in general, for the national capital, for factions of capital (manufacturing, finance, services, etc.), for sectors of capital (particular industries, etc.) or for individual capital (specific companies and enterprises, etc.), and they also educate for functions of capital that cut across these categories of capitals. General education, for instance, is intentionally divorced from labor-power attributes required to work within individual capitals and is aimed at educating for capital-in-general. Practical education tries to shape labor-power attributes in the direction of skills needed within specific factions or sectors of capital. Training, on the other hand, involves educating for labor-power attributes that will best serve specific or individual capitals.

It is important to note that Rikowski has described capital not only as the subsumption of concrete living labor by abstract alienated labor but also as a mode of being, as a unified social force that flows through our subjectivities, our bodies, our meaning-making capacities. Schools educate labor power by serving as a medium for its constitution or its social production in the service of capital. But schools are more than this, they do more than nourish labor power because all of capitalist society accomplishes that; in addition to producing capital-in-general, schools additionally *condition* labor power in the varying interests of the marketplace. But because labor power is a living commodity, and a highly contradictory one at that, it can be re-educated and shaped in the interests of building socialism, that is, in creating opportunities for the self-emancipation of the working class.

Labor power, as the capacity or potential to labor, doesn't have to serve its current master—capital. It serves the master only when it engages in the act of laboring for a wage. Because individuals can refuse to labor in the interests of capital accumulation, labor power can therefore serve another cause—the cause of socialism. Critical pedagogy can be used as a means of finding ways of transcending the contradictory aspects of labor-power creation and creating different spaces where a de-reification, de-commodification and decolonization of subjectivity can occur. Critical pedagogy is an agonistic arena where the development of a discerning political subjectivity can be fashioned (recognizing that there will always be socially and self-imposed constraints).

Revolutionary critical pedagogy (a term coined by Paula Allman) is multifaceted in that it brings a Marxist humanist perspective to a wide range of policy and curriculum issues. The list of topics includes the globalization of capitalism, the marketization of education, neo-liberalism and school reform, imperialism and capitalist schooling and so on. Revolutionary critical pedagogy (as I am developing it with my colleague Nathalia Jaramillo and others) also offers an alternative interpretation of the history of capitalism and capitalist societies with a particular emphasis on the United States.

Revolutionary classrooms are prefigurative of socialism in the sense that they are connected to social relations that we want to create as revolutionary socialists. Classrooms generally try to mirror in organization what students and teachers would collectively like to see in the world outside of schools—respect for everyone's ideas, tolerance of differences, a commitment to creativity and social and educational justice, the importance of working collectively, a willingness and desire to work hard for the betterment of humanity, a commitment to anti-racist, anti-sexist and anti-homophobic practices and so on.

As critical revolutionary peacemakers, as critical pedagogues, in other words, it is crucial to approach revolutionary groups, societies or collectives by relying on dialogue and consciousness-raising among all the groups involved.

I want to say that, while I have been discussing labor, labor power and class struggle, we really need to focus our efforts on fighting racism, patriarchy, homophobia and the devastation of our ecosystems. We need to challenge the European modern colonial capitalist patriarchal world system.

Our pedagogy underscores the importance of anti-racism but at the same time constitutes a radical challenge to an economic system that is based on exchange, value, profit and the rule of market that we must oppose.

Creating spaces for critical learning is difficult, since building recipro-
cal feelings of trust is paramount. In many university settings that I work
in, many students are reluctant to stay in classrooms where they feel they
are going to be the objects of attack and derision. The goal, of course, is to
challenge the experience of students without taking away their voices. You
don't want to affirm a racist, sexist or homophobic voice, but how is such
a challenge accomplished without removing the student's voice entirely?

I try to learn from my experiences working with university groups that
define themselves as progressive, as radical, and I think that is the challenge that we have to take into the twenty-first century.

Questions and Answers

AUDIENCE MEMBER 1: I wonder that we haven't swept Professor
McLaren off the stage ourselves, so excellent, so complete, so total
is his lecture. But I can only ask how coincidental it can be that he
has been excluded from Canada and would have been a professor but
for some offense against one Canadian university president who persuaded all other universities to ban his ability to teach at all in Canada? Otherwise, everything that he speaks of about the University of
Toronto, and the way he handles students, everything makes us at least
brothers, and I thank him and I praise him and I am overjoyed with
that. Now for the question. It's a very short one.

Another Canadian, Naomi Klein, says an incident was heaven-
sent for President Bush because he had been casting around for ten
or fourteen years for an excuse to marshal an international counter-
attack at what was coming to be substantial gains here and there in
mild ways for mild socialism, so that the successes were the genesis
of this massive organization of the world's countries to crush humanity and defeat socialism or anything like it. Perhaps a last comment,
but this is a piece of advice to the younger people here, and I repeat
it everywhere I can. Beware when you begin to succeed in defeating
that enemy, because when you begin to succeed, you will be on the
top murder list for all the forces that surround and oppose you. Watch
out when you are succeeding.

DR. MCLAREN: Yes. Well, this is very interesting, *compañero.* I want to start with a personal anecdote, because it relates to your first comment about me being a professor for one year in Canada, until I was fired. I was fired by way of having my contract revoked, due to a student petition that went around that I was a communist. This was in 1985. A larger group of students who supported me took over the office of one of the administrators and refused to leave until the dean of the university agreed to sign me on for another year. He agreed to do that. The students left and a few months later, they graduated. I was called into the dean's office, and the dean said, "You're out of here."

I couldn't find a job in Canada anywhere. I tried Newfoundland, I tried Halifax, and I tried British Columbia. Henry Giroux, a well-known professor, was at Boston University. He was a brilliant educator; he still is. John Silber was the president of Boston University at that time. He had a hit list that included Howard Zinn and Henry and other professors. Even though Paulo Freire intervened with a beautiful letter, and despite the fact that people from all over the world wrote letters in support of Henry, still he was fired. He ended up at conservative Miami University of Ohio, which hired him because they wanted to put their school of education on the map.

Henry then said, "Peter, you're out of work, come to the U.S." That was in 1985, so I worked at Miami University of Ohio with Giroux for eight years, and then UCLA recruited me. Now Henry is in Canada, at McMaster University. I just thought you would appreciate hearing that.

But you're quite right, the more visible you become, the more you are liable to be attacked.

AUDIENCE MEMBER 2: What bothers me is the concept of religion, or I should say that religion basically defines evil as an actual entity, and I as an atheist reject religion because it does that. Second, I think we only have to go back to Adam Smith's theory of moral sentiments to find an ethical basis for a system that later began to embellish this capitalism. That system itself talks about the importance of setting up a general welfare for people. We don't have to go back to "isms." In addition, since the largest "ism" was debunked in terms of the Soviet Union, we don't have a strong source in the world anymore in terms of strength. We don't have to go back to them, and we don't have to be a Marxist to know that this system is screwed up, but I am afraid that if we do go back to those formal kinds of antagonism, we are going to set up future bloodbaths. Because if we admit to the concept of evil, or at least to the concept that there has to be struggle, I think we have overlooked the fact. We need to go back and read Adam Smith's *Theory of Moral Sentiments* written in 1750 and then *Wealth of Nations* in 1776. You can find a very good basis for American ethics and ethics of capitalism. If we can just hold these guys to their prophets, hang onto them and say, "Hey, you need actual welfare." That's not socialism, that's basically a humanist concept. I think Adam Smith has not been read well enough, and I think I am afraid if we are going back to revive Marxism or some kinds of "isms" in general, or concepts of evil, we are going to be setting up the next bloodbath, because all of the bloodbaths and the violence are religious in origin. I hate to say that, but I think that's true.

DR. MCLAREN: I share your fundamental critique of religion. But let me respond to your comments about socialism. As a Marxist humanist, I have struggled for a socialism premised on participatory democracy and the development of human capacities, on knowledge that is not mediated by capital. I appreciate what you said about Adam Smith, although I do have my critique of Smith's work. I am not suggesting by any means that the Soviet Union should serve as a model. Obviously, I don't feel that. Let me make my point that as a Marxist humanist, one of the first questions that we ask is "Why have so many revolutions turned into their opposite?" That's a question we need to face, and that's why Marxist humanists like myself get attacked a great deal by all kinds of other Marxist groups, because we privilege the centrality of that question.

One of the things that I think many of us have learned over the years is that the failure of so-called socialist states has been the failure of democracy. It was often assumed that when you change the social relations of production, that somehow democracy would automatically follow. Somehow the notion of human development became a secondary goal. I think these are mistakes that many revolutionaries recognize today.

Direct democracy, participatory democracy, is one of the keys, and I know certainly it is one of the keys of the Chavez regimen to bring about socialism for the twenty-first century. That's not easy, by any means. There is a big debate now between the Chavistas and the Zapatistas. Some believe that if you choose state power, you're doomed to fail because you will always exercise "power-over" rather than operate in a modality of "power-with." The Zapatistas have chosen to create autonomous social movements that are not aligned with the state. The Chavistas believe you can rebuild the state from the bottom up. Some of you might argue with me on that in the context of Venezuela, but I am open to questions.

AUDIENCE MEMBER 3: You mentioned earlier the Freire position that the process of pedagogy is sometimes as important as content, and the event that we are participating in today, this wonderful event, is indicative of a long-term relationship that the SGI-USA has with theater. They use theatrical events to bring people together; they use graphics. When you and I first became aware of one another, it was through the Center for Theatre of the Oppressed and Applied Theatre Arts Los Angeles (CTO/ATA) and I thought that it would interesting if you would just give us a little background on Augusto Boal, Theatre of the Oppressed and how that relates to the Freire mandate. I think these patient people are ripe for that information.

DR. MCLAREN: I know Augusto Boal was greatly influenced by Paulo Freire and used Freire's *Pedagogy of the Oppressed* to develop the Theatre of the Oppressed. I have had students who have taken theater workshops with Augusto Boal. I have not taken them with Boal. I believe, still, every year for a few months, he comes to the University of Oklahoma, but I know he has theater groups all over the world. We spoke together only on one occasion, the three of us, Augusto, myself and Paulo. Some people call Boal's work guerilla theatre, but any way you name it, it's a wonderful way of re-conceptualizing, reconfiguring human relationships in the guise of participatory theater, where people come up and assume roles and are open to the possibility of self and social transformation. Peter Sellars, not the comedian from the sixties and seventies, but Peter Sellars, the brilliant and innovative

theater director, has done some marvelous work along the lines of
Boal. He continues to be an inspiration for me. Peter Sellars is located
here in Los Angeles. He is one of the great opera directors and theater
directors of our time.

I would like to be more closely connected to that in my own work.
I am pleased to learn you are involved in theater here. This is absolutely fundamental.

AUDIENCE MEMBER 4: Thank you very much. What political label
would you use in describing the Soka Gakkai?

DR. MCLAREN: I am only just learning about your organization. In what
I have grasped so far, I think it attempts to transcend sectarian political agendas. It seems as though we're talking about making the political more pedagogical and the pedagogical more political, but we're
also talking about making the spiritual more pedagogical and the pedagogical more spiritual. We are talking about making the ethical more
pedagogical and the pedagogical more ethical, so it's a dialectical process. I think you would have to use a verb as opposed to a noun. That's
all I can say.

Thank you everyone, thank you for your participation. This has
been a wonderful meeting for me.

August 18, 2007
Santa Monica, California

Peace in the World Is Everybody's Business

Betty Williams

Recipient of the Nobel Peace Prize in 1976 for her work to bring peace to her native Northern Ireland

Betty Williams' life was changed when she witnessed the deaths of three children caught in the middle of a clash between British soldiers and an IRA fugitive. Deeply shocked, Ms. Williams gathered six thousand signatures for a petition for peace and organized a peace march of ten thousand Catholic and Protestant women and then another march of thirty-five thousand people a week later. These activities gained worldwide media attention. Together with Mairead Corrigan, the aunt of the three children who had been killed, she started Women For Peace, which eventually became The Community for Peace People, to help end violence in Northern Ireland.

In more than thirty years since she was awarded the Nobel Peace Prize for her work to bring peace to her native Northern Ireland, Ms. Williams has devoted her life to fighting against the injustice, cruelty and horrors perpetrated on the children of the world. Ms. Williams has traveled the globe recording the testimonies of children who have been subjected to suffering beyond belief and advocated legislation to protect children. She has called for the creation of safe areas off limits to any form of military attack in every country where children are under the threat of death and destruction. These "Cities of Compassion" will protect children and ensure that they be treated with dignity, respect and love, as well as help alleviate the huge refugee and orphan problems that plague many countries today. As a result of her many years of work in Italy, World Centers of Compassion for Children International is building the first "City of Compassion" for children in the Basilicata Region of southern Italy.

Ms. Williams promotes a message of non-violence and respect for all human rights, particularly for children. This respect for human rights is the third of the eight action areas identified by the United Nations. When confronted with the violent deaths of three innocent children, she responded by finding the common humanity among women, especially as mothers, and brought tens of thousands of people together to voice a shared commitment to the right to live in peace.

Would you all stand up, please? Now I want you to give each other a hug. Didn't that feel good? I'll tell you why I do that. I do it for one reason and one reason only: Arms are for hugging, not for killing.

I am never quite sure what to say because doing what's right just seems to be natural. We should all be doing it. When I meet people who say they can't make a difference, I normally say it is because they don't want to. It's because they don't care enough, because one act of kindness a day can make such a huge difference in our world.

I will tell you, for those of you who don't know, what the beginning of the peace movement was like, because there are many young people in this room, and I am an old, old worker for peace. I don't mean I am any wiser, I am just older.

When our work began in Northern Ireland, it began out of pain and suffering beyond belief. As I stand behind this podium today, you don't see my three little angels, but I never leave home without them.

One day in Northern Ireland, driving home from my mother's house, I heard shots ringout. On that day, I suddenly realized how sick I was, because I could distinguish gunfire. I heard the shots of an Armalite rifle, which is the rifle used by the Provisional Irish Republican Army, and then I heard the return fire of an SLR (self-loading rifle), which was the weapon of the British Army.

As I turned from the main road going onto the road where I lived, a car came careening around the corner, mounted the pavement and slammed into a mother and her three young children. Their names were Joanne, John and Andrew Maguire. Since that day, I have never left home without Joanne, John and Andrew Maguire. The carnage on the streets that day was horrific, even after all these years when I look back on it. It hurts, because you feel so useless and so helpless when you desperately want the children to live, and you know there is absolutely no way to save them. Little Andrew was only six weeks old. He had been lifted out of his pram and was impaled on a railing. Little John was thrown, and little Joanne with her blonde curls was scalped under the wheel of the car.

I was the first on the scene, and I remember I had my daughter. She was in her little car seat, and I ran to see what I could do. Any mother would do that. We would all do that. You go into a store, and you hear a child say "Mommy," and every woman turns around. So you would try to aid the child.

But I couldn't do anything. I remember holding Joanne in my arms and telling her how much I loved her and making a promise to that child, "I will fight the rest of my life to make sure this doesn't happen to other children." It has been a hard fight. It's a thirty-four-year-old fight now.

In Northern Ireland, when that movement started, there was a part of my life that was missing.

I talked to students last week at Soka University of America (in Aliso Viejo, California), and I am on a natural high. I am four feet off the ground since I left. It was the most wonderful experience—them getting to know me, me getting to know them, heart to heart, soul to soul, spirit to spirit, which is the way we should educate. Somebody told me that emotion doesn't belong in a classroom. I disagree strongly.

In Ireland, our work started on pure emotion. I went back to my house that day, and I must have gone into a state of shock, because four hours of my life went missing and I have never gotten them back. I still don't know what happened. I do remember my sister coming into the house and making me a cup of tea, and I was still covered in Joanne's blood.

My next memory is that I was standing in my garage, and I was screaming. A psychiatrist friend told me that must have been my way of getting out of shock. I am really glad that happened. It probably would have cost me a fortune to get it out any other way, you know. But after that, I remember the burning anger. I have never lost that anger. If anything, it has become deeper, because I haven't only been witness to the suffering of the children of Northern Ireland, I have been witness to the suffering of the children of the world.

Our work takes me all over the world, and we see suffering beyond belief. Maybe that suffering would make sense to me if my grandbaby could walk through the doors of this auditorium and declare war on any of you. A child doesn't declare war, and God, Buddha and Allah do not declare war. We declare war, mankind declares war. Mostly *man*-kind.

When the peace movement started, it started on that kind of emotion and that kind of pain. I remember my son was doing his homework, and I pulled some pages from his homework book. He said, "Mommy, where are you going?" I jumped into my car, and I went up into what was supposed to be Provisional IRA territory, and I started banging on doors.

I was yelling at the women, "Sign this!"

One woman said, "What am I signing?"

I very quickly wrote on the top of the piece of paper, "Petition for Peace."

I called a rally then. Well, that's not exactly how it happened, but at the end of five or six hours, we had five thousand signatures for peace. It was rather like being the Pied Piper of Hamlin. All the women were feeling what I was feeling, and I just gave it a voice. We drove around the areas and worked hard to get the signatures, and I came back to my home.

I was sitting on my stairs in my own house, and the house was packed with women. I looked around saying, "How did this happen?" It was a miracle, you know.

So I asked myself, "What am I going to do with these signatures?" I didn't have a clue. Not even a little one. "What am I going to do with these?" I said. "I guess we should let somebody know we have done this."

I picked up the telephone, and I rang our local newspaper, which was the *Irish News*, and a wonderful man who was the night editor. "You're never going to believe this," I said. I didn't believe it myself. Nobody would ever believe this. I told him where I was, where I lived, and what the women of my community had done.

I heard him yell: "Stop the front page! We have a new headline!"

The next morning, it was all over the front page. He asked if I was sure I wanted to give my name and address. I said: "Yeah! I am out, and I am going to stay out."

Non-violence is the weapon of the strong, not the weak. From that first headline, then I was brought into the BBC Television studios, I was shaking like a leaf. I had never done an interview in my life before. I never spoke in public in my life before, so I wasn't expecting any of this. I went into the studio, and a wonderful man named Jon Snow interviewed me at lunchtime. During the interview, I asked the women of Ireland, north and south of the border, and the women of England, Scotland and Wales that if they felt as I did, would they join me in a rally at the spot where the children were killed?

After doing that interview, I said, "Mother of God, what have I done?"

Then my father called, and he said, "I just saw you on television." He knew nothing about what was happening. He said, "What have you done, Betty?" I didn't know what I had done, either, to be honest with you.

I started praying, "Oh, sweet Mother Mary, please let somebody turn up at this rally." But I thought to myself, "No, it's only going to be me."

My father came from a family of eight, and my mother came from a family of twelve, so I knew a few relatives. I got on the phone to call all my relatives, over and over: "Will you be there? Will you be there?"

Well, half of our family was in the IRA, and the other half was, well, you know. Ours was a split family. So my Uncle Bill, who was in the IRA, said, "No way." On the contrary, I knew my cousin Frances would turn up. She had five children, so at least there would be seven of us at the rally. I absolutely had no idea what was about to happen. Even if you don't believe in miracles, miracles do happen.

What happened was this. I was standing at the spot where I had called the rally, and I was thinking to myself, "Oh please, please, God, please, God, let somebody turn up." Buses start to come — Catholic women and Protestant women had hired buses to get themselves to this rally. In one powerful act of love, they wiped out 850 years of mayhem, carnage, bigotry and hatred. How did they do that? They ran into each other's arms, and it became a womb thing. A womb thing. Don't you figure that if God had wanted man to procreate, he would have given them wombs? Go figure.

That's what I love about [SGI president] Dr. Ikeda. He is such a profound man and woman. He has absolutely no fear of his feminine side, none whatsoever. He is wonderful, and he has such love for his wife that it shines. You men who think that I may be anti-man, that's another myth. I love men enough to save their lives.

The peace movement in Ireland grew and flourished because it was born out of great pain and great emotion. We had a series of twelve rallies all over Northern Ireland, Scotland, England, the Republic of Ireland and Wales. When we would have a march in Belfast, we would have a march in Derry, we would have a march in London, and we would have a march in Manchester, and we would have a march in Glasgow, all coordinating with our marches.

And from whom did we learn how to march? My beloved Dr. Martin Luther King. How we loved that man in Ireland, because to be an Irish Catholic was to be a Black American. We couldn't vote, we couldn't own property, we had absolutely no rights.

When he was in Selma, Alabama, I was watching the television saying, "You go, Martin; you go, Martin," not knowing that someday I would very quickly have to buy everything he wrote on how you do marches. Later I did, because I didn't know anything about rallying, but a person who did and who was the closest to our situation was the Reverend Dr. Martin Luther King.

At one point, I was staying in the house of the burgomaster in Berlin, that's the mayor of Berlin. As I was going to bed, he told me that the last person who slept in my bed was the Reverend Dr. Martin Luther King, and the one before that was John F. Kennedy. I sat at the edge of the bed all night, just stroking the pillows. A few times, I would lift the pillow and say, "Martin's head was on this."

If we have to have men as heroes, that's the kind of man I want to have as mine. Six hundred and fifty thousand civilians have been killed since this present Iraqi war began. Six hundred and fifty thousand! Those are not my figures. Those are the figures of *The Lancet* medical journal using credible methodology, which tells us 650,000 of our brothers and sisters in Iraq have been destroyed in this war. This is wrong! This is absolutely wrong!

We have eight hundred thousand injured with only 10 percent of them getting any kind of medical help. I did a trip to Iraq, and we took 15 tons of goods for the children of Iraq.

I will walk you through one story—the story of the children of Iraq. Because of our work in Ireland, which started because of children, everybody thought I was an expert on children. I wasn't then, but I am now. When we went to Iraq, we went to a hospital in which there were two hundred children all suffering from cancer. The mothers' wombs had been infected since the first Gulf War. Children were being born with cancers that doctors couldn't even recognize, different cancers altogether. The doctor knew that he would need five different medications to cure these children. Because of sanctions and embargos, he had only three. When we were leaving the hospital, I said to this doctor, who had been trained at Johns Hopkins, the top training in the world for cancer, "Doctor, how many of these children are going to live?"

He said, "Not one, not even one."

Did those children deserve that? I don't think so.

Saddam Hussein was a horrible despot, an awful human being. When September 11 happened, it will go down in infamy as one of the most ghastly acts of terrorism the world has ever known, but on that same day, 35,615 children in our world died from conditions of malnutrition and nobody said a word. The good news is that, after many years of working in Northern Ireland and worldwide for the cause of children, we are now World Centers of Compassion for Children International, my organization. I should say mine and Rusti Findley's, the wind beneath my wings. We are building the first City of Peace in the world in the Basilicata Region in Italy, beginning this year.

We have to have dreams, and we must have the capacity to make the dream a reality. When people told me in Ireland, "You can never do this," I used to say, "Watch my smoke!" Don't tell me I can't do this, because I know that every single human being is capable of doing magnificent stuff, and there are no ordinary people. All people are extraordinary. God or Buddha or Allah or whatever we want to call that powerful force of love, powerful force of humanity and powerful force of goodness, made no ordinary people in the world. Everybody is different and extraordinary. Have you ever met an ordinary housewife? How many men here can multitask? Not a lot.

To each and every one of you, if you are not already involved in helping to change our world and make it a little bit better, from today make a solemn vow to yourself that you will become involved in changing the future that our world faces. Make that promise to yourself and remember that you are not ordinary. There is nobody in this room who has the same fingerprints. There is nobody in this room who has the same eyes. There is nobody in this room who has the same thought process. You are all absolutely individual. As Jody Williams, my coworker and fellow Peace Prize laureate says, "Violence is a choice; reject it no matter where it comes from."

I said once to His Holiness the Dalai Lama, "When I am with you, I don't know whether I am a good Buddhist or a bad Catholic."

He said, "Same thing; good is good."

I was with His Holiness last year in Dharamsala, and we did a peace jam in the Tibetan village. It was absolutely glorious. His Holiness and I have been friends for many years, for about twenty years. I worked for the freedom of Tibet and for the freedom of Burma, so I got to meet with all these wonderful people. His Holiness has an enormous sense of humor. He really loves a good belly laugh. I said to him the last time we were together, "You know, Your Holiness, it's about time you married me."

He scratched his head, he looked at me, and he said, "I think I need someone a little younger."

If you don't mind, I would like to read this little poem that I absolutely love. It's called "A Dream."

I dreamt of a world without sorrow,
and I dreamt of a world without hate.
I dreamt of a world of rejoicing,
and I awoke to find Christ at my gate.

I dreamt of a world without hunger,
and I dreamt of a world without war.
I dreamt of a world full of loving,
and awoke to find Allah at my door

I dreamt of a world without anger,
and I dreamt of a world without pride.
I dreamt of a world of compassion,
and I awoke to find Buddha at my side.

I dreamt of a world of tomorrow.
I dreamt of a world set apart.
I dreamt of a world full of glory,
and I awoke to find my creator in my heart.

Isn't that beautiful? So let's help our creator, whoever we believe him to be. Let's help him build life and creation and not death and destruction.

This is the Universal Declaration of the Rights of Children. If you agree with it, sign off on it please. We want to take a billion signatures to the United Nations.

We, the Children of the World, assert our inalienable right to be heard and to have a political voice at the United Nations and at the highest levels of governments worldwide.

We, the Children of the World, must live with justice, with peace and freedom, but above all, with the dignity we deserve.

We, the Children of the World, require a Marshall Plan, a Geneva Convention, and a World Children's Court of Human Rights, which meets regularly to listen to the testimonies as to what is actually happening to us. We intend to provide our own testimonies.

We, the Children of the World, demand the right to be taken to safe shelters in situations of war.

We, the Children of the World, consider hunger, disease, forced labor, and all forms of abuse and exploitation perpetrated upon us to be war.

We, the Children of the World, have had no political voice. We demand such a voice.

We, the Children of the World, will develop our own leadership and set an example that will show governments how to live in peace and with freedom.

We, the Children of the World, serve notice on our abusers and exploiters whomever they may be, that from this day hence, we will begin the task of holding you responsible for our suffering.

If you want to learn more about the Cities of Compassion, go to www .centersofcompassion.org. The site also includes the Universal Declaration of the Rights of Children.

September 23, 2007
Santa Monica, California

Nuclear Weapons and a Culture of Peace

David Krieger

Founder and President, Nuclear Age Peace Foundation

Under Dr. Krieger's leadership as president since 1982, the Nuclear Age Peace Foundation has initiated many innovative and important projects for building peace, strengthening international law, abolishing nuclear weapons and empowering a new generation of peace leaders. Dr. Krieger has lectured throughout the United States, Europe and Asia on issues of peace, security, international law and the abolition of nuclear weapons. He has received many awards for his work for a more peaceful and nuclear-weapons-free world.

He is the chair of the International Engineers and Scientists for Global Responsibility, a member of the International Steering Committee of the Middle Powers Initiative and a councilor on the World Future Council. He serves on the advisory council of many organizations throughout the world working for peace and justice.

In his early career, he was an assistant professor at the University of Hawaii and San Francisco State University. He worked at the Center for the Study of Democratic Institutions on issues of international law and ocean governance and at the Foundation for Reshaping the International Order in the Netherlands on the effects of dual-purpose technologies on disarmament, development and the environment.

As phrased by the eighth action area of the 1999 United Nations Programme of Action on a Culture of Peace, promoting international peace and security, Dr. Krieger focuses on individual responsibility in the abolition of nuclear weapons as a key element. He says: "We should all know our rights under international law, which include the rights to life, liberty, security of person and freedom from torture. There is also a human right to peace. We must take responsibility for ensuring these rights for ourselves and others across the planet."

It is a pleasure to be with you in this fiftieth anniversary year of the Toda declaration, in which the second president of the Soka Gakkai, Josei Toda, spoke to 50,000 young members of your organization and called upon them to lead the way in abolishing nuclear weapons—weapons that he characterized as an "absolute evil." I strongly agree with Josei Toda that these weapons are an "absolute evil" and must be eliminated.

I have engaged in a dialogue with your current president, Daisaku Ikeda, which was published in the book *Choose Hope*. I know from our exchange in this dialogue that Daisaku Ikeda carries on the vision of his mentor, Josei Toda, in seeking the elimination of all nuclear weapons from our planet. This is a key element in his vision to create a culture of peace.

For the past twenty-five years, I have been the president of the Nuclear

Age Peace Foundation, an organization that I helped to found in 1982. The Foundation has three principal goals: to abolish nuclear weapons; to strengthen international law, particularly as it pertains to the prevention of war and the elimination of nuclear arms; and to empower a new generation of peace leaders to carry on the struggle for a more peaceful world, free of the overriding nuclear weapons threat to humanity.

One of the key formative events in my own life, placing me on the path to work for a nuclear-weapons-free future, was an early visit to the Hiroshima and Nagasaki Peace Memorial Museums at age twenty-one. At these museums, I learned a lesson that was not part of my education in the United States. In the United States, we were taught the perspective of those above the bombs—the people who made the decisions that led to the creation and use of the atom bomb. It was a story of scientific and technological triumph, a story of victors with little reference to loss of life and the suffering of the victims.

At the Peace Memorial Museums in Hiroshima and Nagasaki, it was a human story, a tragedy of massive death and destruction. It was a story told from the perspective of those under the bombs, and a warning about our common future: *We must eliminate these weapons before they eliminate us.*

Let me share with you ten reasons why I oppose nuclear weapons. These are reasons why I believe everyone should become actively engaged in the struggle against these instruments of annihilation.

They are long-distance killing machines incapable of discriminating between soldiers and civilians, the aged and the newly born, or between men, women and children.

They threaten the destruction of cities, countries and civilization; of all that is sacred; of all that is human; of all that exists.

They threaten to foreclose the future.

They are cowardly weapons, and in their use there can be no honor.

They are a false god, dividing nations into nuclear "haves" and "have-nots," bestowing unwarranted prestige and privilege on those that possess them.

They are a distortion of science and technology, twisting our knowledge of nature to destructive purposes.

They mock international law, displacing it with an allegiance to raw power.

They waste our resources on the development of instruments of annihilation.

They concentrate power and undermine democracy.

They corrupt our humanity.

Nuclear weapons place a dark cloud over the human future, what John F. Kennedy likened to the sword of Damocles. Inherent in these weapons are the seeds of destruction of cities, countries, civilization and even the human species as well as much of life on earth. Such destructive potential creates special responsibilities for all who are alive today, and more focused responsibilities for the leaders of nuclear-weapons states. Nuclear weapons raise profound moral, legal and ethical questions. In essence, these can be reduced to a single overriding question: *Does any country have the moral or legal right to threaten or use these weapons of indiscriminate mass murder in any situation?*

The International Court of Justice answered this question by saying that the threat or use of nuclear weapons is generally illegal. The Court could not conclude, however, whether or not international law precluded the use of nuclear weapons in one circumstance: when the very survival of a state is at stake. But even in this instance, the Court concluded that such threat or use must not violate international humanitarian law, meaning that the threat or use of such weapons must not be indiscriminate, disproportionate to a preceding attack or cause unnecessary suffering.

Unfortunately, the dangers of nuclear weapons have been met largely with ignorance, apathy and denial. This must change. As a species, we must engage the issue of nuclear weapons as though our collective future depended upon our ability to successfully resolve the challenge presented by these weapons of mass annihilation.

Nuclear weapons were invented by man, and it is often argued that they cannot be "dis-invented." Another way of stating this is: The genie is out of the bottle and cannot be returned to the bottle. This perspective is a way of dismissing the problem. It is most often offered by those who possess nuclear weapons to justify their continued reliance upon these weapons and their failure to engage in serious efforts to eliminate them.

It may be true that the genie cannot be put back in the bottle in the sense that knowledge cannot be unlearned, but between the knowledge of how to create nuclear weapons and the implementation of that knowledge in building nuclear weapons is a border that can be respected, controlled and verified. It is a matter of political will, and in the world today the political will for nuclear abolition among leaders of nuclear weapons states is largely absent.

To achieve the necessary political will to eliminate nuclear weapons and establish procedures to ensure that cheating does not occur, it will be necessary for citizens to lead their leaders. Despite long-standing legal obligations in the Nuclear Non-Proliferation Treaty to engage in good faith negotiations for nuclear disarmament, the leaders of nuclear weapons states have not taken this obligation seriously. They have been content with maintaining double standards in which they rely upon their nuclear arsenals while seeking to ensure that other countries do not join the nuclear club. But double standards are not viable. They will inevitably fail, resulting in the continued spread of nuclear weapons.

The spread of nuclear weapons is taking place and raising alarm throughout the world. India and Pakistan made multiple tests of nuclear weapons in 1998. In 2003, North Korea withdrew from the Non-Proliferation Treaty and, in 2006, conducted its first nuclear weapons test. Iran, pursuing its right under international law to enrich uranium for peaceful purposes, has raised concern in the international community that its program is really aimed at developing nuclear weapons. Often ignored in discussions of nuclear proliferation is Israel, which is thought to have a nuclear arsenal of between one hundred and two hundred nuclear weapons, undoubtedly a provocation to other countries in the Middle East. Nuclear proliferation draws attention away from the larger arsenals of the original nuclear weapons states: the United States, Russia, the United Kingdom, France and China. The challenge confronting humanity is not just the spread of nuclear weapons; it is the existence of nuclear weapons. The two problems are interconnected. The existence of nuclear weapons promotes the proliferation of nuclear weapons, and proliferation promotes further development of nuclear weapons as well as further proliferation. It is a reasonable expectation that, as nuclear weapons proliferate, they will find their way into the hands of non-state extremist organizations. Such organizations will not be inhibited from using nuclear weapons by fear of retaliation. They will understand that the more powerful nuclear weapons states cannot retaliate against those they cannot locate. This potentiality should give pause to the current nuclear weapons states, for it suggests a clear way in which deterrence can fail.

There can be no honor in producing, possessing, testing, threatening or using nuclear weapons. Those who take part in nuclear weapons programs and gain livelihood from them risk the destruction of humanity for personal gain. We are challenged as never before in human history. Our responsibility as citizens of earth in the beginning of the twenty-first century is to end the nuclear weapons threat to humanity and to end war as a social institution. Unfortunately, we are far from those twin goals so critical to the future of life on earth. The survivors of Hiroshima and Nagasaki are the ambassadors and prophets of the Nuclear Age. They have seen atomic destruction at close hand. Their testimonies are sober reflections on the unleashed power of the atom. They speak out so that their past will not become our future. But their testimony is not enough. We must act as though the very future of humanity depended upon our success in eliminating nuclear weapons and war. The stakes are very high and the prospects dim, but with courage and persistence we may succeed. And it is that flicker of hope in a dark time that should inspire us to summon the courage to change the world.

In addition to the ever-present threat of nuclear annihilation, we live in a world in which war and structural violence (that is, violence that is built into the societal framework) are prevalent. Each year, war claims countless victims, mostly innocent civilians. It is widely reported that more than 90 percent of the victims of wars today are civilians. In the Iraq war, some 4,000 American soldiers have died, but according to independent polling agency Opinion Business Research, the number of Iraqi civilians killed is reported to be more than 1.2 million. That is a ratio of 1 to 300. It is more aptly characterized as a slaughter than a war. In Darfur, genocide has continued unabated for years, with the international community seemingly helpless to stop the killing.

The structural violence in our world, like war, is a deep stain on the human record. Half the world's people still live on less than two dollars a day, while the world spends some $1.2 trillion on arms. Of this, the United States spends nearly half, more than the combined totals of the next thirty-two countries.

For just a small percentage of global military spending, every child on the planet could receive basic health care, adequate nutrition and an education, but these are not the values we choose to espouse. Something is terribly wrong with our ability to organize ourselves to live justly on our precious earth.

Our world is one in which human life is devalued for many, and greed is often rewarded. It is a world often not kind to children. Each hour, 500 children die in Africa; 12,000 each day. They die of starvation and preventable diseases, not because there is not enough food or medicine, but because these are not distributed to those who need them.

Our world is also not very wise in preparing for the future. We are busy using up the world's resources, particularly its fossil fuels, and, in the process, polluting the environment. So hungry are we for energy and other resources that we pay little attention to the needs and well-being of future generations. Our lifestyles in the richer countries are unsustainable, and they are foreclosing opportunities for future generations who will be burdened by diminishing resources and a deteriorating environment.

Militarism and social progress are inversely related. In 1949, Costa Rica dismantled its military force and instead devoted its resources to achieving a better life for its people. Since then, it has been a stable democracy in a region often shattered by turmoil. The country has a low infant mortality rate, a high life expectancy rate and a literacy rate of 96 percent.

If someone were to observe our planet from outer space, that person might conclude that we do not appreciate the beauty and bounty of our magnificent earth. I hope you will never take for granted this life-sustaining planet—the only one we know of in the universe. The planet itself is a miracle, as is each of us. As miracles, how can we engage in wars that kill other miracles?

War no longer makes sense in the Nuclear Age. The stakes are too high. In a world with nuclear weapons, we roll the dice on the human future each time we engage in war. Nuclear weapons must be eliminated and the materials to make them placed under strict international control so that we don't bring life on our planet to an abrupt end.

Leaders who take their nations to war without the sanction of international law must be held to account. This is what the Allied leaders concluded after World War II, when they held the Nazi leaders to account for crimes against peace, war crimes and crimes against humanity. No leader anywhere on the planet should be allowed to stand above international law.

Every citizen of earth has rights, well articulated in the Universal Declaration of Human Rights and other human rights agreements. We should all know our rights under international law, which include the rights to life, liberty, security of person and freedom from torture. There is also a human right to peace. We must take responsibility for ensuring these rights for ourselves and others across the planet.

We live in an interdependent world. Borders cannot make us safe. We can choose to live together in peace or to perish together in nuclear war. We can choose to live together with sustainable lifestyles or to perish together as our technologies destroy our environment. We can choose to live together in a world with justice and dignity for all or to perish together in a world of vast disparity, in which a small minority live in luxury and overabundance, while the majority of humanity lives in abject poverty and despair.

To build global peace requires our awareness, our recognition of our essential unity with all humanity and our preparations for peace. No nation alone, no matter how powerful, can solve the global problems that confront us. Problems such as environmental degradation, global warming, poverty, communicable diseases and, in recent years, terrorism, to name a few, all require global solutions.

The world is interconnected, and modern communications and transportation have made this impossible to ignore. It is time to recognize that, regardless of where we were born, we are all citizens of earth sharing a common future.

For more than 2,000 years, we have followed the Roman dictum, "If you want peace, prepare for war." But preparations for war have all too often led to war. In today's world, this is a particularly perilous strategy.

We must try a new approach. If we truly want peace, we must prepare for peace. This means that we need to develop global strategies to prevent war, choosing non-violent means of conflict resolution and creating justice by ending structural violence.

War is not the answer to any problem. Every war breeds future violence, making old wounds raw and opening new wounds. War is a surrender to the cycle of violence. It carries the Roman dictum to its logical conclusion: war upon war upon war. And each war in the Nuclear Age contains within it the seeds of nuclear annihilation. If we want to break the cycle of violence, we must prohibit war, all war, as a means of resolving disputes. We must substitute dialogue and judicial procedures for the force of arms.

A culture of peace is one that honors the miracle of life. It is a culture in which human interactions and institutions are based on cooperation and dialogue. It is a culture in which war is not a first resort, not a last resort, not even an option.

It is hard to imagine a culture of peace that would embrace or even tolerate nuclear weapons. A culture of peace cannot be built upon the ultimate threat—the threat to destroy everything. There are some who argue that nuclear weapons have kept the peace, but in fact these weapons do not make the world safe for either peace or war. With nuclear weapons in the world, the possibility of catastrophic war is ever present, and the potential for destroying all we hold dear lurks in the recesses of peace.

A culture of peace requires strengthening peace institutions that use peaceful processes. Among the existing institutions are the United Nations, the International Court of Justice and the International Criminal Court. The United Nations is often blamed for not upholding its own Charter, which calls for preventing war. But one of the main reasons that the United Nations fails to stop violence is that its most powerful member states, those with the veto power in the Security Council—the United States, the United Kingdom, France, Russia and China—prevent the United Nations from acting resolutely for peace. Often these powerful members are the ones who initiate the violence. To succeed, the United Nations must become more democratic, shifting more of its power from the Security Council to the General Assembly, and a new Peoples Assembly needs to be created to give full voice to "The Peoples" of the world, rather than to only the world's states.

The International Court of Justice, also known as the World Court, is the world's highest court. It must be given compulsory jurisdiction over all states, and its decisions must be respected and enforced. Imagine the ineffectiveness of national courts if defendants could simply refuse to show up to their trials, or if there were no means to enforce the decisions of the courts. Again, the most powerful states in the world should lead, and lead by example.

The Rome Statute for an International Criminal Court entered into force on July 1, 2002. This court holds individuals to account for the most heinous crimes committed under international law. The ICC has jurisdiction over war crimes, crimes against humanity and genocide. Once a definition of aggression is agreed upon, it may also add to its jurisdiction the crime of aggressive war. It is a court that brings the Principles of Nuremberg into the Nuclear Age. It upholds the crucial legal principle of individual accountability. Crimes are committed by individuals, regardless of state authority, and individuals must be held accountable for such crimes.

Although the majority of the world's nations are members of the International Criminal Court, including most U.S. allies, the United States is not. The United States has instead pursued bilateral agreements with foreign nations arguing that it needs to insulate U.S. soldiers from the ICC. However, the ICC has a provision that it only takes jurisdiction if national courts fail to do so. Further, it is improbable that this court would ever take jurisdiction of a lower-ranking soldier as the U.S. government claims. Like the tribunals at Nuremberg, it is much more likely that the ICC would be focused on high-level leaders who committed war crimes, crimes against humanity or genocide.

One new international institution that is needed is a United Nations Emergency Peace Service. This would be a 10,000- to 15,000-person UN volunteer rapid deployment force that would be a first responder to suspected acts of genocide or crimes against humanity. It would be a small UN force that would prevent violence from erupting into genocide, as in Rwanda and Darfur.

At the national level, states could also create departments of peace, just as they now have departments of war or "defense." A very good proposal for a cabinet-level Department of Peace has been put forward by Congressman Dennis Kucinich in the United States. His proposal calls for a secretary of peace in the president's cabinet and for assistant secretaries of peace to be high officials in all other cabinet departments, such as the Department of State, Department of Defense, Department of Energy, etc.

To increase the effectiveness of international institutions and to create new institutions at the international and national levels will require committed action by individuals and civil society organizations. We all need to realize that with rights come responsibilities. Change does not occur magically. It occurs because individuals engage with societal problems and take actions to create a better world. Often, change occurs person to person. Each of us can be an agent for change in the world. We are each as powerful as we choose to be.

We can each start by choosing peace and making a firm commitment to peace with justice. This means that we make peace a central issue and priority in our lives and demonstrate peace in all we do. We can live peace, educate for peace, speak out for peace and support and vote for candidates who call for peace. In choosing peace, we also choose hope rather than ignorance, complacency or despair. Hope gives rise to action, and action in turn gives rise to increased possibility for change and to further hope. It is a spiral in which action deepens commitment, which leads to more action.

Like others who have chosen the path of peace—Mahatma Gandhi, Mother Teresa, Martin Luther King, Jr., Archbishop Desmond Tutu and the Dalai Lama—we must realize that it will not be a quick or easy journey. The path will require of you courage, compassion and commitment. The rewards may be few, except your own understanding of the necessity of the journey.

The path to peace will require persistence. You may be tempted to leave the path, but what you do for peace you do for humanity. In the struggle for a better world and more decent future, we are not allowed to give up. Our efforts to create a culture of peace are a gift to humanity and the future. What better gift could we give to our fellow citizens of the planet and to future generations than our courage, compassion and commitment in the cause of peace?

October 12, 2007
New York

Fear and Insecurity As a Cause of Conflict

Douglas Becker

Acting Director, Peace and Conflict Studies, School of International Relations, University of Southern California

Dr. Douglas Becker's expertise covers a wide range of topics, including the prosecution of war crimes, the United Nations and conflict resolution, international law, U.S. foreign policy and U.S. diplomatic history. His most recent publication is *The Bush Administration's Campaign Against the International Criminal Court* (2004, as part of a collected volume). Dr. Becker is an active member of the International Studies Association and was president of the Model United Nations Educators Association, which is committed to aiding university and high school instructors in Model United Nations and United Nations research. He also served on the Board of Directors for the National Collegiate Conference Association.

His lecture particularly addresses the eighth action area of the United Nations Programme of Action on a Culture of Peace: Promoting international peace and security. Dr. Becker argues that we must establish "security through understanding and true peace, rather than provoking fear and then seeking a balance of power to create peace as the simple absence of war." He adds: "We must devise ways to overcome the fear" by first recognizing the problem and then engaging honestly in dialogue about fear and insecurity.

The preamble of the UNESCO Constitution declares, "Since wars begin in the minds of men, it is in the minds of men that defenses of peace must be constructed." Soka Gakkai International President Daisaku Ikeda eloquently writes, "Fear builds barriers of aversion and discrimination in the forms of national boundaries or of exclusion and discrimination on the bases of race, religion, gender, social class, financial status or merely personal preference" (*For the Sake of Peace*, p. 58).

This afternoon I will argue the case for why fear and insecurity compel individuals to commit some of the worst atrocities in human history. I will introduce empirical evidence suggesting that racism combined with fear heightens the level of atrocity and compels even greater killing. I will outline the basic premises of the field of international relations, which is my own field of training, and demonstrate how it reinforces the basic fears, which have compelled this human misery. Considering that those who would practice foreign policy are typically trained in my field, I will suggest that we are what we teach. I will conclude with thoughts on how to overcome these problems posed by fear and insecurity. These proposals, I admit, will probably appear to be modest at best, considering the task at hand.

Many in my field of international relations focus on the question of why states go to war, and why the system itself is based on war. Kenneth Waltz, one of the great international relations scholars, lays out three levels of analysis: the system, the state and the individual, or in his own terminology: man, the state and war. His work focuses on the system, and most of my colleagues seem to focus on the state. I am going to focus on the individual, something on which international relations theory spends far too little time.

Rather than focus on individuals as heads of states, the one area where IR theory tends to be rather strong, my talk takes its cue from Howard Zinn's A *People's History* approach [with multiple perspectives] and applies it to contemporary world politics. Carl Sandburg's poem, "The Little Girl Saw Her First Troop Parade," asks the question, "Do you know... I know something.... Sometime they'll give a war and nobody will come." This poem gave rise to the 1960s slogan, "What if we threw a war, and nobody came?" Now every moral and philosophical system has some variance of that four-word declarative that we find in the Judeo-Christian Bible, "Thou shalt not kill." So why is there so much killing in the world?

There is an impressive scholarship on issues like the dehumanization of others, and this dehumanization enables killing. When you propagandize about the other as subhuman, and you use racist iconography depicting the enemy as something less than human, it serves as a powerful tool to enable this killing. Even if the enemy *is* subhuman, there is no inherent right to kill. We don't have the inherent right to kill animals, for instance. Dehumanization enables rather than compels killing. It is fear that compels us. This is because, in most philosophical traditions, you have the right to kill, to relax that four-word declarative, if your own life or the lives of your loved ones are in danger.

This is a basic human needs approach to human security, and it is most eloquently addressed in Franklin Roosevelt's famous 1941 speech to Congress. He lays out in this speech the four freedoms. It is the president's vision for a peaceful world, and what makes it striking is its explicit reference to fear and insecurity. Alongside his traditional freedoms of speech and religion, Roosevelt adds the need to preserve the freedom from want and the freedom from fear. The basic human needs approach, with its inclusion of the physical and emotional needs of individuals who would fight and support the wars, addresses the true core cause of war.

Now consider what are typically cited as the most basic of human needs: food, water, shelter and security. The first three, which would all fall under Roosevelt's basket of freedom from wants, have compelled states and individuals to fight war. All three of these are tangible and measurable. The amount of average daily calories, access to potable drinking water and the percentage of the population that is homeless are all measurable.

Security is unique in that it is completely perceptual. A person can be in utter peril and unaware of the danger he or she faces. That same person can walk down a safe street in abject fear of consequences, despite the lack of any threat.

As such, fear and insecurity may be manipulated by both scrupulous and unscrupulous political actors and can drive populations to war or call them to peace. Fear is such a powerful motivator because it is so easily manipulated. It is easy to scare people. When those manipulations take the form of racism, this combination provides the sort of combustible mix that has marked human history with horrific atrocity.

The use of race as a means to compel armies to kill is nothing new. The racist typically dehumanizes the enemy with the use of language and removes the moral agency both from the soldier and from the person he is killing. The most damning act of racism is its inclusion of an entire population regardless of ideology, history, personal motivation or any other factor. Simply being a member of the race is enough to convict, often to a death sentence.

Racism alone is not enough to compel violence. The racial descriptions of the other as subhuman are not enough to compel people to kill. It requires fear mixed with racism. Nowhere is this combustible fear and racism more apparent than in the commissions of genocides. Genocides require war. They take place during war. War first provides cover, the fog of war. This makes it easier for those who would commit atrocities to hide what they are actually doing.

How many campaigns of extreme violence take place, literally under our noses, without us realizing until after the killing has taken place? International actors frequently find interventions to stop genocides problematic, simply because of a lack of good intelligence of what is going on in the field, or in another popular parlance, "Who is the good guy, and who is the bad guy?" Genocides also require a certain internal logic of violence. The logic that says it is time to kill or be killed enables the perpetrators to commit this horrific act without moral consequence. They are killing to protect themselves, their family, their home, their nation.

For instance, the killing in Rwanda coupled the racial imagery of Tutsi as cockroaches with descriptions that they were murderers seeking to invade the country. It took place in the context of a civil war, one that would result in a Tutsi victory that actually ended the genocide. German anti-Semitism that led to the horrific, previously unprecedented atrocity of the Holocaust took place under the pretense that Jews were stabbing Germans in the back and would compel that nation to lose its country if allowed to exist. The rape of Nanking was committed in the backdrop of the war in China where Japanese soldiers claimed that they were being attacked by Chinese civilians or soldiers hiding in civilian garb, and that justified the horrific atrocity committed against that city. The Turkish genocide of Armenians occurred during the extreme insecurity of World War I, a time in which the British sought to defeat the Ottoman Empire by destroying it from within. In turn, the Turks attempted to destroy those they believed would be a prime candidate to destroy them from within.

Sadly, it makes little difference whether these accusations are true or not, because the fear is real.

The historian John Dower, in his seminal work on race and war titled *War Without Mercy*, argues persuasively that when two sides in war are racially differentiated, the level of atrocity is considerably higher. One of his most telling statistics is that of slightly under 100,000 Americans who were held as prisoners of war by the Germans, only roughly 1 percent of them died in captivity, largely from battle wounds. In the Pacific, Americans held by the Japanese numbered roughly 26,000, of which 45 percent died. Japan was extremely racially aware and defined itself as a distinctly superior race and as a representative of Asian races against Western colonialism.

John Dower doesn't stop there. He also illustrates the extreme anti-Asian and, in particular, anti-Japanese racism in the United States prior to World War II. There was no subsequent internment of German Americans that mirrored the internment of Japanese Americans. Indeed, the entire American policy of prisoners of war was predicated on the belief that the Japanese would never surrender. This was because of the Bushido, the way of the warrior.

As a result, the United States, and particularly Admiral Chester Nimitz, had a no-prisoner policy, something that never gets reported in the American history texts. It was an effective policy, particularly for the Navy; since they had engaged in an island-hopping strategy, it required a mobile force and prisoners would just weigh them down. When the Japanese discovered the American no-prisoner policy, it compelled its commanders to fight to the death of the last soldier, presuming they would die anyway. It's a chicken-and-the-egg argument, and one that is beyond my expertise as to which of these caused which, but they were certainly mutually reinforcing. It also reinforced the notion that the Japanese would listen to neither reason nor mercy and was an extremely important factor in the decision of the United States to drop the atomic bombs on Hiroshima and Nagasaki.

Germany's own racist policies in the East mirrored Dower's descriptions in the Pacific. Germany's treatment of its Eastern neighbors was considerably worse than its treatment in the West. It should come as no surprise that Germany racially differentiated itself from the East, the Untermensch, or Eastern slobs, as the Germans described them, in a way that they did not in the West.

That is one of many pieces of empirical evidence to suggest that racism in warfare heightens levels of atrocity. It compels individuals to refuse to differentiate between civilian and soldier, which is a fundamental premise behind what we call discrimination. Unlike St. Augustine's Just War Theory, in which you choose legitimate military targets and don't attack civilians, the policy of total war is a very modern concept in which an entire population is deemed a military target. Racism ensures that we simply look at those slanted eyes as guilty. Replace slanted eyes with rags on their heads or copies of the Koran, and you have the horrifically updated version of the painfully familiar sentiments.

The core of my argument is that if security is not provided by some external act or a state, the international system and so forth, humans will provide for it themselves, or at least attempt to do it. This leads us to the security paradox. Perhaps the most important early modern philosopher influencing my field of international relations is Thomas Hobbes, a seventeenth-century Englishman writing in the midst of that nation's bloody civil war. Hobbes identified security as the core interest of all persons. His "natural man" was one who consistently threatened others and who lived in abject fear for his own life, as well as that of his loved ones.

In the absence of a powerful entity to ensure security, we are consigned to a life that is, in his famous phrase, "solitary, poor, nasty, brutish, and short." Hobbes's greatest contribution to international relations is his recognition of the security paradox. He writes that under conditions of what he calls the state of nature, or the absence of governmental authority, because of our extreme insecurity, we have no choice but to arm ourselves for our defense. Because arms have both offensive and defensive capabilities—and they all do, when one person arms himself, he threatens his neighbors—they will respond by arming themselves and creating a cycle of insecurity. Indeed, the more you try to arm yourself, the less secure you will feel. This is the same logic that creates arms races. The United States and the Soviet Union consistently sought to overcome perceptions of insecurity through massive armaments. This led to the perception that peace was kept through the aptly named policy of mutually assured destruction (MAD).

The irony of MAD is that it was based not on rational responses to attack, but instead on the emotional response of anger and vengeance. Remember, mutually assured destruction ensured that if one state attacked the other, so long as there were enough weapons that survived that attack, what we called a second strike capability, they would launch back, both sides would be destroyed, and there would be no victors in war. But if a state launched that first strike and destroyed an enemy, the only motivation for the victim states was vengeance. Nothing is going to save that first state's government or its population. As we now know, probably the entire planet would be destroyed. Nuclear planners understood this because they automated the second strike capability, ensuring computers would launch under the guise that if our command and control structure was destroyed, then neither of the two states could launch a second strike. In reality, there was a distinct question as to whether or not a human would launch that second strike when there was nothing militarily to be gained by it. This is fear rising to the level of complete and utter irrationality. The irony is that mutually shared destruction is described in my field as rational choice.

Indeed, those who argue that nuclear weapons were in fact usable were considered to be proponents of what we called nuclear utilization theory (NUT). The acronym of MAD versus NUT. This irrationality led to the waste of billions of dollars of much needed resources, as well as countless sleepless nights. Personally, I remember being a child of the eighties, occasionally being quite terrified and wondering if I just had enough shovels. I don't know if anybody recognized that. That was the Reagan administration's civil defense policy, in effect, "With enough shovels, we can survive a nuclear attack."

Consider the poignant words of former president Dwight Eisenhower, "Every gun that is made, every warship launched, every rocket fired, signifies in the final sense a theft from those who are hungry and not fed, those who are cold and not clothed. This world in arms is spending not money alone; it is spending the sweat of its laborers, the genius of its scientists, the hopes of its children" (April 16, 1953). And it ensures basic human needs are not met.

Hobbes's recommendation to overcome the lack of security was to create a powerful government; to use his own term, a "leviathan" would be charged with maintaining law and order. Sadly, in international relations, states exist not under the guise of a powerful international organization but under conditions of anarchy. The foundational theory in international relations is termed *realism*. There are four conditions in the international system: states are the primary actors, they all possess offensive capabilities, they are uncertain about one another's intentions, and they exist in a state of anarchy. Hobbes would be proud. Each of these conditions leads the realist to base his assumptions about international relations upon a foundation of fear. This is fear modeled as theory.

At the core, realists maintain that the international system is anarchical. World federalists hold out hope that the creation of an international organization charged with collective security and peacemaking will create a global government that would overcome Hobbesian anarchy. But, sadly, the hope for a global government with the power to ensure a state's security has never been realized. Any survey of the United Nations, with its inability to intervene in conflicts in the former Yugoslavia, Rwanda and Darfur, not to mention Iraq, comes to the same sad conclusion. The United Nations is an organization built on the norm of sovereignty defined as state primacy in control over its own territory.

The United Nations manages anarchy, it doesn't overcome it—or at least it attempts to manage anarchy to varying success. Its interventions are predicated upon state invitation. UN Secretary-General Kofi Annan's pronouncement of a state having a duty to protect is subsumed by the United Nations' respect for sovereignty. Indeed the modus operandi of the

United Nations is that it cannot keep peace if there is no peace to be kept. Hence, it is extremely reluctant to go into Darfur without the invitation of the Sudanese government, a government that may very well be the one committing the atrocities, committing the genocide.

By the way, you may ask why the United Nations is going into Darfur today. If you track the battles in Darfur, they have moved farther and farther west. The United Nations is being invited in because the ethnic cleansing is nearly complete. Consider the role of the United Nations in sovereignty even in a country like the United States with no real threat of the United Nations trying to infringe upon American sovereignty. There is even a political fringe that suggests that the United Nations has plans using black helicopters and special instructions on the backs of street signs to conquer the United States. The United Nations in many places unintentionally instills fear rather than security.

The realists' response to the calls to resolve anarchy via global government, global governance or international law is that the state that faces existential threats must either arm itself or find powerful friends. Hans Morgenthal, who authored *Politics Among Nations* in the 1940s, has become a patron saint of criticism against international organizations. Morgenthal, a German expatriate, witnessed the atrocities of the Nazis. Probably no statement captures the German sentiment of disregard for international law more than the testimony of Hermann Göring at Nuremberg. Prosecutors charged the former Reich marshal with a whole series of violations of treaties, which Germany had signed and ratified, including the famous Kellogg-Briand Pact, which outlawed war as an instrument of violence in the 1920s. Göring's response was that they considered treaties to be, and I quote, "just so much toilet paper."

The realist concludes in the face of rising power and aggressiveness that the state must defend itself, because if you rely on international organizations, you will lose your sovereignty. Since it is the aggressive state that does not respect international law, references to it will fall on deaf ears. For the realist, the only means to ensure peace in this international system is through that ever-elusive balance of power. States are only dissuaded from aggressive war when they believe they cannot win. I remember being in a seminar with a realist professor, and he once asked, "What is it that states in nineteenth-century Europe wanted?" He answered his own question: "Whatever they could take." That is ultimately what a state's interest is.

The only way to maintain peace is to ensure this rough power balance, because, keep in mind, both states have to be convinced that they can't win the war. They have to be balanced or at least have the perceptions that they can't win.

States frequently will take chances if they believe they can win, even if they are not ensured that they will do so. This is a system that is not only elusive but also predicated, of course, on fear. Now unsatisfied with this balance of power as a resolution to war, critics of realism seek to solve the security paradox through addressing the other conditions.

Let's turn to the question of the offensive capability of weapons. Typically the area of nuclear arms control and reduction is cited, particularly recently, as a real advance in peacemaking. The record of nuclear arms reduction has been impressive recently, but it holds little hope that fear can be overcome and that we can ever rid the world of nuclear weapons.

First, there have been impressive cuts in the existing nuclear arsenals of the United States and the former Soviet Union, now Russia. According to treaty obligations that both countries have signed, though still waiting to be ratified, the two states have pledged to reduce their existing nuclear stockpiles by more than 90 percent from what they were at the peak of the Cold War. This means from a high of roughly 22,000 warheads apiece, they have pledged to reduce them to 1,700 apiece. Keep in mind, every warhead packs an impressive punch. Even the smallest of these are roughly ten times the blast of the bombs that destroyed Hiroshima and Nagasaki. The largest of these warheads, which still exist, contain as much as 30 megatons of blast, 30 million tons of TNT, and that doesn't even include the accompanying radiation. If a 30-megaton bomb were dropped on Omaha, Nebraska, we would be killed in Los Angeles. These warheads still exist under the arms reduction treaties, and we are far from even getting down to the 1,700 mark. It's simply a pledge. It hasn't been implemented.

Whenever you have anybody address you who deals with nuclear weapons, the issue of the zero option comes up, ridding the world of nuclear weapons. Proposals for the zero option are always met with the fear-based presumption that some actors would probably hide a nuclear bomb. We call it the bomb-in-the-basement scenario, and it always comes up, I guarantee it. They would use this bomb-in-the-basement either to launch a war or engage in nuclear blackmail. The fear is considered valid, even though the only time in human history where a state had unilateral possession of nuclear weapons was in the mid-to-late 1940s, and U.S. attempts to leverage nuclear power were horribly unsuccessful at compelling the Soviets, for instance, to withdraw from Eastern Europe. Nuclear blackmail doesn't work, so states are considering spending billions on national missile defense, even though such a system has never been proven to work even in a lab.

Even if missile defense worked, fear would compel it to grow well beyond the capacity to shoot down a missile or two, because the enemy may arm itself with multiple weapons. Oh, and by the way, if terrorists got their hands on these weapons, they would probably deliver them via a suitcase bomb. What good is a missile? If terrorists got ahold of a suitcase bomb, what good are 1,700 warheads? It's not going to stop the terrorist from detonating that bomb. Regardless, the Bush administration is currently proposing to Congress the development of what they call reliable replacement warheads (RRWs). These are intended to replace the current warheads that are deployed throughout the United States and Europe.

Arms-control specialist Joseph Cirincione was recently at the University of Southern California, and he derisively called these—and I wish I had coined this term—"Rediculously Redundant Warheads." The administration is also advocating the development of nuclear-tipped bunker busters to be used against potential Al Qaeda targets. The United States is the only nuclear power not to have ratified the Comprehensive Nuclear Test Ban Treaty. India and Pakistan have not as well, but that treaty was negotiated before they officially went nuclear.

Often, the media cite fears of a nuclear-armed Iran or North Korea as justification for new weapons. The United States also continues to deploy nuclear artillery, as well as tactical or battlefield nuclear weapons. Now, lest you think that I am simply highlighting the United States, other states have actually been fearful of developing these weapons, because they believe they will be considered the pariah if they develop new nuclear weapons.

John Ruggie declares that the United States is, what he terms, *the world's leading norms entrepreneur*. What the United States does, the world follows. Leadership has both its privileges and its responsibilities.

This is just nuclear weaponry. Now let's consider how many people have been killed via conventional weapons. I could argue that the AK-47 assault rifle is the real weapon of mass destruction. It is estimated that this weapon kills roughly a quarter of a million people annually. That is a new Hiroshima and Nagasaki every year. There has been no attempt to ban or even limit the production of AK-47s or any conventional weapons. We don't know how many there are out there because they are not all registered, but it is estimated that there are 100 million AK-47s in the world today. States continue to possess offensive capabilities and to provoke fear, and fear is what compels states not to give up weapons.

Let's turn to the issue of state intentions. Immanuel Kant held out the hope that since democracies don't fight one another, if we just increase the number of democracies, we can increase peace—what we call the *zone of democratization*, the zone of peace.

The assertion that democracies do not fight one another is true. Consider, for instance, France and Germany, two states that fought three wars in less than a hundred years, who now would consider war between the two inconceivable. Democratization helped to promote this kind of peace. Some in my field go so far as to call the democratic peace theory an axiom, the only one that we have except for the balance of power in international relations theory. It was the foundation of U.S. President Bill Clinton's policy. It also is the foundation behind the United States' continued presence in Iraq and Afghanistan. It holds up the hope that if people are allowed to decide issues of war and peace, should they trust their counterparts in other nations to have that same choice, they would never choose war. They would always choose peace.

Now there are two challenges to the democratic peace theory. The first is whether or not you can democratize at the end of a gun barrel. It seems oxymoronic to think you can force somebody to be free. It is, of course, the pretext for continued American involvement in Iraq. Setting aside whether or not it is legitimate, the empirical record is pretty shaky. Nations have to want to democratize if they are, in fact, going to do so.

But in Iraq, while elections are held, the nation is gripped in violence. Even more troubling, I think, is the development of illiberal democracy, or democracies that don't necessarily agree with the United States, as evidenced by the elections in the Gaza Strip, the rise of Hamas and the election of Ahmadinejad in Iran. In each case, the election represents an explicit rejection of alliance with the West.

These democratically elected leaders provoke confrontation rather than cooperation, and of course, the United States doesn't respond with anything but confrontation. It raises the interest that Ito Orin raises: When we study the democratic peace theory, if we use American descriptions of whether a state is democratic, we are actually only measuring whether the United States agrees with that state's policy. It simply describes a state as democratic if it is in alliance and undemocratic if it is not.

Now consider illiberal democracy. Democracy as a popular rule of the people doesn't suggest norms of limited government, liberal values, independent legal system and all those other principles that mark liberal democracy. Illiberal democracy must be seen as a challenge to that fourth premise, the centrality of states. The great irony of the war on terror, and we will get into that terminology in just a moment, is that a non-state actor attacked the United States on September 11, 2001. How did the United States respond? By going to war against two states. With the rise of militarized non-state actors, from terror networks like Al Qaeda to militia leaders who would kidnap and recruit children to wage their wars, even to the rise of publicly traded private military corporations like Blackwater, it is clear we no longer live in a state-centric world.

How do we respond to the lack of a state-centric world? The most popular reaction has been described by the author Samuel Huntington as the notion of the clash of civilizations. Huntington argues that the stakes are raised so that state sovereignty or territory is no longer the currency of conflict, it is civilization itself. Sometimes Huntington is described as a proponent of culture clash, that cultures are clashing. Huntington didn't choose the word *culture*. He chose the word *civilization*, because cultures are differentiated, but civilizations are either civilized or uncivilized. Now, instead of fearing for our sovereignty, for our right to govern ourselves, we fear for our civilization. Fear is now fully fused with race, once again creating the combustible mix that leads to horrible atrocities. The stage is now set for a popular acceptance of policies that oppose core American values, such as in the cases of Abu Ghraib, Guantanamo and the Rendition Policy. These aren't done in private. We have candidates winning elections because they are practicing these policies.

Gender scholars have pointed out this ability to secure a population from a dangerous world; that's what we look for in a president. Men are expected to serve as the protector in a dangerous world, and the president is the citizen soldier who is there to protect us. This "man as protector" motif builds fear into the system.

My colleague J. Ann Tickner at USC, in her book *Gender in International Relations*, wrestles with the question whether a woman would ever be elected president, since men do the protecting and we expect a citizen soldier. She came to the sad conclusion that the only way women will build a currency required to govern a country is if they are fully vested in the protection of the country, such as women in combat. I have asked her whether she could conceive of another way. She said, "Not in the world that we live in." However, I hold out hope that there is a better way.

Fear grips the scholarship in international relations. Practitioners of foreign policy study international relations; they internalize the fear. Think about the description of the term *realism*. Apparently, I would be surreal, unreal or typically idealistic, a dreamer or simply hopelessly naïve. Alexander Wendt challenges these presumptions. Anarchy is what we make of it. If we define a fear-based system, it becomes self-reflective and a self-fulfilling prophecy. Our students become the next generation of leaders, convinced that the world is a dangerous place, and they are convinced that the entire civilization is in peril. It should come as no surprise that they act accordingly. We must devise ways to overcome the fear.

First, like a good psychologist, I suggest that recognizing the problem is a good way to overcome it. Speaking honestly about the role that fear plays in our construction of identity internationally will set the stage for redressing this problem. Second, since the combination of race and fear is so combustible, we must recognize racial differences and embrace them. We need a truly honest and racially aware dialogue about fear and insecurity. Rather than deny race as an identifying feature of humanity, we must be honest about it. When realizing the differentiation in fears based on race, we can promote a healing that is so needed among the races. We need to start talking honestly about race.

Since humanity will provide for its own security in the absence of other actors providing it, we must strengthen the institutions we charge with the provision of security. We must promote good governance. As much as we may bemoan a state-centric world and see a loosening of it, states still possess the greatest hope for real democratization and transparency.

But recognize that democracy comes from below, not from above, and that democracy is a moving target. States are not either democratic or undemocratic, they become less or more so. Although the United Nations has not realized its potential in confronting anarchy, it exists because it is needed. We must overcome its institutional biases and historical constraints to allow it to become the institution the world needs, one that promotes security through understanding and true peace, rather than provoking fear and then seeking a balance of power to create peace as the simple absence of war. The United Nations is only one of many institutions, both currently existing and with potential to be created in the future.

Think about who we consider to be the greatest presidents in American history. A survey of scholars laid out their top ten—they actually rank all of them—as follows:

Abraham Lincoln

Franklin Delano Roosevelt

George Washington

Thomas Jefferson

Theodore Roosevelt

Woodrow Wilson

Harry Truman

Andrew Jackson

Dwight Eisenhower

James Polk

What all ten of these presidents share in common, other than being white men, is that they were either war presidents or war heroes. Lincoln, Roosevelt, Wilson, Truman and Polk all led the country in war. James Polk was the American president during the Mexican-American War. The American presidents who were war heroes were George Washington, Teddy Roosevelt, Dwight Eisenhower and Andrew Jackson.

Thomas Jefferson wasn't linked to war, but he wrote the Declaration of Independence, which led to the Revolutionary War. We deem our great leaders to be those who lead in warfare. That is why President Bush reminds us he is a war president. Those who promote peace agreements like Jimmy Carter and the Camp David Accords are derided as naïve as leaders. On that list, I think he was number twenty-nine.

With the rare exception of leaders like Mohandas Gandhi, Nelson Mandela and Martin Luther King, we have a distinct paucity of peace heroes, and we must change that if we are going to overcome this bias of fear.

I also ask you, how many people died on September 11, 2001? What was the most common cause of death? Most of you will say, I think the number was a little more than 3,000 and the most common cause of death was either being crushed by a building or being burned to death. Actually, that number is more than ten times that, as 33,000 children alone died on September 11, 2001, and the most common cause of death was malnutrition. Security is about so much more than physical security from attack, but sadly we limit our discussions of security to just the traditional forms. The human-needs approach to security promotes a new dialogue about the topic and will help secure a world free from fear.

We must promote a conception of interconnectedness that ensures we see all issues as human ones rather than narrow national interests. On September 12, 2001, the French newspaper *Le Monde* declared, "We are all Americans." There are two ways to take that headline. The first is that everyone stands with the United States. That's how the administration took the headline. The other way is we are all Americans because we are all victims of the attack. It was an attack not against the United States but against humanity. There was a wonderful opportunity to recast national security interests to a global security that would criminalize Al Qaeda and treat it as a criminal, as an outcast, rather than militarize it and treat it almost as a quasi-state actor and wage war against it. It was an opportunity wasted.

Think about the term *war on terror*. Have you ever thought about why is it not *war on Al Qaeda*, or *war on terrorism?* Terrorism is a strategy. It is a tactic used by weak actors. Al Qaeda is an actor, and it is a terrorist network. Terror is what we feel that provokes extreme fear. It is almost a war on fear. How strange of a term is that, *war on fear?* But when you hear *war on terror*, it is meant to evoke an emotional response. Language itself is used as a powerful motivator of fear, and we need to change that language.

This is why programs like the Culture of Peace Distinguished Speakers Series that the SGI-USA promotes are so important. Since security is completely perceptual, we choose whether to live in fear. Indeed, as the SGI charter states, this organization promotes "infinite respect for the sanctity of life and all-encompassing compassion, enables individuals to cultivate and bring forth their inherent wisdom and, nurturing the creativity of the human spirit, to surmount the difficulties and crises facing humankind and realize a society of peaceful and prosperous coexistence."

In my own peace and conflict work within the School of International Relations at the University of Southern California—setting aside the fact that the program is in essence me and exists in a basement—I get a handful of students who come through my classes every semester. I hope I get them thinking about these issues, so they can pay it forward in their own scholarship. I hope that some of my students become world leaders or at least influence world leaders.

Many people think that current college students go to school for four years, and they want to graduate into a six-figure job. I can tell you that is not true. A good number of them are working very hard as college students and are graduating to try to change the world, one person at a time. This is a campaign to be waged one person at a time. It may be a cliché, but it is always so poignant. Mohandas Gandhi called upon us to "be the change we wish to see in the world." I share that vision.

In that spirit, I thank you for taking this journey with me and wish you peace, good health, prosperity and the love of another.

Questions and Answers

AUDIENCE MEMBER 1: Can you clarify what you meant by malnutrition, that 33,000 children died in the aftermath of September 11, 2001?

DR. BECKER: By malnutrition, I mean lack of access to water, lack of access to food and other diseases that could be prevented if we arranged access to an improved number of calories, improved vitamins and specifically, food and water to those children. That's what I mean by malnutrition.

AUDIENCE MEMBER 1: I'm not sure of the connection.

DR. BECKER: That's the point, it is not connected. Again, that is our perception. When I asked how many people died on September 11, 2001, I didn't ask how many people died in the terrorist attacks; I asked how many people died that day. More than ten times the number of people who died in the terrorist attacks died—just the children—as a result of malnutrition.

AUDIENCE MEMBER 2: I am curious about acknowledging and accepting the idea of UN reform. What would be your suggestion as to how we would base the governance of peacemaking if it is not to be focused on sovereignty? What would we do or what can we do to have peace more focused other than on sovereignty?

DR. BECKER: There are two ways to approach that. One is normative, and one is specific. The first rule of politics is always answer the question that you want to answer. I do a lot of work on the normative level. [Former UN Secretary-General] Kofi Annan's description of a state's duty to protect was a wonderfully creative approach to the question of sovereignty. He uses contract theory to declare that the reason states have the right to govern is because they provide for their citizens, and if they don't provide for their citizens, they have actually surrendered their right to govern, particularly if they are the ones waging the war on civilians and on their citizens. He said that the state had a duty to protect, and if it wasn't fulfilling that duty to protect, then other actors presumably—and he referred frequently to the unique legitimating authority of the Security Council—would have the right to intervene as justification, for instance, in East Timor or Kosovo.

The mechanism for who makes that determination certainly is problematic and, at a minimum, I believe we need to have a much richer dialogue than we currently do at the Security Council with its five permanent members. Some of it has to do with the development of the non-governmental organization community, and it also has to do with the involvement of other states, other affected actors. I believe if states understood that they would be held accountable for protecting their citizens, they would take that duty to protect more seriously, although as always, the devil is in the details.

AUDIENCE MEMBER 3: My question is this: You said to move beyond fear they have to have the recognition of fear and willingness to confront it. I listened throughout the lecture and you kept using the word *fear*. So the question that came to me was, what are we afraid of, or what are they afraid of? What is it?

DR. BECKER: A great deal of the fear has to do with the fear of a lack of physical security and fear of a lack of security of the nation. However, when you start thinking of issues related to the clash of civilizations, it would be fear that your own civilization could be eroded, that your own civilization could be changed or potentially destroyed. There is the physical and metaphysical existential fear, the idea of a nation and the idea of a citizen.

AUDIENCE MEMBER 3: When you talk about civilization, who decides who is civilized?

DR. BECKER: That is the many, many, many, many, billion-dollar question right now. According to Huntington, he will differentiate civilization on the basis of historical descriptions, but he equivocates. He sometimes uses religion as differentiation, sometimes race and sometimes geography and history. Some of the criticisms of him are his lack of a real definition for what constitutes a citizen as opposed to a state—we know what that is, it exists, it has sovereignty, etc. But that question of who determines it, the language Huntington uses, is simply civilizational differentiation. I believe it is an invitation for any person to declare any other civilization, whomever that might be, uncivilized, which makes the language extremely dangerous.

October 27, 2007
Santa Monica, California

On Equality Between Women and Men and the Role of Cultural Exchange in Creating Peace

Beate Sirota Gordon

Drafter, Women's Rights Articles for the Japanese Constitution

In 1998, Beate Sirota Gordon was decorated by the Japanese government for her service to Japanese culture. She may be better remembered for her contribution to Japanese women's equality when, at age twenty-two, she drafted portions of the post-World War II Japanese constitution that provided equal rights for women.

Ms. Gordon, born in Vienna in 1923, is the only child of renowned Russian pianist Leo Sirota. She moved to Japan at age five when her father was invited to teach at the Imperial Music Academy. Her home became a meeting place for artists, including traditional kabuki actors, modern dancers, painters and sculptors, both European and Japanese. Meanwhile, through housemaids, friends and ladies in her mother's social circle, Ms. Gordon learned about the roles of Japanese women in the remnants of Japan's feudal system.

At age sixteen, Ms. Gordon was sent to Mills College in California to study languages (she was fluent in six languages). Shortly after, World War II broke out, and she lost contact with her parents, who were placed under "village arrest" in 1942 by the Japanese government.

Ms. Gordon was one of only sixty non-Japanese in the United States who spoke Japanese, and her ability to translate was in great demand. On Christmas Eve 1945, Ms. Gordon was the first civilian woman to arrive in Japan after peace was declared. She was reunited with her parents and was given a position on the staff of the Supreme Commander of the Allied Powers, General MacArthur.

Ms. Gordon was one of twenty Americans assigned to research and draft a new constitution for Japan, a monumental task accomplished in only nine days, starting on February 4, 1946. She drafted the women's rights articles as explicitly as possible so that the constitutional intent could not be eviscerated by male Japanese bureaucrats, when they would prepare the new Civil Code at a later time. Also, she knew that American women had been disadvantaged because the U.S. Constitution failed to specifically guarantee women's rights. Two articles on women's rights written by the twenty-two-year-old Ms. Gordon read as follows:

Article 14. All of the people are equal under the law and there shall be no discrimination in political, economic or social relations because of race, creed, sex, social status or family origin.

Article 24. Marriage shall be based only on the

mutual consent of both sexes and it shall be maintained through mutual cooperation with equal
rights of husband and wife as a basis. With regard
to choice of spouse, property rights, inheritance,
choice of domicile, divorce and other matters
pertaining to marriage and the family, laws shall be
enacted from the standpoint of individual dignity
and the essential equalities of the sexes....

Ms. Gordon's efforts directly support the fourth
action area of the 1999 United Nations Programme
of Action on a Culture of Peace: Ensuring equality
between women and men.

Discussion

AUDIENCE MEMBER 1: How did you accomplish such a wonderful thing
in Japan?

MS. GORDON: The funny thing is when I was [helping to draft Japan's
constitution], I wasn't really thinking at all in terms of accomplishment. I was attached to the army, and although we were not soldiers,
we were attached to the army and under army rules. We, of course,
had to do what the army ordered. We did it in the same way as the
soldiers did. You were given a task and you did it. That's it. You don't
even think about it at the time.

One of General MacArthur's top generals called us for a conference, and we were told: "By order of General MacArthur, you will
write the new Japanese Constitution." Of course, we were all stunned.
The Japanese were supposed to write their own constitution. I am
surprised that MacArthur didn't realize how a militarist-born government like Japan's couldn't write a democratic constitution. MacArthur

wanted the Japanese to write it. So he asked three times. Every time it was almost exactly like the old Meiji Constitution, which was as undemocratic as you can imagine. Women had absolutely no rights, not one right. Men didn't have so many rights either, but at least they had some.

MacArthur decided that he wanted the American version of the Constitution completed by February 17, 1946.

Twenty of us were asked from a special section in General Headquarters. It was called the Government Section and was headed by Major General Courtney Whitney, who was the favorite of MacArthur's generals; he had been the lawyer for MacArthur in Manila. They had a long-standing relationship.

It was a very short conference. He said: "You will be given your assignments, and don't forget, this is top secret. You may not speak with anyone, not even in this GHQ, nobody! At night, whatever you have written has to go into the safe, not on your desk, not in your desk, but in the safe, and it will be locked. You cannot talk even to your parents, your brothers or your sisters or anybody about this." Then he said, "You have to do it in seven days."

I was in a small division in the Government Section called political affairs. The deputy chief of staff, Colonel Charles Kades, who practically ran the whole Occupation, and was more important than MacArthur or Whitney or anybody, approached my division. It is not well known that he was so powerful, although the scholars know, but the general public doesn't know. He was an amazing, amazing New York lawyer. He is one of the brightest men I have ever met.

Anyway, Colonel Kades said to us, "You three will write the civil rights section of the new constitution." That was it. He said, "We have some orders about it that you should follow, but it is up to you to write a democratic constitution." He gave us a list of things that had to be in it that had been definitely decided. For example, MacArthur wanted a peace clause. I cannot tell you from whom that came, whether from Washington or how that was, but there was no question to even talk about it.

For women's rights, I was not given many instructions at all. I think American men at that time were not as interested in women's rights as they are now. Don't forget that was a long time ago, and American men were not quite so liberal.

I only knew the American Constitution, and all the other people were in the same boat. We were not legal specialists. We were not even lawyers. There were two or three lawyers among the twenty, but generally they were all ordinary people who were either working for the government or were professors. There were almost no specialists, maybe one or two who specialized in law. Again, they were American lawyers. The American Constitution was their big thing. They were blinded by that. I had been a researcher at *Time* magazine before I came to Japan. There was nobody who knew anything about Japan when I was at *Time*, so I did the research on Japan.

I found out a great deal about how my colleagues were doing research and so on. We had a library, and we had this and we had that, and also a lot of calls to people at *The New York Times*, to people who were experts and speaking to college professors all over the world. We could call anywhere we wanted to find out facts. I put my whole being into this research, because I felt terribly responsible.

Researchers, however, were the lowest as far as status was concerned at *Time*. We were just editorial researchers. We did not earn much money, and we had no power at all, but we took the blame. If anybody wrote a letter to the editor at *Time* and said, "Oh, listen, this fact is wrong," that was the greatest fear that *Time* had.

As soon as civilians were allowed (after World War II), I returned to Japan.

I had learned to be a good researcher. The moment they said, "You have to write on civil rights," I said: "How can I write something like that for a constitution? I have to see constitutional language and many of the thoughts that go into a constitution. I have to go to the nearest library and get the constitutions of as many countries as possible. Then, I will see samples and I will know what to do." I took a Jeep with a Japanese driver. Don't forget, Tokyo was destroyed. After the war, there were hardly any buildings. I asked the driver to find a library. How he found a library, I don't know. I can't even tell you the name because we were just searching. I wanted three libraries. Why? If I went to one library and asked them to show me ten constitutions, they would be rather surprised, wouldn't they? Wouldn't they ask me why a representative of GHQ would want to look at constitutions? Because it was top secret, either I had to lie or I had to figure out another way. I didn't have time to make things up, so I decided to go to three libraries and take three from this one and three from the next one and maybe four from the other. Probably nobody will ask any questions. It did turn out that way. I went to three and I got ten constitutions altogether, and I became very popular in the Government Section, because everybody wanted to borrow my constitutions.

Although we had some very brainy people in this section, this kind of research had not been required from anybody.

We had to finish the draft in seven days, so you can imagine, everybody was looking at the constitutions day and night. Seven days is not much. I found that women's rights, particularly in other constitutions, were so much better than anything the American Constitution had. I was so happy, because I saw many examples and ideas that I would never have thought of. When I read them in the Scandinavian constitutions and the Soviet Constitution and the Weimar Republic's Constitution, I thought, "This is just right for Japan; this should be in the constitution." They also had social welfare rights in their constitutions, not just in the civil codes.

I was happy to see that, in these other countries, they put in what they apparently felt was important, and that was social welfare. They put social welfare rights into the constitution. I decided I would copy that idea. When I got back to the office, everybody borrowed my constitutions, but I could work with one for a while and then move to the next one and so on. I studied these constitutions upside down and inside out just on civil rights. I wrote two pages. The reason I was so worried about social welfare not being in the constitution was that I did not trust that the Japanese bureaucrats, who would later write the Civil Code, would include social welfare.

The Steering Committee cut out all my social welfare rights because, they said, "It isn't in the American Constitution."

I said: "So what? It has been a long time since the American Constitution was written. Social welfare rights in the constitution are essential."

This committee was made up of three men, three older men very high up in government—one was the governor of Puerto Rico. I only

realized recently that they could not see beyond the American Constitution. That was it, and I shouldn't blame them so much for the poor
Japanese women fighting for social welfare rights. One such right,
they have worked through the courts for ten years, and it just passed, I
think about a year ago (in 2006). Now it has to get into the Civil Code.
It has not yet. Can you imagine? I wrote maybe ten or fifteen social
welfare items.

When I defended my stand in front of the Steering Committee,
which was, as I told you, all Americans over forty and all lawyers, they
said to me: "Don't worry, we will be here for a long time as an Occupation force. We will see to it that it gets into the Civil Code." Well,
it wasn't so. The army left in 1952, and the Japanese hadn't gotten to
writing the Civil Code as yet. The Americans had nothing to do with
the writing of the Japanese Civil Code.

I presented this draft, as I said, first to my own committee. I had
two men on the committee, and they were very much in favor of what
I had written. One was married to a woman soldier (we had women
soldiers, the Women's Army Corps). That was very avant-garde at
that time. He was quite liberal in his thinking. The other man who
worked with me was a professor who adored women. He loved Japanese women also. He said, "Anything you write to make life easier for
Japanese women is okay with me."

I was very happy not to have any opposition in my own division.
So, I went into this final meeting with the Committee with great confidence. I was twenty-two years old. At twenty-two, one has a lot of confidence. I went in and the first thing Colonel Kades said was, "Beate,
you have given the Japanese women more rights than we have in the
American Constitution."

I said, "Colonel Kades, the American Constitution doesn't even
have the word *woman* in it, and they have been fighting for rights for
decades."

They were embarrassed, all three of them, but it did not change
their minds. I became so emotional that I cried. It's true, I cried. Colonel Kades later on wrote in a magazine that I cried on his shoulder.
I remember crying, but I do not remember crying on his shoulder!

The constitutional draft went without social welfare rights to

General MacArthur. He signed it, and it went to the Japanese government. Then it evolved through the government, and that was it. Now, the poor Japanese women have the fundamental rights that were left in the draft. They have a basis for equality with men.

AUDIENCE MEMBER 2: What is your determination or dream about what you would want us as the youth to accomplish?

MS. GORDON: It is to encourage women, just as my rights to a great extent have influenced Japanese women. I feel that women in other countries, in America, in China and wherever, who have had a similar experience should try to improve the lot of women. You are the youth, the future of the world, and without peace in the world, we are not going to get anywhere. You have to know a lot about government and politics.

In Japan now, many women are in government on the local level and on the national level. They have even had a justice in the Supreme Court, but there has to be much more. There have to be bigger movements. In America, I don't know very much about the women's movement. I was never involved here, because I changed careers after I came back from the Occupation. I didn't really have anything to do with the Constitution afterwards. It was a Japanese Constitution. Everybody thought it was written by the Japanese. Many people, even now, don't know that it was written by us. That was top secret until 1972, so we couldn't speak about it until then. There was a leak in Japan, and some papers found out that it was we who initially wrote the first draft of this Constitution.

They made fun of the Constitution, saying such things as: "The woman who wrote the women's rights was a young girl only twenty-two years old. How could she know anything?" I did not want to be used as a foil against the Constitution, so my husband and I decided I wouldn't give any interviews, only to two or three American scholars and maybe to two Japanese newspapermen. I never talked about it for fifty years. People keep on asking me why I didn't talk about it. The answer is that I didn't want to be used. Even Americans were wondering about my capability. There is no wonder about it. I grew up in Japan, I was born in Vienna. I knew six languages by the time I was eighteen years old, and I went to an excellent college in the United States, Mills College, which was one of the first feminist colleges in California or, rather, in America. I had already had three jobs before I was twenty-two. They were in government and very difficult—all connected with Japanese.

That's why I want to recommend that all of you learn one exotic language, not to become an interpreter but just to have it as an asset. In my career, I have done many different things. Even though I was a woman, I was able to get good jobs because there were no men who knew Japanese.

At that time in America, there were only sixty Caucasians, not nisei, not second generation, who were considered reliable enough for certain government offices like the Office of War Information or the Foreign Broadcast Intelligence Service. They wanted Caucasian Americans. There were sixty in the United States, that's all! By the way, my husband says that is not true, it was sixty-six, he says. That's what he heard. I could get any job I wanted, really, except the FBI, which I didn't want anyway. For the FBI, you had to be an American citizen, and I wasn't yet, because I was too young to become an American citizen.

I was fifteen when I started college. I had working experience and educational experience. I had been all over the world with my parents, traveling in Asia and Europe. I was not an unprepared twenty-two-year-old woman at all. I had this personal experience of speaking an exotic language. At that time, it was very exotic, Japanese. I tell you all. But you must all study Chinese. Really! I am working on it on my grandchildren. But that is the thing to do, it really is. That is one of the reasons I like to talk with young people.

AUDIENCE MEMBER 3: I would like to ask how your experience with so many different cultures and aspects of society changed your perception of the world.

MS. GORDON: When I was at Mills College, I was head of the French Club. This was during the war. The French had been defeated by the Nazis, as you know, but there was a government in exile in Vichy. All the people who supposedly were patriots went there and had a phony government. However, it was all a pretense. I realized that at the time. Being the president of the French Club, I wanted to help Americans learn a little bit about French culture. The students didn't know anything at that time, really nothing. They just wanted to have a good time. I was sixteen years old. I thought what would attract students would be a cabaret entertainment. We would have red and white tablecloths and maybe do some kind of dance, not exactly the can-can, but something like it.

In that way we would draw them in and then later on we could teach them more important cultural matters. Everybody loved the idea and wanted to do it.

Then I went to my French professor, who was our advisor, an old lady about sixty at the time. She was pro-Vichy and thought of herself as a liberal. When she saw my proposal, she said, "How can you even think of having a cabaret evening when we are suffering so in Europe, especially in Vichy?" I really didn't care about Vichy, you know. She said, "The entertainment can't be exhibitionist, it has to be serious." I said, "All right, we will give a dinner party in the style of the French empire."

I said to the students: "Give me all the sheets you have on your beds, and we will make curtains out of them for the windows and make it look very fancy. We will have some interesting foods and instead of doing a nice cabaret dance, we will dance the minuet."

I had taken dance since I was six. I taught them how to do the minuet. The young people were all very excited. At that time, they had never seen a minuet. Travel to Europe was not that common before World War II, because it was too expensive.

Later, I was head of the International Club, and it was even worse there because they really didn't know much about other cultures, especially about Asia and about Japan, which was almost my native country. They asked me if the Japanese lived in trees and in caves. This was 1939. That was not so long ago.

That these people, who were college students, didn't know that the Japanese not only had their own high culture but also knew a lot about the West did not speak well for Americans. Already in 1885, the Japanese had sent people out to Europe to see what was going on.

They copied the dresses, they copied the dances, and they copied the art. Some Japanese came to study with Gauguin, the famous French painter, and brought that type of painting with oil to Japan. They did not paint with oil before that.

I thought to myself at that time: "I must do something. I don't know yet what it is, but I must do something." Peace was a big thing in my life because there wasn't any in the time I was growing up. Also, I had lived in Japan's militaristic society as a child, and I knew a lot about militarism. I don't have the book knowledge, but I have it from experience. I remember when there were assassinations of the top government officials in Japan, and a man with a bayonet stood in front of my house. Those are all memories I have. I know what it was like. I know that my mother told me, "You must never mention politics in public."

Why do you think that was? It was because the secret police were always after us foreigners. It didn't matter whether you were ten years old or fifteen years old or whatever you were. The secret police visited my house every day, because my father was a pianist and a teacher, and many foreigners and Japanese were his students. They could see by the license plates of the cars parked in front of our house the nationalities of the many pupils. That was suspect.

Also, I was the interpreter for my parents. They didn't speak Japanese. That's why I knew about bureaucrats. If the police wanted some information, which they often did of foreigners, I was the one who went with my parents and interpreted for them. I saw how narrow-minded these people were. Again, much of my knowledge was from personal experience. I was lucky in that I lived in such fabulous surroundings, which gave me a lot of ideas and knowledge that I would never have had otherwise.

I would also like to mention *Time* magazine just once more. When I was a researcher there, they had the best experts on Europe working there, because women couldn't get any other job except jobs like researcher. I cannot tell you what women we had there. I mean brilliant women with doctorates, people who had left South Africa when they were fifteen because of apartheid, that kind of woman, just marvelous. I learned so much from them because, you see, I was the youngest. They wanted to take care of me. Everywhere I went, there were always these people who wanted to take care of me and who told me things that I couldn't have learned in class. This was also their own experience. That is something that I value very much and of course want to share with you.

I don't know when that idea came to me, but I think it was after the Occupation. When I came back to the United States, I thought there must be a way of doing cultural exchange with other countries, maybe with music, with dance and so on, where it is not so much book learning but going to the heart. If the Japanese can understand Western music so well that they are more advanced in listening to modern music than Americans are, then maybe Americans can go to a concert of Mongolian music and appreciate it.

(Editor's note: Ms. Gordon later served as director of the Japan Society and later the Asia Society, both headquartered in New York.)

I brought much music from Asia, at first, only from Japan, and then from all of Asia, music that Americans had never heard before. I knew I couldn't teach very much in one, two or three performances, but maybe I could inspire people to want to know more about the country that had produced that dance or that costume or that mask.

I think that was an idea of mine—to get people thinking about other people in terms of culture and the similarities and dissimilarities, and that you would always find links. I could show you a film, and you would think it was from your country because the movements of the dancer are just exactly the same as you learned. Whether it is modern dance or ballet, I will give you one example and that will be it. You have seen the Chinese shoe for the bound feet for the dancer. Did you ever examine it? It is exactly like a toe shoe for ballet. Things like that I found all over Asia and Europe. Some of the exercises they were doing in India I had done in the German School, which was teaching German gymnastics. It is amazing! I thought if I can inspire interest, that would be wonderful.

The review that I was most happy about was in the *Washington Post*. The reviewer said, "Anyone who saw yesterday's performance of the Mongolian troupe must this morning be in a library looking up Mongolia, because 'Mongolia' is not a household word in the United

States. I am sure they will want to learn more and would like to look at the map and see where these fabulous performers come from. They sing from their throats. It is called throat singing." This was in 1970. At that time, nobody knew about it. I thought, "That is the way to go."

You all must be aware of, and I hope you are doing something about, peace for the world. I know that Mr. Ikeda (SGI president) has written about peace a great deal, and so I know that you probably are trained to some extent. I don't know how active you are as individuals. Of course, my field is women's rights, so I would love for you to be involved with women's organizations in other countries or just to help out in whatever is necessary. For example, when the Afghan Constitution and the Iraqi Constitution were being prepared—I believe they are still being prepared—they asked a very famous scholar in America by the name of John Dower, who wrote *Embracing Defeat*, for advice.

It's a wonderful book. He said, "The Japanese Constitution is no example for a Middle Eastern Muslim country." He said this because Japan's Constitution was created during an occupation. Iraq was not an occupation. It was a liberation. That is number one. The Japanese knew that an occupation is an occupation.

The second thing is that religion was not important in Japan. There was no religious opposition to what we were doing. It never even came up. In the Muslim world, it is different. I don't know what we could do with a Muslim constitution. I really don't, because we would have to change the whole view of life. I looked at the Koran. I know very little about the Koran. I know a little bit because I have been in Pakistan, and I have worked with Muslim people, also in Indonesia. I know about the art. I don't know very much about the politics. I searched for "Koran" on the Internet and out came various interpretations. Every interpretation of the same sentence was different from the next interpretation, the third and the fourth interpretation, and so on. I said to myself: "I am wrong, and John Dower is much smarter than I am. He said the right thing. He said there is nothing that we so-called experts could do about this. I really don't know how they can do anything."

Because of situations like that, you young people have to be as smart as Professor Dower and come up with new ideas, because I would hate to be twenty-two years old right now and be asked to go to Afghanistan or Iraq. In one of the Muslim constitutional drafts, they had women's rights, and then, at the end of the sentence, it said, "but of course, it will be decided by the *sharia*." You all know what the *sharia* is? The *sharia* is a body of law that can decide almost everything. If the *sharia* is going to decide women's rights, you might as well not write them down. So how are you going to change anything? I am sure there are excellent things in the Koran, basically, but the interpretations have changed so much of what it is.

Maybe it will be your job to see how one can teach something as different as our concept of women's rights in a Muslim country. I have no clue, and I have talked to many people about it. They have no clue either. It is the youth who have to do this. We are too old. We don't have the strength, but you are young and fresh and full of hopefulness. For my generation and me, this is a very, very, difficult and tragic time. We apparently did not do the right thing. It is not your fault what is going on now. It is our fault. We are the ones who created this world you are living in now, so don't make the same mistake.

December 10, 2007
New York

Turning Street Warriors into Peacemakers

Gang Intervention in Los Angeles

Bill Martinez

Manager, Youth and Gang Violence Intervention Specialist Training Program, Edmund G. "Pat" Brown Institute for Public Affairs, California State University, Los Angeles, and Co-Director, Unity Collaborative

Jerald Cavitt

Instructor, Gang Violence Intervention Specialist Training Program; Chief Executive Officer, Unity Two Chapter Two

The gang intervention work of Bill Martinez and Jerald Cavitt in particular illustrates the sixth action area of the 1999 United Nations Programme of Action on a Culture of Peace: Advancing understanding, tolerance and solidarity. As Mr. Martinez says, their intention is to "create some forum, some network, some opportunity so these guys will turn to the intervention workers before they turn on one another. It is giving them an opportunity to get together, to talk about the conflicts they see in their community, to deal with those conflicts themselves instead of imposing their wills on one another."

The Unity Collaborative, a network of gang intervention agencies, serves the West, South and Central areas of the City of Los Angeles. Mr. Martinez is also the former executive director of Community Youth Gang Services. His previous experience has ˙ spanned diverse issues, including economic development and redevelopment, public finance, transportation and emergency preparedness planning. He previously served on the Board of the Los Angeles Commission on Assaults Against Women and is a founding member of the Los Angeles County Association of Community-based Gang Intervention Workers, where he is also a member of the board of directors. Mr. Martinez received a master's in city and regional planning from the John F. Kennedy School of Government at Harvard University.

Mr. Cavitt has volunteered in promoting understanding among rival gangs in his South Central Los Angeles community since 1994. After joining Unity Two, a nonprofit gang intervention organization in Los Angeles, he launched Unity Two Chapter Two. In the summer of 2004, he helped negotiate an understanding between two rival gangs, the Swans and East Coast. His gang intervention work takes him to South Central Los Angeles and parts of West Los Angeles, Perris, Hawthorne and Rancho Cucamonga in Southern California.

Mr. Bill Martinez: 'Working Together'

To bring peace to the streets of Los Angeles and the surrounding communities, we rely most on those who previously lived that same gang life— those who were out there running the streets, causing problems, who eventually recognized the harm they did to their communities and that they needed to fix it. They realized it wasn't up to anyone else; it was up to them to resolve the issues they had developed.

I believe we all have a tendency, a bad one, to think about kids as though they are small adults. They are not; they are kids. There is a whole process that kids go through that changes them significantly from when they were children, and it will change again as they enter adulthood. We are finding this out in research. We have always known that, culturally, there is a reason that rites of passage exist in every culture for youth around twelve or thirteen years old. We are finding now that there are actually physiological changes that occur that accompany the emotional and ethical changes that drive who people are.

I want to talk a little about gang intervention, specifically what we call *hardcore* gang intervention. This is a process of working directly with the various neighborhoods in our communities that are themselves promoting violence. As you all know, there are high levels of interpersonal violence, death and other kinds of very difficult, very negative circumstances in our communities. It looks like Los Angeles will have one of the lowest years in terms of gang violence homicides this year (2007) compared to the last several years. It has been on a downhill slope since the mid 1990s. In 2007, we expect there will be less than two hundred incidents for the first time since the 1980s.

A couple of precepts guide what we do. We all believe that violence is a learned behavior. As a learned behavior, it is something we can deal with, we can manage, and we can effectively unlearn.

The other precept is that we are not anti-gang, we are anti-violence. We recognize that if we were to go in and take out an entire neighborhood—and I use the words *gang* and *neighborhood* interchangeably—that gang would be back the next day under a new name and a new guise, because there is nothing to replace it. It is a sociological function. It is part of that transition into adolescence, where you are looking to create independence from your family and create your own network of peers. You are trying to find your identity within your community. If you are in an environment where violence is a regular, everyday occurrence, then the likelihood is that you will find who you are through violent means. We feel it is important for us to work within that structure to create positive change.

In terms of what I mentioned before about treating children as children and not as adults, we also make a distinction between youth violence and organized crime. Most of these kids out there couldn't organize their day, let alone something as vast as the sort of criminal enterprises of which they are a part. We have to recognize that difference and work within that to reach these kids and create the change we are trying to achieve.

Hardcore gang intervention consists of two elements. The first is an individual process through reclamation of individuals; trying to get them back in school, to work, into counseling or whatever else they need to turn their own lives around and make up for the deficits they have faced in the past.

The second element of hardcore gang intervention is a group process. Most of the research will tell you that you should never recognize a group, because doing so gives it legitimacy and pumps it up. We take the opposite tack. We are not giving any gangs anything but the opportunity to live for another day. When we go out and work with them, they want to be able to work with us, so that's how we focus our attention. The violence is rarely from individual motivations, it is more out of a group process, at least the type of violence that we focus on, so we need to change the mindset of that entire neighborhood in order to proceed.

We use a community organizing model that starts by finding out who the leadership is of these various neighborhoods, because in working with those endemic, indigenous leaders and creating the kind of change we are aiming for, the rest of the kids are going to follow along. That is the mechanical tack that we take.

We will mediate conflicts, or they will mediate conflicts. First, I want to explain that I do not work directly in conflict mediation. I want to be very open about that. The people I am fortunate to work with who have lived that life are able to go out there and do that. I am blessed to work with them, and I understand this enough to make this presentation.

To mediate conflicts, we start with the knowledge that there are always shootings going on or other types of conflict. Gang intervention workers will get called out at 1:00, 2:00, 3:00 or 4:00 in the morning. The school calls, the police department calls and neighbors call. The neighborhoods themselves, the members of those neighborhoods, will call and say: "Man, this is about to go down. You better get out here," and they respond. Just so you know, the Los Angeles Police Department estimates something like 40,000 gang members in Los Angeles. The city pays for 61 gang intervention workers. The bottom line is that there is just not enough funding or manpower to go around. But that's what these workers are called on to do. They do it as well as they can, where they can, and they are doing it 24/7.

A lot of that is mediating violence as it occurs. A lot more of it, however, is mitigating those circumstances that allow violence to prosper. A lot of times, it is the nature of those various neighborhoods, which I will discuss in a little more detail.

Who is doing the work? It is primarily people who have lived that life. It is almost exclusively that way. Why is that? Well, they know the players, because many times they are from the same sets. They understand the issues and the dynamics. They understand what the neighborhoods will do and won't do in response to certain circumstances. They also understand what they will or won't do to try to reduce violence.

There are occasions when we know wars are about to break out, and there is not much we can do about it. We have sometimes called LAPD and said, "Look, you want to put a lot of cars on the street this weekend." They don't even have to have officers in them. It works really well. When people see a lot of black and whites out there, they tend to calm down. There is not much else we can do, because, in some cases, the guys just aren't going to listen to anyone. Often, unfortunately, we have to let some things run their course.

We also know that there are some things in which the guys won't participate. In fact, most mediation is not done face to face. It is really a shuttle diplomacy, because we can't get these guys together. A lot of the time is spent running back and forth between different neighborhoods, trying to deal with specific issues and then onto some of the larger issues as they work out all the details. The histories of some of these neighborhoods go back into the 1920s and 1930s. A significant change and rise in youth violence and the gangs occurred in the 1970s. A lot of these wars go back twenty-five, thirty, thirty-five years, so it is not enough to say, "You guys don't have to do this." There is pride and there is family involved in all of this that have to be taken into consideration. People who have lived that life and often are from those neighborhoods understand those circumstances, and they can deal with them and talk to those specifics as they go through this process.

I want to give you an idea with whom we are working. We will call this kid Carlos. Carlos is from a one-parent household. He has a mom. They are an immigrant family. She speaks very limited English. She is able to get some work. She does some part-time work on the side, and she is out of the house a lot. Carlos is raised by an older sister who is left to run the household in his mom's absence. He is a latchkey kid, and he will get out of school about 3:00 or 3:30 and kick it until about 6:00, when his mom might be home, sometimes later if she works that second job. It is in a neighborhood where there is a gang, which might not be strong, but its influence is still there.

Carlos isn't doing well in school. There are a lot of reasons for that. He is in a classroom with forty or fifty other kids. They have got thirty-five books. He has never been good at reading, and he is in a classroom where the individual attention he needs has never been given to him. He is not able to keep up. Research says that if you are not reading at grade level by the third grade, you never will. It is the difference between learning to read and reading to learn. If you are not there by the fourth grade, you are going to have some real problems. Carlos has never been quite up to speed. As a result, he is not having a lot of fun at school.

Actually, how many guys like Carlos do you think are out there? Honestly, I would say there must be 200,000 kids out there, if we are looking at the county of Los Angeles. There was a report done by the United Way about two years ago (in 2005). It was called "One Out of Five," meaning that one out of five kids between the ages of sixteen and twenty-four, I believe, was out of school and out of work, so essentially out of touch with all of our basic institutions that are available and normal for that kid to be involved in. That added up to something like 100,000 kids in Los Angeles. We might say 40,000 of those were gang members, but some of those gang members were in school, so maybe it is 70,000 or 75,000 kids. Others are not gang members, but they still have not been adequately tooled by our major institutions to live a prosperous life, the one that we all hope for them. We have to look at that and say there are a lot more kids out there who are engaged in violence of different sorts. We hear about abusing drugs, sex and kids who cut themselves, sniff, all that kind of stuff. They go unrecognized because they are not shooting one another. There are a lot of things we need to look at that have to be changed. Carlos, unfortunately, is pointed out, because he was willing to engage in violence. He was willing to pick up a gun and shoot someone else, so he gets the notoriety, and everybody else goes unrecognized.

What is Carlos going to do? He is going to get himself kicked out of school. He is going to be the class clown until he gets thrown out. He is not going to do his work. He is going to start ditching classes, and he is going to start finding some of the older guys out in the neighborhoods who will tell him: "Man, you don't need to go to school. That's for punks."

Those are the guys who, three or four years earlier, went through that same thing. They had to make those same distinctions and choices for themselves. They, too, found the older guys who were willing to accept them, and so here is Carlos' new family.

These guys are out there with open arms, saying: "We will take care of you, and we will protect you. We'll give you some fun stuff to do: drugs, sex, all the rest of it. It's there. All you got to do is put in a little work." Who is not going to want that when everything else that you've seen has been set against you?

We're not saying this happens to everybody, but it happens enough, and it is really not that hard to see how these kids get caught up in the life.

Let's bear in mind that a lot of these illegal activities generate money, so a lot of these guys have the cash, the bling, the rest of it. These guys are looking at their moms, saying: "Why do I need to have two or three jobs? All I have to do is kick it with these guys, sling a little, run a little, and I can get the kind of stuff, or if nothing else I can help out so Mom doesn't have to have that second job." There are a lot of different motivations helping these guys get caught up in this whole lifestyle.

One of the things we also have to bear in mind is there are so many homes where there is only the mother. It is a social phenomenon that has become more prevalent over the years.

There was a National Geographic program on recently called "Killer Elephants." I think it was in South Africa where they tried to control the elephant population by sending all the baby elephants off to be raised elsewhere until they got to adolescence, around their twenties, and then they put them all back into the park. Administrators said: "We have cut down on the numbers. We control them, and they are nice and healthy." What happened? What did they do? The adolescent elephants started killing the rhinos and all the other big animals that they saw as threats or rivals to them. The solution that administrators came up with was to introduce adult male elephants to show the adolescents how to socialize, not only among themselves but also with all the other species out there. It was remarkable.

We are in a society where our kids don't have that opportunity to socialize to the levels we need. We don't have it in the households where we need it, and all the guys on the streets are saying: "Hey, that's cool. Come on, we've got your back. You can do those kinds of things."

There are a lot of other issues, such as learning difficulties, these guys are dealing with. They often go undetected or unfunded because our schools don't have the money to do the job. I have heard some school district officials say that if they really funded every kid that needed special support, it would bankrupt the school.

Just so you know, the federal government is supposed to be paying something like forty cents on the dollar for every kid in some kind of ADA class. Instead, they spend about twelve cents on the dollar. Despite the federal mandate, about a quarter to a third of the need goes unfunded. Then there are a lot of mental health factors. Obviously, there are a whole lot of kids who are just generally going to have some issues, but then we have to look at issues like post-traumatic stress disorder. We have kids living in war zones, and we are asking why they are not growing up normally. We have got levels of violence equivalent to Beirut. Think about what that is like, and think about what we are doing for these kids. Absolutely nothing! There is no mental health support available to these guys. They just go from one day to another, and it becomes numbing.

There is a quote about grief in Joseph Conrad's *Heart of Darkness*: "Even extreme grief may ultimately vent itself in violence—but more generally takes the form of apathy." That is what we see in a lot of these kids. A lot of these kids are the walking wounded. They are soulless. They are just trying to get by from one day to another. We often hear comments like "What do I care? I am going to be dead by the time I am twenty." It is what they see and what they believe.

There is a process called *phenomenology*. It is a sociological process that basically says your experience defines your reality. If that is what they see around them, then that is what they expect is going to happen with them. We have to look at that and ask what are some of these conditions. There is violence as a regular occurrence that affects their sleep, and it affects their preparedness for school, and it affects their being able to come and go to school. Bullies are another form of violence, although not necessarily gang involved, but they are very important. A lot of kids are going to clique up because of the bullies. It is a form of protection for them. It is a known decision-making tool. So much of this history is passed down from generation to generation within the gangs, and they deal with it through violence. When somebody comes and shoots at you, or if somebody only disses you, you respond in a violent manner. It is what is accepted. There is a very limited knowledge of alternatives because there are very few elders who understand what those alternatives are.

We look at the hardcore intervention people, the street mediators, resolving conflicts on the terms of the kids in the street. It is very important. You can't walk in and say, "Hey, you guys, you shouldn't be doing this," because that ain't going to fly. Our approach is more like: "We know why you are doing this, but you gotta stop. We can help you. We can give you alternatives."

Shuttle diplomacy, going back and forth, is a key, because these guys are not going to sit down. It's not like you can send representatives. This isn't the United Nations, although we probably deal with as many conflicts and as many casualties as they do. The form of mediation that goes on is unique. We are currently creating some curricula specific to that point.

What we also do, as an approach to mitigating a lot of these issues, is what we call a *peace process*. It is essentially trying to create some forum, some network, some opportunity so these guys will turn to the intervention workers before they turn on one another. It is giving them an opportunity to get together, to talk about the conflicts they see in their community, to deal with those conflicts themselves instead of imposing their wills on one another.

There have been some historic events in the last fifteen years that have held. There has been a truce up in the San Fernando Valley that, until recently, had maintained a strong network of participants. The Harbor area of Los Angeles, since about that same time, has had a truce that includes some thirty-five or forty different neighborhoods.

It is important to recognize that we can mitigate the violence in some situations when we find out the difficulties and try to work them out, but actually getting all the participants to sit down at a table requires some very important events to occur. In almost all cases where we have had truces, there has been some overriding reason to get a whole lot of people who otherwise wouldn't.

Just recently was the second anniversary of the execution of Tookie

Williams. [Editor's note: Stanley Tookie Williams was an early leader of the Crips in the 1970s. He was convicted of the 1979 murders of four people and sentenced to death. In 1993, he became an anti-gang activist while on Death Row. He renounced his gang affiliation, apologized for the Crips' founding and was nominated for a Nobel Prize for authoring several books intended to help disenfranchised youth. He was executed on Dec. 13, 2005.]

Leading up to that anniversary, a lot of the neighborhoods, particularly the Crips sets, were saying, "Tookie changed; we need to change, too." They have been trying to work out these relationships among themselves. It has yielded something very powerful, but if it weren't for Tookie, these guys wouldn't have come together.

It doesn't always take a martyr. It could very well be like the Harbor peace, where they said, "Can we all try and not shoot one another over the holidays?" That was in 1992. It lasted, and some components of that are still in existence today.

Getting the kids all together can be very difficult, but it is the kind of thing that the intervention workers have been very effective at doing over the last several years. I think, honestly, a lot of the results are showing up in the drop in gang-related homicides. The intervention workers are getting so much better at reaching out that a lot of neighborhoods that haven't been involved will come to them now, because they want in. It is a great tribute to the work and the time that these guys have put in over the years.

A couple of things we have also been doing is to provide some training. I am involved in training at California State University Los Angeles. What we are trying to do is link theory to practice by bringing in experts in these areas. Again, it is studying a theoretical academic area and then drawing parallels to the work that they are doing every day on the streets. It is important to standardize the knowledge base among the various participants around the city, because a whole lot of different agencies and a whole lot of different communities and cultures are involved. It is not just the Mexicans, and it is not just the blacks. We have Filipinos, we have Asians, we have whites, we have a whole lot of people who are engaged in this violence, but there are certain standards that we can all live by and that drive our work.

We are actually trying to create a profession for gang intervention, because I think it is important that we recognize the value such workers provide to us. At the same time, it is not the kind of thing you go to college to do. We have to look at the value of each individual's experiences on the street, and we add to that knowledge what we think is going to be useful to them out in the field. Again, we focus a lot on mitigation or mediation and also on community organizing, so we can look at those elements and see what is in that community that we can try to improve and fix so it just makes it a whole lot easier for them to do their job.

A lot of this is culminating into something very new. We have just created something called the Council of Community Violence Intervention Professionals. It is essentially the next generation of an association of which I was part in the 1990s. It is saying we all have to be working together, because we can be in our own cliques as anybody out there on the street. We are trying to get our act together so that we are more effective and can better coordinate our services. That is a little bit about what intervention is all about.

I want to ask Jerald Cavitt to come up. Jerald spends his time on the streets. He is one of those 24/7 guys. We wanted to give you a sense of what it is that intervention workers do on a regular basis to keep kids from killing kids.

Mr. Jerald Cavitt: 'Not Just a Gang Issue'

This is not just a gang issue. This issue includes what is going on before and after the gang. The kids are not learning; the kids have nothing else to do; and the kids have no hope. Some of the guys out in the street, if you ask them, they have a life expectancy of seventeen or eighteen years.

The system has also let them down. No matter what the problem is or what a child does, that child comes from somebody's community, that child comes from somebody's family. Every kid deserves a chance. We all at some time needed to be forgiven for something as an adolescent. Most of my adolescent life, I wanted to apologize for something I had done, as did most of the people I knew, maybe because that is what adolescents do, and that's why they are not called adults.

The youth now involved in gangs for the most part inherited a gang. We have two to three generations of kids who just inherited an association to gang and street life not by choice but by household. Everybody around you is dancing. Your neighbor is dancing. The guy up the street is dancing. Pretty soon, you are going to dance.

When two generations of kids turned to gangs over the past thirty years, there was a closed eye to the problem. People in some places did not want to recognize the problem.

The problem didn't start so bad. The problem has been here for decades, but nobody seemed to recognize when it turned into a civil war. Over the past thirty years, we have had more body bags here because of gangs in the United States than for U.S. soldiers in Iraq, and I should have been watching. This is a public safety issue, if we care about the safety of all the public.

We don't make excuses, but at some point we have others we need to hold accountable for all the deaths of all the kids. I see it, probably more up close than most people. I have whole billboards of murdered kids. Billboards—I mean big, huge, full with little pictures of kids who have been murdered in the city.

The teaching starts at home. Let's make no mistake about that. Kids do, for the most part, as we teach or allow. That makes us responsible as parent figures. It takes a village, they say, to raise kids. I think a village ought to want to be involved in raising the kids. If, as a village, you raise the kids right, you raise your neighborhood right.

I think that kids who go to school in some neighborhoods, we should pat them on the back, give them a big hug for even attempting to go and upon returning from school. You see, some kids must go through four or five different neighborhoods when they walk to school, and five or six times before they get to school, somebody asks them where are they from or where they live. Pocket check. They take your phone and show you a gun. These are our twelve- and thirteen-year-olds who are going to school. How horrified would that make us, as adults, to run into this? For a child who goes to school just to learn, this happens every day, at least five days a week. Let's make no mistake about it; this happens more so than not.

I have a program at some of the schools. I try to get there in the mornings, when I have time, but we have teams of people who help with safe passage to cut down on some of the stuff that I just talked about.

I see the stares from some of the kids. The kids in certain neighborhoods and certain parts of the different cities, at thirteen, have been to too many funerals. They have watched too many other kids die. By the time they start school, that look is often evaluated as a learning disorder, and they are sent to the office. The parent is told that there is a learning problem with the child. If the parents sign a paper, they can get some assistance, and that will take care of some of the money for the bus costs and other things where they have to go. The parents need the money, sign the paper, and now here is a mental health issue. There is some mental issue there, but it is not usually the one authorities think it is: it is a post-war syndrome. If you think about everything that goes on here, you must know that this exists.

When time allows, we do special things with special kids. I not only want to work with the kids who are not doing so well, I want to help reward the kids who are doing well. We need to let them know that we really appreciate them, going steady on, in spite of all of the resistance that they run across as children, just to make it through the twelfth year in school. We haven't gone to hardcore intervention. We are talking about the kids who may just need to be appreciated more, not misunderstood more. You see, when we don't appreciate them or we misunderstand what they are going through, then they turn to somebody in a group of people with whom they can talk, people who won't misunderstand them, who won't judge them for what they are going through. He/she winds up being your next gang member. It starts at home. The signs are on the walls, also.

You may shake your head and say, "Ah, no." Then it is time to sit down and have a talk. It is time to let the kids know we care, because somebody else is telling them that they care, and somebody else is putting a pistol in their hand, and somebody else has got them in a neighborhood or com-munity gang. Sometimes it is just to get through some of the stuff that they go through as a community. Just because you live in a certain place or go to a certain school, people think you may be affiliated with a [gang], or you may have ties. I tell a kid every day: "If you need me, I will be here. Call me or let somebody call me."

Hardcore gang members don't care about kids getting an education. They care about numbers in the neighborhood. They care about who is the next person who is going to help them run some dope.

We go to the communities where there is a problem. I get calls from law enforcement individuals who recognize that there are some issues they can't deal with, and they are not social workers. They need commu-nity intervention here, because the community at large sometimes doesn't have the conversation for suppression. Things are going to slip away from suppression, and before long, there is a big huge thing going on.

Instead, we can pick up a phone, make a call and see if we can contact somebody with a level head in the community who will either enable these kids to go to school and avoid war around a public school. This needs everybody who really cares, starting with the parent in the house.

I want to touch on hardcore gang intervention. If we don't focus on the hardcore gang members, they will have the kids as the next gang members. I went through Bill's class, first at Cal State University, on gang intervention. It is a program that spells out the many steps in this process. I got attached to conflict-resolution and the mediation part. I, in turn, after a couple of years, came back as a co-instructor, and I am currently a co-instructor of the same class.

We do conflict resolution through talking with people who are about to get in cars with AK-47s and 9 mm guns to do some stupid stuff. You hear about the shootings, but a close-up look is very different. It's like the difference between looking at the sky with your naked eye and then through a scope. That's the magnitude of this situation. I look at it through the scope, and it's just real vicious out there. For the most part, it is our kids who have been left out there for the picking, after we allow them to be disenfranchised by the school system, which regularly expels the kids. I would like to save him, but if he did something that wrong, let him go through the process—let him go to court and stand up—but should he be denied the right to an education? I can think of some politicians who have done a lot worse than a lot of these kids, and yet they haven't been thrown out of City Hall.

We have a program where we get kids who have been expelled. We try to get them immediately into another school, because each time a kid is expelled, most of the time the parents are working two jobs and don't have time to take off.

We try to do a re-entry program with the kids. First, we sit down with the principal of the school where the kid was thrown out. They are throwing little girls out at an alarming rate now also—this is not just boys being boys. This is something that affects the whole structure of our family, the structure of our being. This determines which way these kids will go. If you stay in school, you may associate yourself with these people. If you don't, and you are out for a couple of months, then you may associate yourself with those people. Is the price worth that?

A flick of the pen, and kids are written off. We don't write kids off, we deal with kids. We deal with kids as kids. We are the adults and the parents.

For the most part, the kid wants to be understood. If I can't understand, then I will sit down again and say, "Make me understand this." Don't feed our kids to the wolves. The wolves are waiting.

There is an alarming rate of prison entries. Prisons are not just run by the State of California or the federal government any more. Prisons are now in business with Nike and Proctor & Gamble. That makes it corporate; that makes it business. Nike doesn't have to pay someone $15 or $20 an hour to make a shoe. Instead, it pays 7 cents an hour to inmates in prison. Nike started with one big company, and now it is a multi-billion- or multi-trillion-dollar company. How many prisons will Nike mount their operations in? If those prisons are not filled, then that costs Nike money.

Prisons back East have not been as full as they have been on the West Coast, particularly California. I found out a while back that prisons in Virginia and other states are negotiating to get prisoners from California to fill their jails. This creates a problem for me, because they have to go through poverty-stricken neighborhoods to fill the prison system.

These are issues that we as adults and parents, as anyone who cares, have to address. Maybe you think it doesn't affect you. Maybe this problem didn't knock on your door today, but what about tomorrow?

There are people who don't like me to say this, but I don't care much for what they don't like. I walk a straight line, and I do what I know is right. I walk with my God and that makes me all right. If you don't tell somebody what you know, are you partially to blame? Kids are evaluated at age eight. Just a few people know this. At age eight, our kids are evaluated in schools to see who is going to make it to prison in ten years. They build prisons accordingly from the evaluation.

What is really going on? We have to get involved. We all can't do the same thing, but all of us can do something. We all can do something about this *if we want to*. They don't want us to. We can turn around this civil war that has been funded. I am not going to touch on this long, but this gang war has been funded.

Law enforcement does a good job of going through neighborhoods during wartime or when two or three people get killed. They will take a neighborhood and all the guns. Before the sun goes down the next day, the same neighborhood is armed to the teeth again. I don't like that. All this adds up to something.

It takes money. Even if they try to work two or three jobs or try to sell a little dope, these kids don't have the finances to buy shiploads of weapons. How do weapons get sold and so readily disposed? I know when I put some of these things together, it makes me believe that somebody is funding this war.

Here's what a typical day might be like for me: I get up any time of night. I get called at 3:00 or 4:00 in the morning. I even get calls from Bill at 3:45 a.m. He will say: "Hey, Jerald, I got a call from downtown. Something is going on. Can you check it out?"

Sometimes I call and wake somebody else up with something. I will get a number on somebody where something is going on. I tell them I need to get up. I need to come talk to them. If somebody is dead and the police have taped it off, then my conversation is: "Can we sit down and talk before somebody goes and does something stupid?" I try to do that before they get in a car, and two or three more people get killed, because they have automatic weapons—the same weapons they use in Iraq, the very same AK-47s.

I blame people who don't care about certain communities. Certain communities and certain kids are expendable because jails have to be filled and guns have to be run and people have to have jobs, so a certain amount of chaos must go on. Is this something we can think about intelligently? What do you think?

I believe kids in any community have a right to go to school without fear of harm and not be hungry.

We can't do much about what goes on in the house, but at some point, when you see a kid at the bus stop and he may be looking strange, he may just want you to say something to him. Something grave may be going on that is wrong in his house.

Bill also touched on a real sensitive topic about Stanley [Tookie] Williams, who was executed. Maybe the trial was right [in convicting him], and maybe it wasn't. I have read a lot of stuff on the trial. I know that witnesses were let go, charges were dropped and cases were dismissed in order to induce witnesses to testify against him. There was a lot of shady stuff in the court documents. I don't know what went on behind the scenes. But he was nominated for the Nobel Peace Prize. I know that he reached out and touched kids all the way in New Zealand, getting them to stop and rethink what they were doing.

Now you've got Crips and Bloods in New Zealand, because across the world, people act on what goes on in Southern California. It's a domino effect, either positive or negative. He reached out and saved some lives, thousands of lives. If you ever check the emails on his website, some of the conversations persuaded kids to talk to their parents. I could go on about that, but I am not preaching about him. I am not speaking about him and what he did prior to his execution. What I am speaking about are the lives of the kids that he touched through his books and through everything else.

Could his life have been spared? Would it have been so wrong for him to spend the rest of his life in prison, if he was saving so many kids? Then another inmate was pardoned thirty to sixty days later. This is not about black, white, Latino; it is about humanity and right or wrong. If everybody should be judged, everybody should be judged equally. If nobody should be judged, then so be it. Educate mine and, if I can, I will help educate yours.

Our kids are scared, whether they say it or not, in most of these schools. They are literally scared, just in the time they travel to and from school.

I was involved in a peace agreement, a mediation table, and we had to do a lot of conflict resolution. In these two communities, every year, there were between twelve and seventeen bodies between the two rival gangs. With blessings, we finally got both gangs to the table and we worked out things. They wanted this and they didn't want these cats to do that. All that is okay if we can just stop the shooting. Well, for the past four years, neither side has lost a life. In four years there hasn't been a death between them.

December 15, 2007
Santa Monica, California

A Journey Toward Peace

From the Intrapersonal and Interpersonal to the International

Paula Garb

Co-Founder, Center for Citizen Peacebuilding, University of California Irvine

In addition to being the co-director and co-founder of University of California Irvine's Center for Citizen Peacebuilding, Dr. Garb is the associate director of international studies, associate adjunct professor of anthropology and lecturer in anthropology and political science. She is a facilitator and researcher of citizen peacebuilding projects. Dr. Garb spent seventeen years living and working in Moscow. She received her master's in anthropology from Moscow State University and later completed her doctorate in anthropology at the Russian Academy of Sciences Institute of Anthropology. She ultimately secured a job as a field producer for CBS News in Moscow, where she worked until she came to UCI in 1991.

After returning to live and work in the United States, she has studied the mobilization of activists around environmental problems associated with the nuclear weapons complex in Russia and the role of citizen initiatives in the ethnic conflicts of the Caucasus. Since 1995, she has been promoting

citizen peacebuilding activities and research. Her
primary project has focused on facilitating and
studying peacebuilding efforts between Abkhaz
and Georgian academics, journalists, representatives of nongovernmental organizations and
politicians. In 1999, she initiated a coordination
network of peacebuilding projects and organizations working in the Georgian-Abkhaz conflict and
continues to foster the network. Garb has been
using her long-term and in-depth experience and
research data from the Georgian-Abkhaz conflict
to examine and compare how citizens are helping
to resolve disputes in other conflict zones, such as
Kosovo, Bosnia and Herzegovina, the Middle East,
Cyprus and Northern Ireland. She draws on these
experiences for courses in conflict resolution that
she teaches to Los Angeles gang intervention
workers and UCI students. Her work has also led to
a number of publications.

Dr. Garb highlights the eighth action area of the
1999 United Nations Programme of Action on a
Culture of Peace: Promoting international peace
and security. She particularly focuses on empowering each individual to make a difference in his or
her own environment and points out the effect this
can have on international relations.

[Editor's Note: The Caucasus is one of the most linguistically and culturally diverse regions on earth. The nation-states that are comprised by
the Caucasus today are the post-Soviet states of Georgia, Armenia and
Azerbaijan. One territory in the region that claims independence but
is not acknowledged as a nation-state by the international community is

Abkhazia. On the contrary, the international community views Abkhazia as part of the state of Georgia. As the Soviet Union began to disintegrate at the end of the 1980s, ethnic tensions grew between the Abkhaz and Georgians over Georgia's moves toward independence. Many Abkhaz opposed this, fearing that an independent Georgia would lead to the elimination of their autonomy, and argued instead for the establishment of Abkhazia as a separate Soviet republic.]

I am going to start with a story and then tell you a little bit about what I have learned recently about stories and how they can contribute to both peace and violence.

My first story is about the people of Abkhazia and Kabardinia. These are two small ethnic regions tucked away in a forgotten paradise of the world in the Caucasus in the former Soviet Union. These are two of the 130 to 150 or 200 ethnic groups, depending on how you are counting them, that were part of the former Soviet Union. They were very small ethnic groups. The Abkhaz population was never more than around 90,000; so don't feel bad that you have never heard of them.

This story was told to me by an Abkhaz writer, a fiction writer. He was telling me about how he was doing what people in the Caucasus do a lot, sitting around a table heavily laden with great food and wine and drinks. People were toasting one another, saying gracious things to each other over these long toasts. One man stood up who was a Kabardinian. He talked about how great it was that these two groups were meeting and representing both peoples, and he said, "You know, we may actually be relatives." This begins the story that this writer told me about the violence between Abkhaz and Kabardinia in the 1700s.

These are regions with a culture of blood revenge. That is, family members are obligated to take revenge against any dishonor or violence committed against their family. Because of these traditions, both groups understood that they had the potential to wipe each other out over this conflict. What they decided to do to stop the violence was not unusual for these cultures, but what was unusual about it was the scale of it and the particular poignancy of the act. They identified young women with small infants in both communities and brought them, blindfolded, up to a hillside. They were hugging their children. At a certain designated moment, they were to cross over and exchange babies and never know where their own infant went. This was a way to make these two communities related, so that they could never fight again.

It's hard for me to tell this story without getting teary-eyed. I am a mother myself, and I can't imagine what it would take for me to make such a sacrifice for the sake of peace and to know that this would be the ultimate solution to a very difficult situation.

In the Caucasus, I worked as a cultural anthropologist—collecting gossip, as I say. When you study contemporary society as an anthropologist, you are in effect collecting interesting stories about how people experience the world and give meaning to it. I was fascinated by story after story like this about how, for example, it only took a woman to take off her scarf and to throw it into the middle of a fray between two men or on a battlefield where two sides are fighting for the fighting to end instantly. No negotiation.

I found that these situations, these blood feuds wouldn't go on and on, in fact, because they had these mechanisms to stop them. Our notion of blood revenge tends to involve barbarians killing one another. Actually, in all my studies where blood revenge is practiced, traditionally this conflict resolution mechanism quickly goes into effect.

In the Abkhaz communities, I was told that if someone feuding on the other side expected the next strike to be against them, they would identify an extended family member, anybody who was somehow related to this family with whom they were feuding, and try to get close enough to pick up a baby and place it symbolically to the breast of any woman in their group. That would end the fighting. The child would not even have to take the breast. It would just be the symbolic taking of milk from the other side. The saying among these people is that milk is stronger than blood.

You could never have milk siblings fighting each other. Blood siblings might fight, but not milk siblings. That is the ultimate end to any conflict. Again, this is representative of this relatedness.

You probably can imagine how I, at the age of thirty, a young, single mother, already married and divorced, living in the Soviet Union in this exotic place, being an anthropologist in the field, how this could stir me.

That's where I want to begin my journey, talking to you about the personal lessons I have learned along the way as well as how I have gone back and forth noticing the personal in the international and the international conflict in the personal. We are just talking about bigger, more complicated conflicts when we are talking about the international, but there is so much, as I probably don't need to tell this crowd, that comes from the interpersonal, starting with the self and working out, and that certainly has great benefits. If we just change ourselves, we can change dynamics without ever having to tell other people what to do or not do or create any other kind of activity but just the peace within ourselves.

I know, of course, that how we interact with creatures of all kinds, human and others, and what energy we go into the world with is largely going to make changes without us explicitly having to do something.

I was quite impressed by the creative and effective ways that these people resolved their conflicts. In particular, it was the authority and the respect given to the elders that helped people move along through life, stage by stage, getting more important to their society instead of less important. Very critical to giving respect to the elders in a society like that is the elders giving respect to the younger ones—it had to work both ways.

This changed a lot of what happened in my interactions with my children. I brought them with me into the field, where they saw, having lived both in the United States in a modern, urbanized context and then living in Moscow in the Soviet Union, again an urbanized, modernized approach where the older you get, the more you get pushed aside. It was wonderful to see them admire how this society worked with intergenerational respect and then experience the respect that they got from the elders as well.

Some of the lessons I learned are as follows: I already mentioned one—the enormous sacrifices that ordinary people are willing to make for the sake of peace. Also, I learned about relationships and how creating relatedness with others helps prevent bad deeds done to others, violence being the worst of it. We certainly know of many other ways humans are abusive to one another. We are abusive in speech, in action, in withholding communication, as well as in communication.

By this time, I was divorced. I was a single parent. I had to look back at the ways I had been in my marriage and some of the things that I could have done differently had I lived in this community or had I been brought up with a different way of thinking about conflict resolution. I was focusing on my dissertation for my master's as an anthropologist at Moscow University. I was doing it on child rearing in the Abkhaz rural areas.

Then I stumbled across these councils of elders. I started out my study being very interested in child rearing and also in living long lives. Did I mention that this was part of a study to look at the long-living peoples of this area, who lived over the age of ninety in larger percentages than most other territories? In the Soviet Union, in Azerbaijan, we also found communities like that, not only in Abkhazia in Georgia. Of course, such communities exist in other parts of the world as well.

I was interested in gerontology, and I was interested in child rearing, but these councils of elders, these incredibly poignant ways of getting around conflict—preventing it, rolling it back and creating peace—took me in a whole different trajectory. I left behind the child-rearing studies, and I left behind the gerontology studies and began working on conflict resolution, looking at culture and conflict, how people in different cultures fight, and how they make up in different cultures.

I lived another ten or so years in the Soviet Union after these experiences. I came back to the United States in 1989 and 1990, discouraged with the Gorbachev reforms. It looked like the rejuvenation of Soviet society and a social democratic stable society was not going to happen. It was turning into really ugly nationalism and ethnic conflicts. The vacuum left by a weak central power left open a lot of space for political and ethnic entrepreneurs to do a great deal of damage and spread many stories about each other, so that it was possible for former neighbors and relatives to pick up guns and shoot at one another and create havoc.

Meanwhile, my beloved Abkhazia was turning into a war zone. [Editor's Note: The war in Abkhazia between 1992 and 1993 was waged chiefly between Georgian government forces on one side and Abkhaz separatist forces supporting independence of Abkhazia from Georgia on the other side. Ethnic Georgians who lived in Abkhazia fought largely on the side of Georgian government forces. Abkhazia's population of ethnic Armenians and Russians largely supported Abkhazians and many fought on their side.] From 1992 to 1993, in a territory of about 500,000 inhabitants, 90,000 of them were Abkhaz. Imagine a territory no larger than New Jersey where within a little more than a year, 20,000 to 30,000 people were

dead in urban warfare on the beautiful shores of the Black Sea. Sometimes when you look at the videos of people in camouflage with rifles
going through this paradise, it just makes you feel as though humanity has infinite capacity for evil. I resist that thought. I resist that way of
thinking, and I resist that story, so I will carry on with the evolution of my
own journey.

During the war, I found it impossible to relate to the warfare. My
father had been a Jewish war refugee from the civil war of the Soviet
Union, and he had seen his parents tortured before being killed. As a ten-
to twelve-year old, he had been heavily traumatized in the civil war of
Russia, which then became the Soviet Union. He left as an orphan with
his older brother to the United States. My father, who had experienced
such violence at a young age, somehow came out of it a completely non-
violent person and a very softhearted, kind man who talked about pac-
ifism, although not as a complete way of being for him. He fought in
World War II, and he believed that there were causes that one could fight
for, but generally, there is something in my DNA about not being able to
pick up a gun or support people who were fighting.

My friends, my dear friends, the Abkhaz, were out there fighting,
and I couldn't bring myself to help them with that. All I could manage
to do was to have clothing and food sent out there. I was so relieved in
1994 when the cease-fire became final, and I thought: "That's why I had
to learn all of this mediation and conflict resolution. This is where I can
play a role."

I went back to the region completely in the story of the Abkhaz victim-
ization by the Georgians. Completely! But I knew that I could not help
my friends if I stayed stuck in the story that the Georgians were the invad-
ers and the Abkhaz were the victims, pure and simple. I knew theoretically that I had to create a new way of being in the region. Believe me, it
was painful.

First of all, I was afraid to go to Georgia proper. There was a cease-fire
line held by Russian peacekeeping forces and monitored by UN forces,
and held to this day, so that neither side can go to the other side, at least
not easily and not without peril.

All during the war, I had been making a plea to the international community in writing and in every other venue I could about the plight of the

Abkhaz and the potential genocide. I was afraid to go to Georgia proper; I was afraid something might happen to me there. But when I went to Georgia, the custom of hospitality of the Caucasus kept me from knowing that they hated me. They treated me as though they didn't know who I was and that I had always favored the Abkhaz side in the war. I thought: "Hmm, I got away with it. They don't know who I am. I guess they didn't read what I was writing."

It took four years of going back every several months. I was trying to work with journalists, academics, members of new non-governmental organizations—that is, the opinion makers on both sides. According to a theory of one of my dear colleagues, John Paul Lettera, if you work with the middle echelon of the non-governmental sector, these are the people who talk up. In other words, they have people in high places who listen to them, and they can talk down because they are still not so far away from the grass roots that they don't understand what is going on there. When you leverage that community, you can get peaceful talk going up and down, and it is faster and easier.

I have been testing that theory for quite a while. I can tell you that even with the most patient and multiple projects that are in the area—not only mine, but several other major organizations and major projects who have been in it from the beginning for the long term, bringing non-governmental actors at all levels together—it seems as though it is still very hard for people to go to a meeting, have some breakthroughs in their understanding of where the other side is coming from, and then go back home and feel safe to tell everybody.

A lot of that information and much of that personal transformation that takes place stays within this middle sector. It goes a little bit up and it goes a little bit down, but here we are in 2008, and we are no closer to a peace agreement than we were in 1994. I can talk about all of the major breakthroughs that we had, intellectually, on both sides to help them understand, but there is more work to do.

In my own breakthrough, I began at some point not only to understand intellectually the side of the Georgians but also to feel their pain with the same intensity that I feel the pain of my Abkhaz colleagues. Still, you may hear a partiality that I am still trying to overcome, because we do get stuck in our stories of victimhood and who is the bad guy and who is the good guy and what they did to us.

The international community involvement in this conflict includes the U.S. government and the other six or seven major countries that form the negotiation team—including Britain, France, Germany—all under the auspices of the United Nations. The stated purpose of this negotiation team is to restore the territorial integrity of Georgia, which means they go to the negotiation table with the Abkhaz on one side and the Georgians on the other side and they say, "We are here." It is in all of their documents. They don't have to say it. It is essentially going into a mediation as a third-party neutral, supposedly, and saying, "We're going to solve this conflict so that you agree to go back to live in Georgia." It is a nonstarter. Part of the reason this particular conflict is stuck in place, in the opinion of many of us who have been doing this work for a long time, is because the international community will not at least pretend to be third-party neutrals.

For the Abkhaz, it is always: "What is it you don't understand about the word *independence*? We are an independent country, de facto. We don't care if you recognize us or not, and we have nothing to talk about." That is the basic conversation that goes on in these official talks, over and over and over and over. The result of living day in and day out in a territory with a frozen conflict is that now, in the last four or so years, my dear colleagues are all turning inward against one another. It is: "You're going over to meet the Georgians. You are no good. We will not vote for you." And then on the other side it is: "You're going over to meet with the Abkhaz. You're ready to give them recognition. We won't have anything to do with you or your political party."

The one positive thing that we can make a claim to, those of us in the non-governmental movement, is that we have built up a large constituency of people on both sides who understand what a resolution would look like and basically agree.

Instead of having all the illicit trade that is going back and forth over this border, where bribes are taken by both sides and trickle up to the top leaders, open it up to free, honest trade. The Georgians would have to be the first to say okay. Then the international community will say: "This is a border. We are going to put our customs people here; they are going to put their customs there, and we are going to get rid of all those folks who are stealing UN cars." They are stealing cars on both sides. They take the license plates off, they take it to the other side, and they get away with it.

I discovered this about eight years ago, when we were several years into our non-governmental process and were still struggling with some of the animosities across the divide. We found out that these warlords are cooperating well with one another across the divide. It was discouraging for a while, but then I heard my colleagues on both sides, the Abkhaz and the Georgians say, "We have to keep walking, even if we are standing in place." You know how joggers will keep jogging in place? Well, we feel like we need to do that to keep our energy up.

But it is sad to see my colleagues now divided among themselves. When I first started out, there was quite a bit of unity. In unity, there was strength, and now they are losing a lot of that strength.

I would like to turn now to a discussion of how I see wars closer to the experience of people in this room; that is, the wars about which you know more than the Abkhaz-Georgian war. I would like to talk about how I have come to understand the power of story-making in peacemaking and in making war.

I go back to the Soviet invasion of Afghanistan. The United States and the Soviets were trying to woo the Afghans in the pre-Soviet era, in the late 1970s, by giving aid. The United States was giving aid, and the Soviets were giving aid. They were competing in this arena. At some point, the Soviet military command—and we still don't understand what the motivation was and whether or not they believed this to be true—convinced the politburo that Hafizullah Amin, a leader in Afghanistan, was going to allow the United States to establish missiles in Afghanistan.

In fact, no such plan was happening. The United States was not interested in this area, other than that small kind of aid. However, a huge story was made up. I don't know whether the Soviets believed it to be true or whether it can be attributed to the historical xenophobia of the Russians, which lasts until today and which says basically that anybody who is not Russian can't be trusted.

I lived in the Soviet Union for twenty years. I loved my Russian companions, and I loved very many things about the Soviet Union. The xenophobia was one thing that propelled me out of there, because I felt as though no matter how I tried to go native, I could not be accepted. I did not want to spend the rest of my life feeling like an immigrant among xenophobic people.

A recent example is Iraq and the stories we heard about Saddam Hussein, what he was attempting to do, and what that would mean for the world. In the Afghan-Soviet war, probably 30,000 Soviet soldiers were killed and maybe tenfold that many Afghans over a made-up story. With Iraq, I think we can talk about quite a bit of storytelling. Saddam Hussein's story was to the international community: "If you come and fight us, we are going to go after you. We have all this equipment. We have all this military might." This was a story to be told domestically. Maybe he believed it, and maybe he didn't, but he intended it to scare the rest of the world. When it turned out that the Iraqis could barely put up a fight, people wondered what in the world was Saddam Hussein thinking. Did he believe his own words, or did he not?

Again, I am going to give a recent story in my life, where I was walking a treacherous line.

I found myself telling a story, making up a story, and potentially getting into a situation where an already delicate relationship with my younger son could have become even more delicate.

We were in Moscow. We had all decided that we couldn't stand doing New Year's one more time outside of Russia. The Russians have a really great way of celebrating it, and we wanted to all be there together. We had a wonderful reunion. My son was staying with his wife's parents. I heard things that made it sound to me as though he thought his wife's family was great, but his own family was not so great. This story had been building up in my head, and I was imagining that this was the narrative he was giving everybody, because he was making toasts to family: "Family is great. I am understanding on this particular trip how great it is to have a supportive family," he would say, and all the time I thought he was talking about his in-laws, and I was taking the punches.

I was so thrilled to find out that I had made up a story (that my son had turned on his whole family), and it wasn't true. Believe me, it was a struggle. I think that had he not, the next morning, given me the opportunity to hear what he really meant, I probably would have found a way, another time, to get clarity. It certainly would not have done my nerves any good, and maybe I would have spewed a bit of irritation at other people who had nothing to do with what was going on inside of me.

When I realized I had made up the story, we laughed about how I do this, and how damaging it can be to relationships. At that point, my son said to me, "You know, Mom, all your life, you have done this."

I was able to say: "You're right. You are really right." He was so floored that I got the greatest hug of my life.

He cried on my shoulder, and he said: "You know what, Mom? I do that, too, in my family."

I am paying a lot of attention to the stories that are out there in the international arena, the stories that get told in our own minds about bosses.

There are two people of authority with whom I deal, and I have to remember that they are just people who are living their lives. I am making up the story myself about who they are, but if I just treat them like the people I need in my life and around me, we can keep up our communication.

I want to end with some good news that comes from anthropology. It comes from my own experiences and my own understanding. Throughout history, most of the time, most people have resolved their conflicts peacefully. The first story I started out with is an example. There are many more. I worked in Northern Ireland during the troubles. I was in Azerbaijan and Moscow and other places during troubles. There were plenty of times when things got dicey. I can say that, in all of those places, I can count on one hand the number of times I heard that violence was going on around me. In other words, most human beings, even in the diciest places, have the experience of resolving conflicts peacefully without violence.

Some more good news I would like to end with is that the International Peace Academy in New York has come out with a recent study that shows that, between 1992 and 2005, violence in wars between countries dropped by 40 percent. There is Rwanda, there is Iraq, there are other places where there is internal conflict and things are horrible. Coups have dropped dramatically since the 1960s. There are indicators that things are not quite as bad as is sometimes portrayed when we pick up the newspaper or listen to the news.

What are the explanations for this? At the top of the list are the proliferation of non-governmental grassroots organizations and the vastly increased UN diplomacy. I understand that the goal in the United

Nations is to have all staffers, no matter what their work is, complete an intensive course in conflict resolution so that they can understand these principles and live by them. Another explanation is the change in thought about the place of war in international affairs. There seems to be a growing recognition that war is a lousy way to resolve differences.

People around the world are no longer satisfied with leaving it up to their governments to prevent, stop or mitigate violence. How we know this is the exponential increase in non-governmental organizations all over the world that are organizing to make a difference at the non-governmental level. There are more non-governmental people in the world than there are governmental people. That always can give me some hope as well.

Another thing about these organizations is that they are actually in touch with one another. They are collaborating. They are learning from each other. They are spending time acting together. In the Georgian-Abkhaz arena, there are several organizations that began working there at the same time. At first, we all felt kind of crowded, that one of the other organizations might get the funding, not us, or they are going to do it the wrong way and muck it up for us. The United Nations looked at us that way, too; that is, the UN negotiators. The first UN negotiator we met with when I first came in there to say, this is what we are going to do, we are going to do some citizen diplomacy. He said: "Citizen diplomacy! You're not diplomats. You haven't been trained as diplomats. Here we are working very hard for an agreement, and now you guys are going to come in and be diplomats too?" So, I changed the word. From then I started talking about citizen peacebuilding, so as not to get that particular word, that trigger going.

With each new negotiator, we found more and more welcoming. In fact, the latest negotiator is trying to hire one of the directors of another non-governmental organization, Conciliation Resources. This is a guy who has been working with politicians on both sides at the very highest levels. So, there you have the United Nations trying to bring in somebody who has been doing non-governmental work in order to better inform their efforts, and the same kind of development of knowledge of the conflict and sophistication of the nuances by the various ambassadors in the U.S. embassy.

Questions and Answers:

AUDIENCE MEMBER 1: Thank you very much, Ms. Garb, for coming today and being so honest and refreshingly open about your personal experience. It is provocative for me, and I have reflected on my own personal experience.

I want to get your insights about the kind of frozen circumstance you were describing in the Georgia-Abkhazia situation. It sounds like it is in transition, and I am wondering what you imagine might be the next break in that situation?

DR. GARB: There are so many of those frozen conflicts around the world, and several of them are in the former Soviet Union. Kosovo is the one that we hear about the most. As you probably know, the Kosovars have already declared that they are an independent country. They have been frustrated with the international community for not finalizing what they had been promised. Largely that is because of the fear that the Russians and the Chinese will not vote for independence. Until they come to a conclusion that Russia won't stop Kosovo independence, it is a place that these people and people in other frozen conflicts are looking at and saying, "If Kosovo can become an independent country, why can't we?"

If you look into each and every one of those frozen conflicts, these criteria fit in almost every case to one degree or another. What happens to Kosovo officially may be the breakthrough for Abkhazia-Georgia and the others in the former Soviet Union.

I feel firmly that until the Georgian side is willing to allow the international community to become more neutral in its facilitation, there will not be movement in that situation. You know, war was tried once, and it didn't work, so there is no chance that war again is going to solve the problems.

AUDIENCE MEMBER 2: Thank you for all of your ideas. It seems to me that you are seeing the solution as the breaking of small groups into their own nations based on their cultural and religious unity. I am concerned that we, worldwide and in this country as well, are moving more to separate entities. I watched it as a university student as we moved from integrating and starting to become less mindful of race and religion and now we have the campus people wanting to have the Asian dorm, the Italian dorm, and so on. It was a very interesting separation that I have watched taking place in the last few years. I can't help being concerned that it is the wrong direction. I just wondered if you had a comment on that.

DR. GARB: It is a worrisome trend, and I find myself asking the same kinds of questions. Over the years, I have watched my Abkhaz friends and the citizens of that area that I felt from the cease-fire time were angels. I have watched them as they get the upper hand. There is one particular area in Abkhazia, which is a mostly Georgian population. I watched the Abkhaz treat the Georgians the way they didn't like being treated by Georgians when the Georgians had the upper hand. This caused me to ask the same question and to be less certain that the answer was a divorce.

I believe the answer is an amicable divorce, where the borders become transparent, and where healthy relationships are able to develop again, where there can be a meeting across the divide, but it is tricky. How can we both separate and integrate at the same time? I am working at a university and know exactly what you mean, in terms of ethnic groups and also we have been trying to be interdisciplinary for as long as I can remember. Yet, all of the bureaucratic and institutional mechanisms are set up against us being able to work with our colleagues in different disciplines. The answer is one of nuance. In this particular case, I see no other resolution but a recognition of the de facto situation, calling it a transition, which is legitimate.

Even my Abkhaz colleagues today will say in hushed whispers and only carefully that they could foresee a time in ten or twenty years when they would agree to live within Georgia, but they need to see a stable Georgia. They need to see a Georgia where nationalism doesn't frighten them. Things have to change on both sides.

Another great insight I got sitting in a seminar in Northern Ireland listening to representatives of the non-governmental organizations that worked in Northern Ireland before the peace agreement and continue to do the harder work after the Belfast Peace Agreement, the harder work of reconciliation.

I heard speaker after speaker, and they all spoke separately. I don't know even if they knew one another, but I kept hearing the same thing about the breakthrough being when, for instance, the paramilitaries said: "We need to change ourselves. Maybe we are doing something wrong." And realizing they needed to stop thinking about what the other paramilitary was doing wrong. It seemed as though that *ah-ha* moment that created peace was when they stopped pointing the finger at the other side. That has not happened in the Georgia-Abkhaz dialogue. My colleagues are still stuck in "You're to blame." Not "What can I do?" No one asked that question.

I am about to be sixty. Most of the people who are in the project on the Abkhaz and Georgian side are in their fifties or forties at the youngest. Now I am shifting over to the college students, because I am seeing that my colleagues are stuck. There is much more openness among the college students.

AUDIENCE MEMBER 3: (Asks whether Abkhazia was always part of Georgia)

DR. GARB: This is the story that the Georgians have, that the Abkhaz always were part of Georgia. The Georgians, being great hosts, allowed this myth to come up in the Stalin era. This myth allowed the Abkhaz to live in their house, and now they are taking it away from them. The vast majority of Georgian citizens today still think that it is true, even though it was a Stalinist history that was told. The Abkhaz have just the opposite story, that they were, for the most part, never part of Georgia, that only under Stalin did they become part of Georgia.

AUDIENCE MEMBER 4: It was just a story that the Soviet Union took over?

DR. GARB: It depends on whom you believe. You go to Israel/Palestine, you get a similar thing. There are some of these conflicts where it is a little easier to say who was there first, but mostly it is not easy.

If we start with the Soviet period, Soviet Georgia was not the same Soviet Georgia it was in 1921. What they had in 1921 was called the Caucasus Federation or something. I fall in that category of people who say that Abkhazia was not under Georgia, it was an equal entity within this larger entity, and all these ethnic entities stood side by side. It was only afterwards that it got incorporated as an autonomous republic.

When the Georgians left the Soviet Union and re-established the pre-1921 constitution of their independent Georgia, there was no mention whatsoever of Abkhazia in this constitution. So the Abkhaz said: "Good, you are going to say the pre-1921 constitution is valid. We weren't part of you then. You don't mention us there, so bye-bye."

The Georgians argue, "No, you weren't mentioned there, but everybody knew you were there." It is hard, even as an academic, to say for sure.

AUDIENCE MEMBER 5: This has been a real eye-opener for those of us who are far past sixty. I wonder what is your thinking about the possibility of joining the West Bank and Gaza in the future? Does this make any sense at all? There has been some talk, the little that I know about it, of possibly building a tunnel or building a bridge between the two. This is very important for the Palestinians.

DR. GARB: This is not an area where I have as much depth of understanding. It is a complicated place. The only intelligent thing I can say about it is that the two-state solution, that is, an Israeli state and a Palestinian state, seems to be the only possible resolution of that conflict. Now, what will constitute the Palestinian state is still a complex matter because of what has happened in the Gaza Strip.

AUDIENCE MEMBER 6: If they are not joined, wouldn't there still be a possibility of a lot of conflict?

DR. GARB: I am hoping that they will all talk it through. This is another situation where the war weariness, the toil, the human toll that conflict takes, that these multi-year conflicts take on the people, is that they begin to turn against one another. I think that is what we have seen in the Palestinian territory.

AUDIENCE MEMBER 7: I would like to ask you if part of what you are talking about is the overcoming of ego and narcissism, because all of the activities that are necessary require joining and require seeing a larger purpose than one's own life. I just don't know how you over-come and how you make peace attractive to a narcissist, or if you just ignore them and go ahead and go to people who are willing to work together.

DR. GARB: I am still learning. I find that when I can't relate to someone else in possibilities that are positive, I do well with avoidance, but I do better when I recreate who that person is in my own mind, and I cre-ate a story about that person, which allows me to then go forward and interact. The most I can do, and this is what I always tell my students, and I probably don't have to tell you, but this is about as far as my con-trol goes, and that is just with me.

So, if I am in my life—you know, the possibility of peace, love, fun—then hopefully people around me will appear to me to be more peaceful, loving and fun. That is the possibility I create in the world for myself. Not that I don't stumble a lot on that one.

Definitely, in all of these conflicts, hearing my colleagues point the finger at the other side has become wearing on me.

I will tell you a story of my other son. My older son announced to me a couple years ago that he and his wife were divorcing. This was a marriage made in heaven. I could see no good purpose coming from this, but it was their decision. He watched me live my life, so most of the things that I didn't think that they were learning from me, I see them doing, the better ones as well as the not-so-better ones.

I talk to her and I talk to him. For a long time, I would hear him say, "She, she, she." I would hear her say, "He, he, he." I am not hear-ing that anymore. I tell that story to my Georgians and the Abkhaz, too, that I can see no exit from that conflict as long as neither of them wants to look at themselves and see what they are doing in that rela-tionship to cause problems.

I guess that is all we can do. There is one other idea I want to leave you. One of my peace colleagues said, "We need to come up with something for the peace movement like the environmental move-ment, that moment when it became a huge shift in thinking among the masses." She cites recycling—when people can see something that an individual could do—as one of those things that help that shift. Otherwise it is just so big, we feel overwhelmed: "What can I do, what can I do, what can I do? I can't do anything. I am going to watch TV."

So far, this is the best I have come up with—if each and every one of us reaches out to that family member or friend or colleague that we stopped speaking to long ago or that we hold resentments against. If we would just do that, and everybody would do that, maybe that's the equivalent of recycling.

January 19, 2008
Santa Monica, California

Paths to Peace Through Compassion, Cooperation and Sustainable Development

Jeffrey D. Sachs

Director of the The Earth Institute and Quetelet Professor of Sustainable Development at Columbia University

Jeffrey D. Sachs is widely considered to be the leading international economic advisor of his generation. For more than twenty years, he has been in the forefront of the challenges of economic development, poverty alleviation and enlightened globalization, promoting policies to help all parts of the world benefit from expanding economic opportunities and well-being. He is also one of the leading voices for combining economic development with environmental sustainability and, as Director of the Earth Institute, leads large-scale efforts to promote the mitigation of human-induced climate change.

Dr. Sachs is also Quetelet Professor of Sustainable Development and Professor of Health Policy and Management at Columbia University as well as Special Advisor to United Nations Secretary-General Ban Ki-moon. From 2002 to 2006, he was Director of the UN Millennium Project and Special Advisor to UN Secretary-General Kofi Annan on the

Millennium Development Goals, the internationally agreed goals to reduce extreme poverty, disease and hunger by 2015. Dr. Sachs is also president and co-founder of Millennium Promise Alliance, a nonprofit organization aimed at ending extreme global poverty.

In 2004 and 2005, he was named among the hundred most influential leaders in the world by *Time* magazine. In 2007, he was awarded the Padma Bhushan, a high civilian honor bestowed by the Indian government. Sachs lectures constantly around the world and was the 2007 BBC Reith Lecturer. He is author of hundreds of scholarly articles and many books, including *New York Times* best sellers *The End of Poverty* (Penguin, 2005) and *Common Wealth* (Penguin, 2008). Sachs is a member of the Institute of Medicine and is a research associate of the National Bureau of Economic Research. Prior to joining Columbia University, he spent more than twenty years at Harvard University, most recently as Director of the Center for International Development. A native of Detroit, Michigan, Sachs received his B.A., M.A., and Ph.D. degrees at Harvard University. His work supports several of the eight action areas identified by the United Nations Programme of Action on a Culture of Peace, especially the third: Promoting sustainable economic and social development.

There is no one person who bends history; we are all going to have to do this job. The good news is that we can do it. We do not have to wait for the politicians, or the so-called leaders; we are lucky enough to be living in an age where we have the capacities, technologies and tools to do absolutely wonderful things as individuals and as a global community. The world today is interconnected in absolutely fundamental ways. Our connections are becoming more and more immediate and the possibility of a truly global community exists now more than ever before.

Let me give you and an example. Earlier this week at Columbia University, I was thrilled to put into motion an idea that I have dreamt about for a while: the global classroom. The technological advances in the past year or two have made this possible and just last Tuesday, I gave the introductory lecture for a semester-long class taught by faculty from about sixteen universities around the world. Simultaneously, in real time on the Web, we had Columbia, Emory and Georgetown universities join along with the Institute of Development Studies in Sussex, England, the Canadian International Development Agency, Ibadan University in Nigeria, Mekelle University in Ethiopia, University of Malaya in Kuala Lumpur, Tsinghua University in Beijing, University of International Business and Economics in China, Lee Kwan Yew School of Public Policy in Singapore, the Energy and Resources Institute in India and Universidad Internacional del Ecuador! There were rooms of students all around the world looking at one another and learning in one common space. It is exciting and wonderful, and I think it should make us sit back and think about the possibilities of all that we really can accomplish right now.

The homework assignments in this global class have students from Columbia working with students in Ethiopia, and the students in Malaysia working with the students in Kyoto to discuss climate change. They work as groups and have to understand one another. They see each other around the table, and they brainstorm together. This, I think, is the whole spirit of our time. We have the capacity to do things that were once unimaginable and that are so important.

We also have the capacity to destroy as never before. This is the paradox of technology. We have learned throughout history that technology can do wonderful things, yet it can be equally unimaginably destructive. In the end, it comes back to humanity and choice, and it comes back to values and commitment.

Today, we have the capacity to use technology to address and end a scourge, that of extreme poverty. We have within our hands, within our time, within this generation, the realistic ability to end extreme poverty.

This shocks a lot of people. It seems utopian and naïve. But the fact is, if we actually spent a little effort on it, the problem would turn out to be vastly easier to solve than we might imagine. The hardest part of all of this is just being focused. It is not the costs, it is not the unimaginable difficulties of certain places, and it is not the harrowing challenges of economics or the environment or finance. The main challenge is really our ability to focus on what is within our reach right now. That is what I want to tell you a little bit about today.

I want to begin with one of my favorite remarks of John Kennedy. I find that going back to a spirit of an earlier time helps us move forward from the period of bad leadership that we have found ourselves in recently. We live in an age of pessimism and cynicism and "can't do" spirit. Washington goes out of the way to prove that they cannot do things, and I think that is a deliberate ploy because it is not that hard. If they can-*not* do it, they have to move aside, so we can.

I am always reminded of the optimism and the sense of purpose that we have had in great leaders, and in my view, John Kennedy and Robert Kennedy were two of the greatest. At another time of great pessimism about the Cold War and the possibility of spiraling into an outright hot war with the Soviet Union, John Kennedy gave a speech, which I regard as one of the greatest speeches of modern history. I want to read to you from this speech, because I think that it resonates so well for us today. He said:

> First examine our attitude towards peace itself. Too many of us think it is impossible. Too many think it is unreal. But that is a dangerous, defeatist belief. It leads to the conclusion that war is inevitable, that mankind is doomed, that we are gripped by forces we cannot control. We need not accept that view. Our problems are manmade; therefore, they can be solved by man. And man can be as big as he wants. No problem of human destiny is beyond human beings. Man's reason and spirit have often solved the seemingly unsolvable, and we believe they can do it again. I am not referring to the absolute, infinite concept of universal peace and good will of which some fantasies and fanatics dream. I do not deny the value

of hopes and dreams but we merely invite discouragement and incredulity by making that our only and immediate goal.

Let us focus instead on a more practical, more attainable peace, based not on a sudden revolution in human nature but on a gradual evolution in human institutions—on a series of concrete actions and effective agreements which are in the interest of all concerned. There is no single, simple key to this peace; no grand or magic formula to be adopted by one or two powers. Genuine peace must be the product of many nations, the sum of many acts. It must be dynamic, not static, changing to meet the challenge of each new generation. For peace is a process—a way of solving problems.

(From his commencement address at the
American University, June 10, 1963)

What I love about this speech is how he goes on at length to talk only to the Americans about our own views. We were in the middle of the Cold War, in the middle of so much attack and vilification of the other, yet his speech was only about what we believe and how we should be looking inward. It goes on to give massive praise. He says, "As Americans, we find communism profoundly repugnant as a negation of personal freedom, but we can still hail the Russian people for their many achievements in science and space and economic and industrial growth and culture and in acts of courage." He goes on to speak with great praise of the Russian people, and he repeatedly calls on us to think about how we can set a path for others to find peace with us.

The outcome of this particular speech was absolutely startling. Nikita Khrushchev heard it and immediately declared that it was the finest speech of any American leader in modern times. He called the American envoy Averell Harriman and said, "I want to make peace with this man." Six weeks later, the first partial Nuclear Test Ban Treaty was signed (Aug. 5, 1963). That is what can come from reaching out to find connection with others. It is a demonstration of what is possible and practical when we overcome fear and search for the true human connection.

Today, people believe that solutions to other problems are impossible; that poverty cannot be solved, that climate change cannot be addressed, and that issues of the environment cannot be addressed. As John Kennedy said, "That is a dangerous, defeatist belief." He is right—it leads to the conclusion that we are doomed. None of these problems is beyond solution if we overcome the fear, which is the greatest obstacle of all, and understand the nature of the challenges, the power of the technologies that we have and the practicality of our solutions.

What is this problem of absolute poverty? How can it exist in the twenty-first century, in a time of incredible capacity to produce, to grow food and control diseases? How can it be that ten million children died last year (2006) because they were too poor to stay alive? And how can it be that we are not yet addressing this issue?

Two million children died of measles, although there is a measles vaccine that could have saved every one of those children. One to two million children died of malaria, although malaria is a 100 percent curable disease, cured by an 80-cent medicine. About two million children died of respiratory infection because they lacked the 10 cents for an antibiotic. About two million children died of dehydration from diarrheal disease because they could not get simple oral rehydration therapy to keep them alive until the infection passed. That is how simple and how ludicrous the problems are. Millions of utter tragedies. They are absurd tragedies in the sense that they were completely within our control to prevent.

The problems of extreme poverty are the core difficulties of people who lack the basic tools and basic means of staying alive and climbing out of poverty. It is not a matter of blaming the poor, because the poor that I have seen are among the hardest working, most focused on the future, and most loving of their children of anybody in the world. They simply lack the most basic means because, for example, the clinic is 20 kilometers away and the water source is not even a well, just an open spring, which is dangerous to drink from. They cannot afford the five dollars that it would cost for an insecticide-treated bed net to protect from malaria for five years.

Probably the hardest thing for us to understand is what it means to have nothing. Nearly one billion people are in that state on the planet, a condition you cannot escape without a helping hand. When you have nothing, no bank is going to lend you the money, and you cannot save your way out. You need every ounce of your energy, your income and your food supply merely to survive. You cannot tighten your belt when you do not have a belt, and you cannot pull yourself up by the bootstraps when you are barefoot. They cannot do it on their own. What we do not understand, what our leadership refuses to see, are the necessary steps to move from a state of such powerless existence to a place where people can save and invest for their future. They are such small steps. In fact, the first step would be almost unnoticeable in terms of the effort required on our side, a tiny fraction of what we waste in war and on the Pentagon.

I did not understand what it meant to have nothing for a long, long time. I worked in many poor places, but I had not worked in the poorest places and could not imagine what they were like. I began to work in tropical Africa in the mid-1990s, about thirteen years ago now. Even though I was experienced and well traveled by then and had been a tenured professor at Harvard University for quite a while, I was stunned by what I saw. I just had no idea. I had never seen children die right before my eyes. I had never been in clinics where patients were three to a bed. I had never been in a hospital without running water and electricity. It was my naïveté. I did not understand how small things make the difference between life and death.

I was overwhelmed when I began to work in tropical Africa, even after having worked in India, China, Bolivia and many other poor places. Nowhere had I seen the truly extreme nature of disease: the pandemics of AIDS, the resurgence of malaria as a result of spreading drug resistance and much more. I had never experienced so much death around me before and could not have imagined so many people dying without heroic actions being at least attempted. It took me three or four years to understand we were doing nothing to help because we put up a wall of confusion around ourselves. We want so much to believe that we are helping. We have a well-ingrained habit of patting ourselves on the back, but we do not conduct a searching analysis.

When I started working in Zambia in 1996, the first thing I was told was that ten of our counterparts in the Central Bank had died in the last couple of months. When I inquired about the doctors and the medicines, I was told, "There is nothing like that."

"What do you mean?" I asked. "People just die without having a doctor?"

"Oh, yes, they do."

"There are the medicines!" I insisted.

"Well, no, not here."

So what was happening? It took me three years to untangle rhetoric from fact, to realize that as late as 2001, with more than thirty million infected, not one African was on anti-retroviral treatment funded by a Western government or an international agency. The whole Clinton administration came and went without one person being funded for medications. It was already well-known that the medicines were lifesavers, yet not one person in Africa was on a U.S. government program or a European program or a World Bank program.

It took a long time to realize this fact because there were so many speeches, so much professional concern and so many declarations regarding all our efforts and everything we were doing. I only fully understood in 2000, when I was flying to Durban for the International AIDS Conference. I was reading a World Bank paper, which did not mention anti-retroviral medicine. In a four-page scientific paper, the words "anti-retroviral medicine" were not even mentioned because donors did not want to acknowledge the medicine, as if it was some secret. What the article did say was that the World Bank would help to finance bereavement training. It would help enterprises to restructure. It would advise on how to have human resource programs in the midst of a high-disease burden. At that point, I questioned a lot of colleagues and it turned out that the Western world was spending $80 million, roughly three dollars per infected person per year, to address this issue up to 2001.

The problems of AIDS, malaria or food insecurity are not grand problems of cosmic uncertainty. They are not the great mysteries of the universe. They are the mysteries of our inattention. The inability to solve this problem does not rest with our technologies. It lies squarely with us and with our understanding. As I have looked at these shocking realizations, what has amazed me is our incapacity to understand and to act with the power we have.

I have almost given up on Washington. For a long time, I hoped that someone would sign a check and we would get programs going. I have realized that it is not going to happen that way. I have realized that it is going to happen when we understand the stakes, the opportunities, and when we make direct connections. I have realized that whether it is a global classroom, a temple to a community, a city to a city, or an individual to an individual, we need to turn the tide on a large scale. The beautiful part is that making a difference does not require us to overturn our lives. It does not require self-abnegation to the point of living an ascetic life. It just requires our attention, our awareness—nothing more.

Let me focus on malaria for just a moment, because it is the perfect example of a scourge we can end. Malaria is a mosquito-born, tropical disease. The parasite, which is a protozoan, lives in the mosquito and is transmitted to a human when the mosquito bites. That person gets sick, and then another mosquito comes to bite that person and pulls up the parasite and goes on to transmit it to somebody else. This transmission requires warm temperatures, making it a tropical disease. It turns out, for absolutely accidental and fascinating reasons, that in Africa malaria incidence is by far the worst in the world. This is not because Africans are uncaring, corrupt and do not know how to get their act together, but because of the kind of mosquito they have, the high temperatures and the ample mosquito-breeding sites.

[Editor's Note: Anopheles is a genus of mosquito. Of the approximately 400 anopheles species, 30–40 transmit the Plasmodium parasite that causes malaria. Anopheles mosquitoes usually enter homes between 5:00 p.m. and 9:30 p.m. and again in early hours of morning. They start biting by late evening with the peak of biting activity at midnight and the early hours of morning. By keeping the windows and doors closed between 5:00 p.m. and 10:00 p.m. and again in early morning, one can prevent the entry of these mosquitoes into homes. Protection can also be provided by wearing garments that cover the body as much as possible and by using mosquito nets while sleeping.]

There is one type of mosquito (anopheles), that transmits malaria, but there are many kinds of anopheles. As it turns out, Africa has the only kind that does not bite other animals, it only bites humans. Africa's problem is a burden of nature. It is not the fault of the poor, and it is not to be blamed on the poor.

One hundred years ago, even ten years ago, we did not have the tools to help. Now, thanks to modern processes, for example, making bed nets that protect against mosquitoes, help is here. The bed nets drive mosquitoes out of the hut since they are repelled by the smell. The nets are made in an ingenious way that includes a mosquitocide, and thus it protects the child from being bitten. A company invented a way to put the insecticide right into the resin that is used to weave the net. For five years, when you wash the net, the mosquitocide keeps coming out from the resin and keeps providing a protective cover. If you protect everybody this way, you can drive the malaria burden to zero.

How hard could this be? The nets cost five dollars—that's all! Five bucks and they last five years. Do you think we could manage this? We know there are roughly 500 million people in the malaria region of Africa, and that the average size of a household is five people. That's 100 million households. The average number of sleeping sites in the household is three, so three bed nets are needed for five people. Three bed nets for 100 million households, or 300 million bed nets that cost five dollars equals $1.5 billion.

Here is another denominator. Every minute, the United States spends $1.2 million on the Pentagon. Every day, we spend $1.7 billion on the military. It costs $1.5 billion for five years of bed net coverage versus $1.7 billion per day of military spending! It seems to me that 22 hours of the Pentagon budget would fix this problem. My longstanding policy recommendation is that the Pentagon take next Thursday off. If they did, and we could use the money to give every African family in a malaria zone protection against malaria, our security would be raised profoundly in terms of goodwill, in terms of understanding and in terms of human connection.

It is clear that the health problems of the poor have solutions—like bed nets against malaria. Issues for agricultural productivity also have simple solutions. A while back an agronomist took me, a complete city boy, out to the fields and said, "See the yellow on that maize stalk. It should be green. The yellow is an indication of nitrogen deficiency, because this farmer is too poor to buy a bag of fertilizer." That's all.

Two hundred years ago, you didn't need to buy fertilizer. The population was one-tenth the size it is now, and when the soil ran out of nitrogen, you moved to another area. It was called slash-and-burn or rotation agriculture. Now the population in the world is 6.6 billion and the old ways just aren't an option. But, if you take out the nitrogen, the potassium and the phosphorus, every year, without putting them back, you get massive crop failures.

Farmers in Africa have the yield of about 1 ton per hectare. That is about one third or one quarter of what it should be, and it is not enough to feed the family, much less to have a surplus to take to the market to earn a profit.

Certain things are utterly unimaginable, but true. One of these things is that the World Bank, headquartered in Washington, let African farmers farm for twenty years without fertilizer. Twenty years ago, the World Bank said that the problem of African agriculture is government intervention. They advised that the government get out and let the markets take over. They were wrong. Unfortunately, the market runs away from people who have no money. If you are investing in a business that is specializing in customers who have no money, I suggest you get into another business. The market is not designed to solve the problems of people who have no money.

For twenty years there was no fertilizer. I was a latecomer to this—what did I know about fertilizer? I am a macroeconomist. I had to learn about malaria. I had to learn about AIDS. I had to learn about fertilizer. The mistake I had been making until then was thinking that someone must be taking care of these problems. The reality is that we were letting people go hungry year in and year out. Then when an extreme famine came, we would ship food from Iowa at about eight times the price it would cost to give a bag of fertilizer in the first place! If you give a 50-kilogram bag of fertilizer to a farmer with half a hectare farm, he can triple his production. This can happen within one season, not years of training and a generation of change, just a bag of fertilizer.

In September 2006, the World Bank issued a report in what is called its Independent Evaluation Office. If I had to paraphrase the 150-page review of their twenty years of agriculture work, the title would be "Sorry," because the report quite honestly said, "Well, we blew it for twenty years. Nothing we recommended worked. We said the market should get involved but there was no market."

Let me close by telling you what we have done and mention what you might do.

A few years ago, my colleagues and I worked with Kofi Annan, then UN secretary-general, and we decided that we needed action; we needed to put the policies in place that would save lives. I went knocking on the doors of the White House and 10 Downing Street and other places for help. I explained this to a benefactor, a wonderful trustee of Columbia University, Gerry Lenfest, complaining about the lack of financial support and all the rest, and he said, "Well, what if you actually did this, how much would it cost to help a village?"

I made some quick calculations, and he took out a checkbook. He wrote a $5 million check and said, "Go get it started."

We started in Western Kenya, in a place called Sauri Village. One of the most incredible days of my life was meeting with the community in Sauri in the summer of 2004. I recounted it in my book, *The End of Poverty*. People had walked many kilometers to come, and we sat in the sweltering school hall. I asked them questions. I asked them about malaria. Everybody had it. I asked them, "How many of you have bed nets?" There were two or three hands out of the 250 or so people in the room.

I have heard so many rumors from Washington and elsewhere, all of them wrong, like, "Maybe they don't like bed nets." "Maybe they are too hot and they bother people." I asked this roomful of people: "How many of you know what bed nets are?" I thought that maybe they don't even know. Every hand went up, of course. I asked, "How many of you would like bed nets?" Every hand stayed up, and people got very excited.

A woman in the front row stood up and, through the interpreter, said, "But, Mister, we can't afford bed nets."

They are poor, that's all. They know what bed nets are. They know malaria is killing them. They would love bed nets. They just can't afford them.

We talked about fertilizer the same way, and they knew exactly what the situation was. This wasn't about changing some deep cultural habit somehow, it was just about poverty. I said something about electricity and a man raised his hand, stood up, and said, "Professor, I am chairman of the electricity committee." Wonderful! But there was no electricity anywhere. He explained through an interpreter that they had been told in 1997 that electricity would be coming, so they formed a committee. But electricity never came.

There is nothing that can't be done in a straightforward fashion, in partnership, to address these problems. We have launched a program that we call Millennium Villages, of which Sauri is one. These are villages committed to meeting the Millennium Development Goals, the goals to fight hunger, poverty and disease by 2015. The Millennium Villages now cover about 600,000 people across Africa.

Governments, NGOs and companies are all partnering on the Millennium Villages Project. Sometimes companies are vilified, but some of these companies have key technologies that can work toward human betterment. The first company I talked to was Sumitomo Chemical, which makes wonderful bed nets. The chairperson immediately said, "I will provide bed nets for every sleeping site in all of the Millennium Villages for free." He delivered 360,000 bed nets for free. It didn't take twenty years to see the results. It took a few days to cover all the sleeping sites. They didn't go missing, they weren't stolen, and they didn't end up in safe deposit boxes. There weren't bribes. There wasn't any theft. There were bed nets protecting people from mosquitoes, and the malaria burden went down.

The point is that there are solutions. They are within our hands. We have no time to lose; our safety depends on it. Our security depends on it.

We can take action. I would like everybody in one way or another to help partner in the cause of meeting the Millennium Development Goals. One way that you can do it is something as straightforward as helping to provide bed nets. There is an organization I helped to start, called Malaria No More, that can help you do that. The Web address is www .malarianomore.org. It is led by a wonderful philanthropist named Ray Chambers. He is raising tens of millions of dollars for bed nets and helped to get *American Idol* to Africa last year.

Another way is an organization that I co-founded with Mr. Chambers called Millennium Promise, which is devoted entirely to achieving the Millennium Development Goals. Because of the beneficence of wealthy people who support the organization itself, we can say that every cent anybody contributes goes directly to villages. It is used to empower people through a holistic approach, addressing malaria, AIDS and tuberculosis, through a clinic, safe childbirth, safe drinking water, a bag of fertilizer, food supply and microfinance. It is an organization that helps with the transition from subsistence to cash earning, so that communities can escape from poverty once and for all.

I met with heads of state last week (2007) in Ethiopia, Mali and in Liberia. The words and the ideas are spreading. President Toure of Mali is an absolutely wonderful person. He has seen the village that we started in Segou, Mali, and asked for more. This past week, we opened the Timbuktu Millennium Village with the most incredible hospitality you can imagine. We are now working with the government on scaling up to 166 communes.

I believe we are capable of ending poverty and changing the world. I have no doubt that by doing so, we can make the most important connection of all, across every racial divide, religious divide, linguistic divide or any other divide you can think of including class. Human-to-human contact is so powerful. It is the essence and the path to peace on the planet.

Let me end with one statement from that miraculous peace speech by John Kennedy. I find these words to be the most beautiful spoken by any American president of modern times. He said: "So let us not be blind to our differences, but let us also direct attention to our common interests and to the means by which those differences can be resolved. If we cannot end now our differences, at least we can help make the world safe for diversity. For in the final analysis, our most basic common link is that we all inhabit this small planet. We all breathe the same air, we all cherish our children's future, and we are all mortal."

Questions and Answers

AUDIENCE MEMBER 1: What I am wondering about is population and the environment, the growing population. What happens to the capacity of the environment to provide for us?

DR. SACHS: Thank you very much. That's in my next book, *Common Wealth: Economics for a Crowded Planet* (published in 2008). We are 6.6 billion people on the planet, and on the current trajectory the United Nations projects that we will reach 9.2 billion people by the year 2050. All of that increase is projected to take place in today's poorest countries, because that is where the fertility rates remain so high. People don't have access to family planning. Their children die in large numbers, so they compensate by having lots of children, almost like an insurance policy.

One of the things that has been learned throughout history is that if children survive, the fertility rates come down, and eventually the growth rate of the population diminishes. There are practical reasons for saving the children, beyond the obvious moral ones: doing so will help to make a reduced fertility rate possible and thereby help slow population growth. It is very important.

AUDIENCE MEMBER 2: I am a student at Baruch College. I am from Togo, West Africa.

DR. SACHS: I was there last year.

AUDIENCE MEMBER 2: I know what it is to be hungry and to wake up in the morning with no food, nothing, and go to school, study and come back home and ask "Mommy, what do you have?" You don't have anything, and then you have to continue to study. Once again, thank you. I have two questions. The first one is this: What is your legacy?

The second question is this: We are aware of the situation; and some of my friends and colleagues will put our efforts together, and we will create an organization that will support the poor people in Togo particularly in West Africa. You are ahead of us as a professor. What kind of help can we get from you?

DR. SACHS: Wonderful! I can give you a lot of help, I promise. Let me say one word about a very important point you made about going to school hungry. If we can help children to have a meal at school, not only will the children go to school, but their ability to study, as you know, soars because they can concentrate.

In that village in Western Kenya, before we arrived, a wonderful headmistress said that when she first came to the district, the school was rated something like 170th out of 200 schools in the eighth grade exam—very miserable results. She realized the kids couldn't focus because they were starving. She said, "I am going to give a school meal, at least for the eighth graders during the national exam year." In two years, that school rose to number two in the district. It is incredible. She says the kids come to school thinking that they are coming for food. The meal transformed the life possibilities of the kids. In all of the villages we work in we promote a school feeding program for every child. A biscuit in the morning, some milk or a piece of fruit can change a child's life, make it possible to study and meet some of the basic nutritional needs.

I want to see student groups like yours flourish everywhere, and we are committed to giving the support we can. What I would encourage you to do is contact me through The Earth Institute website at www. earth.columbia.edu. Sometimes you have to try two or three times. There are a few hundred or a thousand emails a day, so sometimes things get a little bit lost in the screening, so you have to be persistent. That's a key trait for life anyway. I'm sure you are. What we will do is find ways with Millennium Promise to see how we could give you some advice or some ideas.

One thing I am trying to do is to start Millennium Villages in Togo. Togo is also very interesting in that while it is utterly impoverished, as you know better than I do, it has the potential of a very lush rainforest economy. I was in a wealthy rainforest economy a couple of weeks ago in Malaysia. They grow rubber and palm oil and wonderful fruits and so forth. Togo could do all that as well. I am asking the Malaysians to give some help to Togo. Better palm, better rubber trees, better fruit trees.

I am not sure what you meant about the question of our legacy. We are the generation, the first one in history, that can end extreme poverty. The year 2025 is our rendezvous date. The year 2015 is the Millennium Development's halfway point. By the year 2025, we will end extreme poverty. That is our legacy.

AUDIENCE MEMBER 3: I am a student at a community college in Brooklyn, but I am moving on to Hunter. I never really was a college person. I always wanted education, but I wanted to be a do-gooder as my career. You talked about the different ways to help.

I am asking you how I can have my life as a do-gooder, to go to Africa, to help people, to teach people as my life.

DR. SACHS: First, you are on the right track. The most important thing is to care and to want to do it. Don't lose that focus. There are many ways to do this; there are many, many ways. There is not one path. There is not one profession. There are many ways, and it can end up being through the arts or it can be through public health or through agronomy. It could even be through economics. You never know. Keep the focus.

The truth is that I don't know anything. I am just an economist. I know how to multiply two numbers and follow the dollars. What I became good at was finding the experts. It was my colleague who said it's nitrogen that farmers need. It was my colleague who said the solution is insecticide-treated bed nets. They gave me the ideas.

Become an expert or be very good at finding them, one of the two. There are so many ways to contribute, and it is more about the spirit of wanting to contribute and honing your skills and keeping the focus, and not saying "Well, I will do that after I earn my first $50 million." Of course, go ahead and earn it (then you can do even more) but the point is, don't delay. Get involved, stay involved, and keep the focus. You will learn a lot over time. You will be better at it later. Everybody makes mistakes, starts out one way, or learns new things.

What I feel so satisfied about personally is how lucky I am to have stayed focused on what I was doing, for years and years. It helps to build life and ideas around it, friendships and knowledge and experience. That is what I would recommend.

AUDIENCE MEMBER 4: SGI President Daisaku Ikeda stated, "This century is the century of women." I wanted to ask you how do you see the role of women?

DR. SACHS: I like to think that men still do have something to contribute, although I think we do have a terrible tendency to mess up things. There really is something weird about our half of the species, I must say. We are a little bit less caring. We are a little bit more aggressive. We are a little bit less good at cooperative problem solving. We find that women play a huge role in making the Millennium Villages move forward. We are constantly asked about gender empowerment and so forth. It becomes absolutely natural that once you start focusing on developing health and education and opportunities, the women come to the leadership. It is one solution for Africa's problems: Let the women take over! I believe that.

I met recently with President Ellen Johnson Sirleaf, who is the first woman president elected in sub-Saharan Africa. She is the president of Liberia. She is a wonderful leader. She is very brave and very competent, and she exemplifies for me what could be in terms of quality of leadership.

In fact, from a technical and economic point of view, all societies where women are facing severe discrimination are also economic failures. It is basic human arithmetic, which is if 50 percent of the population is hugely disadvantaged, you are trying to accomplish things with half the ability. Moreover, when women don't have choices, the children suffer, because women everywhere are the principal caregivers. When women face discrimination, which is pervasive, and they don't have access to income, the results first and foremost fall on the children. The empowerment of women is an extremely serious matter for practical economic development issues.

AUDIENCE MEMBER 5: We talk a lot about your work in my program at school. I have so many questions, and it is very hard to pick one. I work at UNICEF in early childhood development. We are having a week-long consultation this week. My boss said, "When you meet Jeffrey Sachs, please ask him about the early childhood summit."

It has been shown that if you invest in the early years, it has results and benefits for the rest of anyone's life, and that there are returns on investment economically in terms of the national picture if you invest in the early years. I was just wondering what your perspective on the importance of early childhood development has been and what you have seen in your experience.

DR. SACHS: I think the investments start for anybody before birth. There is a tremendous amount of evidence that the health of the mother during pregnancy affects the whole lifecycle of a child. Indeed, at least it is hypothesized, that very early nutritional deficiencies in the uterus can lead to cardiovascular disease late in life. Therefore, investing in a healthy early upbringing is a vital investment.

An astounding proportion of children die in the first twenty-eight days of life. This is not because of intrinsic physiological reasons, but because of simple ignorance about how to keep a child alive. Ignorance such as leaving children exposed or cutting an umbilical cord with an unclean knife, leading to tetanus, or putting a child on the dirt ground, or lack of exclusive breast feeding. People need help to know what to do. They need guidance. We need community health workers, which poor countries can't afford. One of the most crucial things, which is very important for UNICEF, is free access to all of these services. We cannot charge for this basic health care and expect that poor people will be protected. My main message is that we need to raise our voice about the importance of these interventions and insist that the only standard that is humane and decent for the world is universal access.

It is bizarre that people don't understand this and act on it, and that's where you have to come in—to raise awareness and consciousness. Our world has struggled to have the rich be willing to give even

1 percent of their income for the poor. This country came close only once with the Marshall Plan. But right now we spend only 0.17 percent of our income on development aid. We spend nearly 5 percent for the military. I put it to you that a world in which the rich can't find themselves willing to give 1 percent of their income when a billion people are at the edge of death from poverty, is intrinsically a world that will never find peace. We need to overcome this profound disconnect.

AUDIENCE MEMBER 6: The fact that you have so much conviction and determination in such a cynical world and time, I am really curious as to what your influences are, if you have a mentor or where you get this drive to actually go in front of the United Nations and tell them that you can cancel these people's debts. How do you do that?

DR. SACHS: You just have to be stubborn, very persistent and very hard-headed. With all successes that I have learned about, read about and studied, I have found that nothing comes easy in this world, for whatever reasons. Persistence may be the most vital ingredient of success. Things that seem so obvious to us now were long struggles, such as the end of slavery, for example. We went for millennia not recognizing it for the unbelievable moral crime that it is. Then, when the movement against slavery started in England in the 1770s and the arguments were so compelling, it still took sixty years to bring it to fruition.

I have set a shorter timetable. By 2025, we have to be done with this agenda, because we have other things to do, so we really should be ending extreme poverty by 2025. These are long struggles. They are not simple. The kind of problem that we are talking about is different from many other problems in the world. Let me say why.

If you are a scientist, the problem is really quite different. The problem with science is understanding. If you have understood something that is correct, you don't have to convince everyone else it is true. They will come to learn that over time.

I always love the line of Albert Einstein when he published his theory of relativity, which, by the way, just had another unbelievable triumph of confirmation last week published in *Science*. He got an irate letter from traditional physicists who gave a hundred reasons why his theory was wrong. He wrote back and said something like "you don't have to send a hundred, one would be enough." With science it is not a matter of piling on, it's either right or it's wrong. It turned out to be right at least as far as we know.

If you are a business person, it is also different. When you have a good product, you don't have to convince everybody that it is a good product; your customers will buy it. If it is good, other people may disagree, but you are not dependent on a majority vote; you are dependent on selling your goods.

If you are a musician, you want your fans and you want people to listen and to hear, but you don't have to convince everybody. You spend your time with your music and you are gratified when people like your music. You aren't out there all the time saying, "You have to like it."

This problem is actually different, and this is the odd thing. This one, we actually do have to change minds, because in the end, we need a collective action. No one person, even Bill Gates, is going to solve this on his/her own. No president or prime minister is going to act until he or she is forced to do so. There are no leaders among our politicians, almost none. There are many followers, and that is not all bad. Followers follow the public. It is our responsibility, because we are the public. As I get older, I am less and less interested in Washington but more and more interested in Iowa and Kansas, and I am interested in what people think everywhere, because that is what is going to count in the end. It is a little bit different from a scientific principle, and it is a little bit different from a business product, and it is a little bit different from artists who create for themselves or for their community.

AUDIENCE MEMBER 7: What do you think it will take to get people to take action? You ended your book saying, "One person at a time," but it just seems that so many of my peers, including myself, have felt doubt. Until I got this book. You really pointed out how it is possible and you stated how it could be done from the level of how "we" can take action.

DR. SACHS: Right. I think what is very helpful is to be specific about things people can do, and to organize around specific ideas and goals.

I certainly find my own inspiration in that. Ending poverty is a big and an amorphous idea. For me what is helpful is to put it into specifics, to talk about actual things that can be done.

I find that when there is better understanding about that, people are much more likely to engage as well. People don't have the right orders of magnitude and they don't understand the practicalities. I think the way to get action is to think through problems and put them onto a level at which people can respond. What do I mean by that? Right now, what I find quite exciting is that on campuses all over the country there are more students engaged in these issues, probably ten times more, than a decade ago.

What are students doing about this? They are raising funds for malaria bed nets. That is actually a wonderful, very straightforward, very practical and extraordinarily important thing to do. If one wanted to do nothing more, I would say to a friend give ten dollars for a bed net. If we got 300 million people to do it, the job would be done. A worldwide effort is absolutely possible.

I really have seen a surge of interest. I actually think that we are on a very powerful path of progress right now. That is another reason why I am a bit stubborn in this. I don't find it hopeless at all, not only at a conceptual level but also at the practical level. I see a lot of progress right now.

I am going to a conference at Yale in the spring for something called "Unite for Sight." The conference is organized by a student group, which is raising funds and expertise to restore eyesight from diseases and to provide corrective glasses for poor people. It is one student's idea.

I had a little interview yesterday about a very clever website and project called Kiva. Does anyone know about it here? Kiva is an international microfinance project. I think it is www.kiva.org, if I remember correctly. You can get online and find a list of people with requested microfinance loans. They are very poor people, their story is told, and you are invited to give a loan. This networking has created a low-cost channel for your contribution to go through a microfinance unit and then over the next six months you get a progress report of what the individual has done. For example, they report that they have opened up a little shop or have a stall on the street. This was unimaginable a couple of years ago.

I think that there is not just one way to do this. There are innumerable new and creative ways to do it. I do believe that we have to find all of our linkages, whether it is through SGI, or whether it is through student groups or artistic groups. Kanye West, I am sure, is very interested in these things. I know Wyclef is and many others. If we just keep expanding the reach of this, it will actually work.

AUDIENCE MEMBER 8: I am a student in school and I see so many false ideas of success among my peers. I see that there is this kind of drive that I can already see in adults, and that it started from there. It is saddening to me, but I feel that if we had more communication with other nations, it would bridge that gap of humanity. So many of my friends, I can see them going down the road with the thought of "This is my dream; I have to achieve this dream of success." Once they reach it, they probably would ask what was it all for. I feel that to try to battle this, we need success less as individual and more as universal or global. I think that few people see that and there are many people around this world that want that. How would you try to change this idea of success?

DR. SACHS: I would listen to you more. I think you put it perfectly. I couldn't have put it any better than you just did.

Why don't we help to get your school online with a school in Africa? That way you can talk to students in a very different place in very different circumstances. We have some sites where computers are just coming in; we could probably get a Web cam going and help you start this connection. One thing that is very important is following through. That's where stamina really counts. We just have to make sure we do it, because if we actually do what we say we do, we will solve the problem.

AUDIENCE MEMBER 9: I did my internship with the United Nations. I did an internship with twenty more students. Our three fields of work were going to be the Millennium Development goals, environmental stability and problems and projects that we can solve in our local communities. We had great successes working as a group and networking among those universities, but we were frustrated from the breaks we were receiving from the United Nations. I did my internship with the Department of Public Information and working with NGOs from all over the world. Even though people were interested in our projects, everybody was saying that there were too many bureaucratic obstacles that need to be overcome before our ideas find any influence at any stage to be developed.

How do we overcome this? You mentioned that we have to work one by one in our local communities, but then we also need peace via political will. Which comes first and how do we balance between them and not lose our inspiration?

DR. SACHS: Well, let me say that I spend a lot of my time at the United Nations as a special advisor to the secretary-general, who is a wonderful person. The United Nations is a very difficult and bureaucratic place. Of course, I am a great fan of the United Nations, and I think we must get it right, because it is vital for our survival that the United Nations works effectively as an organization. I think of it like a plumbing system where the pipes do not fit together. We spend an incredible amount of time on plumbing—one leak springs loose and then the next one springs loose. It is amazingly difficult to get these new linkages right in traditional organizations. They are not well designed for the twenty-first century. The building itself has to be renovated because it's sixty years old and just not equipped for all that it needs to be.

In general, the greatest fear of bureaucratic organizations is messing up, not failing to do something. It is sad but true. Bureaucracies are vastly more concerned about avoiding problems and mistakes than they are about solving problems, even when they are filled with wonderful people. They get a lot of criticism when there is a mistake and they don't get congratulated when they solve a problem. With any initiative, the first ninety-nine responses are "what if," and "that might not work" and "no, we shouldn't try because we might fail." As a result, there is a tremendous bias against action. In the meantime, the status quo is a disaster. We can't wait for these organizations. I have spent a lot of my life trying to make this work, but not always through organizations because I think we have to find many different pathways to accomplishment.

AUDIENCE MEMBER 10: I feel that I may be asking this personal question, but I would feel disappointed if I don't ask it. As a young adult, what advice can you give in saving and investing in terms of money, in terms of time and in terms of energy and ourselves? I want to get guidance on a personal and economic level how to spend and invest our time, our money, our wealth and energy wisely and efficiently.

DR. SACHS: I don't know if I am the right one to ask. I myself was wrapped up in these issues a long time ago. I found them very captivating. What I tell my students, for example, is "don't work on a problem you are not interested in and remember why you came into the field." Don't let a professor tell you "oh, that's too hard." They can give you advice, but don't lose the drive that got you into this in the first place. That is extremely important.

I love the fact that I have loved what I have been doing professionally now for thirty-six years, never with a regret. I have had a lot of frustration, but never with regret of what I am doing because, for me, the drive has been the compelling nature of the challenges. It is a privilege to work on them and it feels very fulfilling.

Of course, having a supportive family is for me the most important thing. My whole family is engaged. My daughter is doing human rights law, and my son is very active in political issues. My twelve-year-old daughter is completely immersed in watching the election campaign and raising money for bed nets and other things at her school. My wife somehow forgives the endless travel and the long hours and everything else, and she is a full partner in every way.

I am not saying I'm a paragon in any of this. I have lived very comfortably but I am also not compelled by a tremendous amount of attention to material things. Again, I don't want to be misunderstood or paint some false portrait, but I think that being very focused on this approach to life, which I was lucky to inherit from my parents and my community early on, helps to balance things. I think balance is extremely important.

January 24, 2008
New York

From a Culture of War to a Culture of Peace

Irving Sarnoff

Founder, Friends of the United Nations

During years of human rights activism and outspoken opposition to abuses of human dignity, Irving Sarnoff saw repeatedly how solutions and a pattern for a world at peace were already provided for in the Universal Declaration of Human Rights and other fundamental documents of the United Nations. The task, he realized, lay in getting the declaration widely known, understood and applied.

Mr. Sarnoff has consistently worked to put this concept into action. He has served as founder and director of the Southern California Alliance for Survival, the Southern California Peace Action Council, the Mississippi Assistance Project and the Interfaith Council for the United Nations.

Mr. Sarnoff stood as a delegate to the World Assembly of Religious Peaceworkers in Tokyo and the World Assembly for Peace in Prague. He acted as executive producer for a series of events in support of the United Nations, culminating in 1982 in Peace Sunday at the Rose Bowl, attended by 100,000 people.

In 1985, Mr. Sarnoff founded the Friends of the

United Nations, whose purpose is to promote the
spirit and vision of the UN Charter and to encourage participation from all sectors of society in the
United Nations' goal of a peaceful, flourishing
planet.

This organization works with the United Nations
and UN nongovernmental organizations, sponsor-
ing briefings throughout the United States on the
work of the United Nations. Through coalitions
created with artists and the entertainment industry, the advertising industry, educational workers
and legislators, Friends of the United Nations helps
to keep people informed of UN activities, goals and
accomplishments.

His message to support voter registration and
involvement in democratic efforts supports the
fifth of the eight action areas defined by the 1999
United Nations Programme of Action on a Culture
of Peace: Fostering democratic participation.
"Registering to vote," he says, "is good citizenship;
it is not a political thing."

I feel that, at this critical moment in the history of our planet, this organization, the SGI, can be crucial in helping to mobilize the sentiment
that lies deeply within all of us—to move from war to peace. It will not
be easy, because the culture of war has been embedded in our psyche for
so many years, for so many decades. To move away from that is a monumental task. I do believe that the SGI as a community can make a major

contribution, particularly the youth within the SGI, to help turn the situation around.

Most young people, particularly in this country, have no idea what war is. In some ways, it is an abstraction. We say "to transform a culture of war into a culture of peace," because it has not been part of our experience.

How many people are aware of the bombing of the World Trade Center? Everybody is probably aware of that. Everybody probably knows that 3,000 people perished in that one incident. If you multiply that, and instead of 3,000 people dying, let's say there were 15,000 people in the World Trade Center at that moment who lost their lives.

Got that picture? Horrible! Now, think for a moment what it would be like if six hours later there was another bombing and 15,000 more people lost their lives. Then, think, again, six hours later, another 15,000 people lost their lives, and then again, six hours later, another 15,000 people. Imagine if that went on every six hours, twenty-four hours a day, for four years. That was the total number of casualties in World War II.

That is not to even talk about the destruction of cities, the fire bombing of Dresden, the fire bombing of Tokyo, nuclear weapons destroying cities and the rebuilding of whole countries that suffered from the bombings. That is the culture of war that we are trying to transform.

When World War II was over, the horror of that experience was so emblazoned on the mentality of the people on the planet and the nations and the governments that they came together and formed an organization called the United Nations. The United Nations was not born out of a dream of peace. It was born out of a nightmare of war, the second global war.

In World War I, millions of people were killed, almost all of them in Europe. That system came out of another system that was essentially based on a culture of war called colonialism. Colonialism imprisoned whole nations of people. The western powers of England, France, Germany and Belgium imprisoned and owned chunks of real estate all over the world. The cost of that to those countries is a legacy that still haunts the body of human beings on our planet. In some ways, that colonialism ended with the end of World War II.

As a result of ending that colonial system, the United Nations, which was formed by fifty-one countries in 1945–46, grew until today there are

192 nations that are part of the UN system. The charter of the United Nations indicates the path to transform a culture of war into a culture of peace. Many years ago, I found out what the United Nations was, what it was doing and what its mission was. I decided that, since most people did not know anything about the United Nations or what it was doing, one way that I as an individual could contribute to a culture of peace was not only to support the United Nations but to try to inform and educate people about what it is and what it does.

It is not taught in the school system. Most people in our country do not know, literally, anything about the United Nations. The government and the media do not paint the United Nations in a positive way. Many people have a negative view of what the United Nations is.

Here is an international organization, the only international organization that represents officially every single nation on earth, 192 nations. That is an incredible accomplishment, which grew out of the whole history of humanity. There has never been an organization functioning for so many years that represented all of the nations on earth with a commitment to never allow future generations to experience the scourge of war. This is the longest time in history that there has not been a world war. In some part that is because the United Nations has provided a forum for dialogue among nations and among people.

Because it has provided that kind of a place for dialogue, it has prevented a major conflagration from taking place. It has not been successful in stopping other smaller wars, although it has tried. The United Nations probably has as good a record of stopping smaller wars as not being successful in other sort of wars. Some of that is because most of the wars today are wars within a country rather than wars between countries. Because of the UN Charter, it is very difficult for the United Nations as an international global institution to interfere in the internal affairs of a country.

People sometimes accuse the United Nations of interfering in the internal affairs of individual countries. It is not permitted to do that. Having established the United Nations, however, it became clear to the people involved that one needed more than a charter commitment to prevent war. It was also necessary to have a way of working on those issues that lead to war—the economic issues, human rights issues and political issues. It was in the process of doing that that the United Nations established a number of programs, agencies and other forums through which they could address the issues that cause war.

UNICEF is a UN program directly funded by the General Assembly that deals with the welfare of children. It was established right after World War II. There is a United Nations environment program that deals with environmental issues, and there is a UN development program that deals with providing funds for the undeveloped countries in the world.

There are several agencies in the UN system that deal with everyday things that affect every one of us. For example, if you mail a letter to go anywhere in the world, one of the reasons it gets there is because of the International Postal Union, an agency of the United Nations. If you travel on a plane, you do not have to worry about the safety of the landing and take off because there is a standardized method to which all countries adhere. That is organized by the international agency on air travel based in Montreal, a UN agency. A UN agency called the World Meteorological Organization, based in Geneva, provides global weather reports. There are hundreds and hundreds of satellites transversing the globe. Those satellites enable you to get on your cell phone and talk to somebody anywhere in the world. The organization of those satellites is organized by the International Telecommunications Union, a UN agency based in Geneva. If you take a cruise on a ship, the World Maritime Agency, based in London, is involved with providing the rules and regulations to do that.

That is how the UN family helps provide a better way of life, creating, in a sense, the basis for a culture of peace. The basis of a culture of peace is the interconnection among all of us on a personal level, whether it is violence in the family or on a global, nationwide and international level.

One of the other things that the United Nations developed was a human rights system through which we can define what human rights are. In 1948, Mrs. Eleanor Roosevelt, the wife of the U.S. president, was assigned the job of chairing the Commission on Human Rights. Out of this commission grew a document called the Universal Declaration of Human Rights. Because of that declaration, a number of covenants were negotiated and signed, placing the thirty articles of the Universal Declaration of Human Rights into a legal framework. Today, there are many covenants and treaties that have been adopted because of that declaration.

I do not know how many people have ever even heard of the Universal Declaration of Human Rights. It is not taught in the school system. It is amazing that this document, the Universal Declaration of Human Rights, which actually codifies all of the individual human rights with which every single person is born, has not been made more public. It is one of the things that my organization, the Friends of the United Nations, and the SGI have played a role in—educating people about the Universal Declaration of Human Rights.

One of the things that the United Nations is accused of is not doing much and that all they do is just talk. This is important, because it is true that one of the things that the United Nations does, especially in the General Assembly and other places, is that it provides a forum to talk. When there is no forum for talking, for dialogue, then what begins to happen is that we move away from a culture of peace to a culture of war. There is no way to solve the problems that people have without dialogue.

It is no accident that at the conclusion of SGI President Ikeda's 2007 Peace Proposal, he calls upon the creation of a culture of dialogue. He calls it *dialogic*. It is very interesting that he calls it *dialogic*, because the previous period also had a different sort of an issue, but it starts with the word *diablo*, which is "devil." You can go from diablo, *diabolic*, to dialogic. That goes to the essence of what President Ikeda was saying: to move from no dialogue to a world community in which dialogue is embraced as fundamental to solving problems.

The General Assembly is a unique body where every single nation on earth, big or small, has a vote. Through the General Assembly, there are a number of things that happen and various committees that are formed out of those 192 representatives. One of the things that happens is that they pass conventions, treaties, declarations and so forth. The Universal Declaration of Human Rights was passed in the General Assembly. They have also passed conventions on the rights of children, conventions on the abolition of racism, conventions on the abolition of sexism and conventions on the rights of refugees. They have passed more than 120 conventions and treaties that came out of the dialogue at the General Assembly.

What happens is that when the General Assembly passes a convention or a treaty, it automatically goes to every one of the 192 member states. If that member state then passes that convention, it is ratified. If the General Assembly ratifies that convention, such as the convention on the rights of refugees or the convention on the rights of children, then it becomes the law of that country. The United Nations is involved in creating international law. More international law has been created by the United Nations in its existence than has been created or developed in all of the history of human civilization. It all happened through the dialogue at the General Assembly.

What we are talking about is creating a movement away from this insanity of war. War is insane! You have to start from that concept, no matter where it happens. Sometimes there are reasons for it, but when you look deep, it is a form of some sort of insanity. It ends up with the insanity of creating nuclear weapons, which have the ability to totally destroy all of civilization. How crazy can you get? How many nuclear weapons do you need in order to feel secure? Right now, there are about 20,000 to 25,000 nuclear weapons on the planet. Now some countries are thinking about producing more or increasing the efficiency of some of our nuclear weapons stock.

To transform this culture of war into a culture of peace, we are talking about a gigantic job. Everybody thinks, "What can I do?" or "What can our little group do to contribute to that transformation?"

One of the reasons I am fascinated by coming to the SGI is because I know that the young people in the SGI, not just here but throughout the country and throughout the world, have the passion and the commitment because of your studies of humanity and Buddhism to make a change that could be dramatic. It is no small job. I usually address the people in the audience who are considered our young people. My generation was very involved in creating the culture of war. Even though we may not have fought in it, we contributed to it; our tax money went into it, our nations and our media. Our generation was rather locked into it. It is hard to move that generation into making a passionate commitment to move away from the culture of war and to transform it into a culture of peace. It is a gigantic job!

I will tell you just how gigantic it is. If you include all the secret things and all the nuclear development, our military budget is approaching somewhere around $1 trillion. Some places will deny that and say it is really only $500 billion, but that does not include Iraq or Afghanistan or the development of nuclear weapons, which is handled by the Department of Energy. The development of nuclear weapons does not appear on the military budget. The military budget does not include the money spent by the CIA and sixteen other intelligence agencies that are part of the war budget, because that information is generally considered secret. If you put all of that together, you end up with a military budget that is somewhere around $1 trillion. That military budget exceeds the military budgets of all the countries on the entire planet put together.

I am not saying that we should not defend our country and other countries against terrorists and terrorism, but there is another way of looking at terrorism. If you are a mom or a dad, and you get up in the morning and there is no food for your children, that is terrorism. If you get up in the morning and, in your village, there are no people around to take care of the children because they all died from AIDS, that is terrorism. Every day, 30,000 children die. This is preventable. Every single day, children die from AIDS and from other diseases because they have no access to fresh and safe drinking water. It is another type of terrorism.

In the year 2000, all the heads of state came together at the United Nations to discuss that issue. It was Bill Clinton, our president, and the presidents and heads of state of 190 countries. They put out a declaration called the Millennium Declaration in which they recommitted their countries to work to make the United Nations the premier continuing organization working for a culture of peace in the world. That was their commitment in the year 2000. That was the basis of that declaration. As part of that declaration, they also made a commitment to an agenda to achieve eight goals by the year 2015 called the Millennium Development Goals.

The problem is that not many people have heard of the United Nations Millennium Development Goal campaign. This is a campaign started in the year 2000 to be achieved by the year 2015 to cut the number of children dying every day by 50 percent. This is preventable. Other goals include cutting the number of people living on less than one dollar a day by 50 percent, providing universal education for boys and girls worldwide and providing a framework in which to raise the status of women and empower them to be part of creating a better world.

We are now halfway through the Millennium Goals. Go home and get on your computer and search the Internet for Millennium Development Goals. You will find out what the goals are, what people are doing to achieve those goals, and how close we are to achieving those goals.

For example, there are 1.5 billion people on the planet who do not have access to fresh water. This means that people have to walk six or seven miles sometimes to get water for their family or their children. The water bearers are the women. In the process of going from the village to get the fresh water to bring it back for survival they are subjected to violence and rape. Their children are not in school because they must sometimes help them provide the fresh water.

Two and a half billion people on the planet do not have access to toilets. We can build the most sophisticated nuclear weapons in the world to destroy an entire city in a matter of seconds, but we are not capable of providing toilets for people who don't have them. There is something wrong somewhere. That goes to the essence of moving from a culture of war to a culture of peace.

I believe we can make that change, and I think the reason we can make it is that we have in our power, particularly in this country, a structure that can help put these things on the agenda. I will almost guarantee you that not one single person that is running for elective office at the national level will ever once mention the United Nations or ever once mention the Millennium Development Goals.

President Clinton and President Bush have committed our country to supporting those goals. If our country does not contribute to these goals, they won't happen. We are the wealthiest country on earth. Reducing that trillion-dollar defense war budget by, say, 10 percent, that would free up a few hundred billion dollars every year that could solve most of the problems that the United Nations is trying to address through the Millennium Development Goals.

But the candidates won't address it, because they do not see it as an important issue. The way to change that is at the grassroots level. If they knew there were thousands, even millions, of young people in our country who want to achieve those goals, you would begin to hear a different story. That means becoming active and becoming involved. Those goals are not political. They are part of a commitment made by our country and by 190 other countries to make the world a better place. We have it in our power to make that happen.

How do we do that? We can do it by having a gigantic voter registration campaign. Registering to vote is good citizenship; it is not a political thing. The SGI youth could inspire themselves and other young people to begin registering to vote and to become aware of the promise and the pledge that our government made to fulfill those Millennium Goals. We are not talking about something these governments didn't do or didn't know about. They passed it. They know what they passed. They are just not doing anything about it, because they know that, at the grassroots level, nobody knows about the goals and nobody cares. Their whole emphasis is getting everybody afraid of terrorism, but they don't see that terrorism is also children dying, no fresh water and no toilets. To me, those are all terror.

We can turn it around by creating this movement of people who are committed to voting and to voting for candidates who will place on their agenda the fulfillment of the Millennium Development Goals, which our country has already pledged to do.

SGI youth throughout this country can lead the way and inspire young people on campuses and in communities to know about those goals and to support candidates who will place those goals on their platforms whether they are Republican or Democrat. It doesn't really make any difference.

One of the reasons I am honored to be here is because I think we can inspire that to happen. If we want to move from a culture of war to a culture of peace, that is one way to do it. The other way is to begin the process of educating yourselves and people everywhere about what the United Nations is.

It may seem like a giant institution, but the United Nation's budget is less than the budget of the Tokyo Fire Department. The number of people who work in the United Nations system in all the different agencies and all the different programs are fewer than the number of people who work globally for either McDonald's or Disneyland; under 50,000 people.

If you want to get serious about going from a culture of war to a culture of peace, you have to take this institution, the United Nations, which is the only institution that we have, and begin saying to the political leadership, "If you think this is an important institution and can accomplish these things, you need to begin funding it. You need to begin having more people on staff. You need to begin doing the things that will make that institution a more credible place. "

Questions and Answers

AUDIENCE MEMBER 1: It has been a wonderful lecture to listen to, but
as you young people can see, I am much older than you are. I was
thirty-two in 1945 when the United Nations was coming to be born. I
had some small part in writing part of the charter of UNICEF. What I
want to say is that we have two things that we can count on. We knew
people in our own country and in other countries, in Europe and here
in the United States and so on, who were passionate that their brothers
and sisters should have the deal that they had, worldwide, no exceptions. There was that passion, and with it went an understanding that
if that was going to come about, it had to begin in the hard work of
knowing why that was not already happening. You had to have people who were willing to work hard at writing law, the charters of both
the United Nations and UNICEF, who understood people in other
nations and who cared; people who lived their lives with the passion
that the world should finally come to be like a decent home where
everybody had what each one needed.

AUDIENCE MEMBER 2: You talked about voter registration and that the
youth of SGI should take part in that, but I know many of us are not
U.S. citizens. In terms of making the change that you spoke about—
our education system, the Millennium Development Goals or how
the United Nations isn't taught in our school systems—could you go
further into education? For us, I believe, the culture of peace really
encompasses education.

MR. SARNOFF: In whatever country one is a citizen, that country signed
on to the Millennium Development Goals. Wherever you live, you
can encourage that country to live up to the pledge that it made to
those goals.

My other concern has to do with the specific wording, "Fostering
a culture of peace through education." If in the school system there is
no teaching about what the United Nations is internationally or what
the various covenants and declarations that are part of the legal system of international law, we are functioning in a wasteland of a lack
of knowledge. I think if we can somehow influence the school system
to begin teaching about the accomplishments and the activities of the

United Nations, it will make a major contribution to changing the way people look at a culture of peace versus a culture of war.

We know what homeless people are. At the international level, they don't call homeless people *homeless*, they call them refugees. The United Nations has an agency called The International High Commission for Refugees. They take care of almost 25 million refugees. That means feeding them, providing tents, providing blankets and providing schooling for the children. Most of the refugees, at least 80 percent of them, are women and children.

Iraq is a country of 26 million people. There are now 2 million external refugees who have left Iraq to go to Syria, Iran and Sweden. There are also 2 million people in addition to those 2 million refugees that are internally displaced, who have left Baghdad and other places where there is violence. In a country of 26 million people, there are now 4 million refugees. A lot of solving those problems is now going to fall on what is called the international community.

Let me touch on one other thing because you hear these words often. They are very important to how you understand the world. There are two words. One is called *unilateralism*, which means going it alone. The other word is *multilateralism*, which means doing something together. You are powerful here in the SGI because you have a community. If you didn't have a community called the SGI, it would diminish not only the SGI's power, but it would diminish the power of each one of you individually. Because you have a community, you have strength and you have power. At the international level there is a community. It is a multilateral community, and it is called the United Nations. When we ignore that and we do something that is unilateral, we end up with war. If you go back in time three or four years from now, you say why did we go to war? There were millions of people on the streets saying go through the United Nations. Unilaterally, we decided to not go through the United Nations, and that was a major error. The secretary-general at that time described the war as an illegal war. That is the difference between community and going it alone. You have power because you have a community. You have power as an individual because you have a family. As we go up the structure, our ability to have power involves education, and it involves the maintenance of community.

AUDIENCE MEMBER 3: Is it only in the United States where the United Nations isn't taught in the schools and its initiatives promoted? Is the United Nations being promoted through the media and taught in school systems in other countries?

MR. SARNOFF: You know, that is a difficult question to answer. It sort of depends on the country. A lot of the work of the United Nations is involved in assisting people in countries in what is called the under-developed world. So you will find a very large number of programs of the United Nations and the whole UN system that are taking place in Africa and Latin America and different parts of Asia. The people in those countries see the UN in a different light because in many ways the UN is the difference between life and death. It is a program that is assisting children, women, or working on malaria, AIDS, or one of these other things in their country.

The thing that they see quite often is a UN institution; the World Health Organization, UNICEF, The World Food Program, they are all UN agencies. That is what they see. They have another sort of view of the United Nations. In the more developed countries, particularly in the Scandinavian countries and in Canada, there is more knowl-edge about the United Nations than there is in this country.

In Japan, there is a very strong SGI organization, and there has always been a lot of support for the United Nations as a system. Finan-cially, Japan, as a nation, is one of the strongest contributors to the UN system. I think it is the second largest contributor next to the United States when everybody pays his or her dues. In many of the other countries including Japan, there isn't a lot of promotion through the media about the UN system. The media has a way of presenting things from a very negative point of view. Somebody once told me, and I think it is true. The United Nations has a lot of days, like the interna-tional day for water, and the international day of solidarity. I think on the 21st of this month, which is in a couple days, is the international day for dialogue and diversity. I have a list of all those days.

Every year, on September 21, there is the International Day of Peace. They try to promote thinking about peace at home, peace within yourself and peace within the community. When that day happens at the United Nations, they ring the Peace Bell. The Peace Bell was the gift of the children of Japan who contributed coins. The coins were melted down and made into this bell. Every year on September 21, the secretary-general goes out and rings the Peace Bell and makes a little speech. One year, they planted a tree. I don't think anybody in the press even noticed. A number of months later, the tree died. Somebody either forgot to water it, or it was a weak tree. That got headlines in papers all over the world: "UN Peace Tree Dies." There is an attitude among the press about focusing on the negative. We must focus on the positive.

May 19, 2007
Santa Monica, California

Appendix A

Declaration on a Culture of Peace

United Nations Fifty-third Session Agenda Item 31: Resolutions Adopted by the General Assembly

The General Assembly,

Recalling the *Charter of the United Nations,* including the purposes and principles embodied therein,

Recalling also the *Constitution of the United Nations Educational, Scientific and Cultural Organization,* which states that "since wars begin in the minds of men, it is in the minds of men that the defences of peace must be constructed,"

Recalling further the *Universal Declaration of Human Rights*[1] and other relevant international instruments of the United Nations system,

Recognizing that peace not only is the absence of conflict, but also requires a positive, dynamic participatory process where dialogue is encouraged and conflicts are solved in a spirit of mutual understanding and cooperation,

Recognizing also that the end of the cold war has widened possibilities for strengthening a culture of peace,

Expressing deep concern about the persistence and proliferation of violence and conflict in various parts of the world,

Recognizing the need to eliminate all forms of discrimination and intolerance, including those based on race, colour, sex, language, religion, political or other opinion, national, ethnic or social origin, property, disability, birth or other status,

Recalling its *resolution 52/15* of 20 November 1997, by which it proclaimed the year 2000 as the "International Year for the Culture of Peace," and its *resolution 53/25* of 10 November 1998, by which it proclaimed the period

2001–2010 as the "International Decade for a Culture of Peace and Non-Violence for the Children of the World,"

Recognizing the important role that the United Nations Educational, Scientific and Cultural Organization continues to play in the promotion of a culture of peace,

Solemnly proclaims the present Declaration on a Culture of Peace to the end that Governments, international organizations and civil society may be guided in their activity by its provisions to promote and strengthen a culture of peace in the new millennium:

ARTICLE 1

A culture of peace is a set of values, attitudes, traditions and modes of behaviour and ways of life based on:

(*a*) Respect for life, ending of violence and promotion and practice of non-violence through education, dialogue and cooperation;

(*b*) Full respect for the principles of sovereignty, territorial integrity and political independence of States and non-intervention in matters which are essentially within the domestic jurisdiction of any State, in accordance with the Charter of the United Nations and international law;

(*c*) Full respect for and promotion of all human rights and fundamental freedoms;

(*d*) Commitment to peaceful settlement of conflicts;

(*e*) Efforts to meet the developmental and environmental needs of present and future generations;

(*f*) Respect for and promotion of the right to development;

(*g*) Respect for and promotion of equal rights and opportunities for women and men;

(*h*) Respect for and promotion of the right of everyone to freedom of expression, opinion and information;

(*i*) Adherence to the principles of freedom, justice, democracy, tolerance, solidarity, cooperation, pluralism, cultural diversity, dialogue and understanding at all levels of society and among nations; and fostered by an enabling national and international environment conducive to peace.

ARTICLE 2

Progress in the fuller development of a culture of peace comes about through values, attitudes, modes of behaviour and ways of life conducive to the promotion of peace among individuals, groups and nations.

ARTICLE 3

The fuller development of a culture of peace is integrally linked to:

(a) Promoting peaceful settlement of conflicts, mutual respect and understanding and international cooperation;

(b) Complying with international obligations under the Charter of the United Nations and international law;

(c) Promoting democracy, development and universal respect for and observance of all human rights and fundamental freedoms;

(d) Enabling people at all levels to develop skills of dialogue, negotiation, consensus-building and peaceful resolution of differences;

(e) Strengthening democratic institutions and ensuring full participation in the development process;

(f) Eradicating poverty and illiteracy and reducing inequalities within and among nations;

(g) Promoting sustainable economic and social development;

(h) Eliminating all forms of discrimination against women through their empowerment and equal representation at all levels of decision-making;

(i) Ensuring respect for and promotion and protection of the rights of children;

(j) Ensuring free flow of information at all levels and enhancing access thereto;

(*k*) Increasing transparency and accountability in governance;

(*l*)   Eliminating all forms of racism, racial discrimination, xenophobia and related intolerance;

(*m*) Advancing understanding, tolerance and solidarity among all civilizations, peoples and cultures, including towards ethnic, religious and linguistic minorities;

(*n*) Realizing fully the right of all peoples, including those living under colonial or other forms of alien domination or foreign occupation, to self-determination enshrined in the Charter of the United Nations and embodied in the International Covenants on Human Rights,[2] as well as in the Declaration on the Granting of Independence to Colonial Countries and Peoples contained in General Assembly resolution 1514 (XV) of 14 December 1960.

ARTICLE 4

Education at all levels is one of the principal means to build a culture of peace. In this context, human rights education is of particular importance.

ARTICLE 5

Governments have an essential role in promoting and strengthening a culture of peace.

ARTICLE 6

Civil society needs to be fully engaged in fuller development of a culture of peace.

ARTICLE 7

The educative and informative role of the media contributes to the promotion of a culture of peace.

ARTICLE 8

A key role in the promotion of a culture of peace belongs to parents, teachers, politicians, journalists, religious bodies and groups, intellectuals, those engaged in scientific, philosophical and creative and artistic activities, health and humanitarian workers, social workers, managers at various levels as well as to non-governmental organizations.

ARTICLE 9

The United Nations should continue to play a critical role in the promotion and strengthening of a culture of peace worldwide.

107th plenary meeting
13 September 1999

1. Resolution 217A (III)

2. Resolution 2200A (XXI), annex.

Appendix B

Programme of Action on a Culture of Peace

United Nations Fifty-third Session Agenda Item 31

The General Assembly,

Bearing in mind the Declaration on a Culture of Peace adopted on 13 September 1999,

Recalling its *resolution 52/15* of 20 November 1997, by which it proclaimed the year 2000 as the "International Year for the Culture of Peace," and its *resolution 53/25* of 10 November 1998, by which it proclaimed the period 2001–2010 as the "International Decade for a Culture of Peace and Non-violence for the Children of the World";

Adopts the following Programme of Action on a Culture of Peace:

A. AIMS, STRATEGIES AND MAIN ACTORS

1. The Programme of Action should serve as the basis for the International Year for the Culture of Peace and the International Decade for a Culture of Peace and Non-violence for the Children of the World.

2. Member States are encouraged to take actions for promoting a culture of peace at the national level as well as at the regional and international levels.

3. Civil society should be involved at the local, regional and national levels to widen the scope of activities on a culture of peace.

4. The United Nations system should strengthen its ongoing efforts to promote a culture of peace.

5. The United Nations Educational, Scientific and Cultural Organization should continue to play its important role in and make major contributions to the promotion of a culture of peace.

6. Partnerships between and among the various actors as set out in the Declaration should be encouraged and strengthened for a global movement for a culture of peace.

7. A culture of peace could be promoted through sharing of information among actors on their initiatives in this regard.

8. Effective implementation of the Programme of Action requires mobilization of resources, including financial resources, by interested Governments, organizations and individuals.

B. STRENGTHENING ACTIONS AT THE NATIONAL, REGIONAL AND INTERNATIONAL LEVELS BY ALL RELEVANT ACTORS

9. Actions to foster a culture of peace through education:

   (a) Reinvigorate national efforts and international cooperation to promote the goals of education for all with a view to achieving human, social and economic development and for promoting a culture of peace;

   (b) Ensure that children, from an early age, benefit from education on the values, attitudes, modes of behaviour and ways of life to enable them to resolve any dispute peacefully and in a spirit of respect for human dignity and of tolerance and non-discrimination;

   (c) Involve children in activities designed to instill in them the values and goals of a culture of peace;

   (d) Ensure equality of access to education for women, especially girls;

   (e) Encourage revision of educational curricula, including textbooks, bearing in mind the 1995 Declaration and Integrated Framework of Action on Education for Peace, Human Rights and Democracy[1] for which technical cooperation should be provided by the United Nations Educational, Scientific and Cultural Organization upon request;

   (f) Encourage and strengthen efforts by actors as identified in the

Declaration, in particular the United Nations Educational, Scientific and Cultural Organization, aimed at developing values and skills conducive to a culture of peace, including education and training in promoting dialogue and consensus-building;

(g) Strengthen the ongoing efforts of the relevant entities of the United Nations system aimed at training and education, where appropriate, in the areas of conflict prevention and crisis management, peaceful settlement of disputes, as well as in post-conflict peace-building;

(h) Expand initiatives to promote a culture of peace undertaken by institutions of higher education in various parts of the world, including the United Nations University, the University for Peace and the project for twinning universities and the United Nations Educational, Scientific and Cultural Organization Chairs Programme.

10. Actions to promote sustainable economic and social development:

(a) Undertake comprehensive actions on the basis of appropriate strategies and agreed targets to eradicate poverty through national and international efforts, including through international cooperation;

(b) Strengthen the national capacity for implementation of policies and programmes designed to reduce economic and social inequalities within nations through, *inter alia*, international cooperation;

(c) Promote effective and equitable development-oriented and durable solutions to the external debt and debt-servicing problems of developing countries through, *inter alia*, debt relief;

(d) Reinforce actions at all levels to implement national strategies for sustainable food security, including the development of actions to mobilize and optimize the allocation and utilization of resources from all sources, including through international cooperation, such as resources coming from debt relief;

(e) Undertake further efforts to ensure that the development process is participatory and that development projects involve the full participation of all;

(*f*) Include a gender perspective and empowerment of women and girls as an integral part of the development process;

(*g*) Include in development strategies special measures focusing on needs of women and children as well as groups with special needs;

(*h*) Strengthen, through development assistance in post-conflict situations, rehabilitation, reintegration and reconciliation processes involving all engaged in conflicts;

(*i*) Incorporate capacity-building in development strategies and projects to ensure environmental sustainability, including preservation and regeneration of the natural resource base;

(*j*) Remove obstacles to the realization of the right of peoples to self-determination, in particular of peoples living under colonial or other forms of alien domination or foreign occupation, which adversely affect their social and economic development.

11. Actions to promote respect for all human rights:

(*a*) Full implementation of the Vienna Declaration and Programme of Action;[2]

(*b*) Encouragement of development of national plans of action for the promotion and protection of all human rights;

(*c*) Strengthening of national institutions and capacities in the field of human rights, including through national human rights institutions;

(*d*) Realization and implementation of the right to development, as established in the Declaration on the Right to Development[3] and the Vienna Declaration and Programme of Action;

(*e*) Achievement of the goals of the United Nations Decade for Human Rights Education (1995–2004);[4]

(f) Dissemination and promotion of the Universal Declaration of Human Rights at all levels;

(g) Further support to the activities of the United Nations High Commissioner for Human Rights in the fulfilment of her or his mandate as established in General Assembly resolution 48/141 of 20 December 1993, as well as the responsibilities set by subsequent resolutions and decisions.

12. Actions to ensure equality between women and men:

(a) Integration of a gender perspective into the implementation of all relevant international instruments;

(b) Further implementation of international instruments that promote equality between women and men;

(c) Implementation of the Beijing Platform for Action adopted at the Fourth World Conference on Women,[5] with adequate resources and political will, and through, *inter alia*, the elaboration, implementation and follow-up of the national plans of action;

(d) Promotion of equality between women and men in economic, social and political decision-making;

(e) Further strengthening of efforts by the relevant entities of the United Nations system for the elimination of all forms of discrimination and violence against women;

(f) Provision of support and assistance to women who have become victims of any forms of violence, including in the home, workplace and during armed conflicts.

13. Actions to foster democratic participation:

(a) Reinforcement of the full range of actions to promote democratic principles and practices;

(b) Special emphasis on democratic principles and practices at all levels of formal, informal and non-formal education;

(c) Establishment and strengthening of national institutions and processes that promote and sustain democracy through, *inter alia*, training and capacity-building of public officials;

(d) Strengthening of democratic participation through, inter alia, the provision of electoral assistance upon the request of States concerned and based on relevant United Nations guidelines;

(e) Combating of terrorism, organized crime, corruption as well as production, trafficking and consumption of illicit drugs and money laundering, as they undermine democracies and impede the fuller development of a culture of peace.

14. Actions to advance understanding, tolerance and solidarity:

(a) Implement the Declaration of Principles on Tolerance and the Follow-up Plan of Action for the United Nations Year for Tolerance[6] (1995);

(b) Support activities in the context of the United Nations Year of Dialogue among Civilizations in the year 2001;

(c) Study further the local or indigenous practices and traditions of dispute settlement and promotion of tolerance with the objective of learning from them;

(d) Support actions that foster understanding, tolerance and solidarity throughout society, in particular with vulnerable groups;

(e) Further support the attainment of the goals of the International Decade of the World's Indigenous People;

(f) Support actions that foster tolerance and solidarity with refugees and displaced persons, bearing in mind the objective of facilitating their voluntary return and social integration;

(g) Support actions that foster tolerance and solidarity with migrants;

(h) Promote increased understanding, tolerance and cooperation among all peoples through, inter alia, appropriate use of new technologies and dissemination of information;

(i) Support actions that foster understanding, tolerance, solidarity and cooperation among peoples and within and among nations.

15. Actions to support participatory communication and the free flow of information and knowledge:

   (a) Support the important role of the media in the promotion of a culture of peace;

   (b) Ensure freedom of the press and freedom of information and communication;

   (c) Make effective use of the media for advocacy and dissemination of information on a culture of peace involving, as appropriate, the United Nations and relevant regional, national and local mechanisms;

   (d) Promote mass communication that enables communities to express their needs and participate in decision-making;

   (e) Take measures to address the issue of violence in the media, including new communication technologies, *inter alia*, the Internet;

   (f) Increase efforts to promote the sharing of information on new information technologies, including the Internet.

16. Actions to promote international peace and security:

   (a) Promote general and complete disarmament under strict and effective international control, taking into account the priorities established by the United Nations in the field of disarmament;

   (b) Draw, where appropriate, on lessons conducive to a culture of peace learned from "military conversion" efforts as evidenced in some countries of the world;

   (c) Emphasize the inadmissibility of acquisition of territory by war and the need to work for a just and lasting peace in all parts of the world;

   (d) Encourage confidence-building measures and efforts for negotiating peaceful settlements;

   (e) Take measures to eliminate illicit production and traffic of small arms and light weapons;

(*f*) Support initiatives, at the national, regional and international levels, to address concrete problems arising from post-conflict situations, such as demobilization, reintegration of former combatants into society, as well as refugees and displaced persons, weapon collection programmes, exchange of information and confidence-building;

(*g*) Discourage the adoption of and refrain from any unilateral measure, not in accordance with international law and the Charter of the United Nations, that impedes the full achievement of economic and social development by the population of the affected countries, in particular women and children, that hinders their well-being, that creates obstacles to the full enjoyment of their human rights, including the right of everyone to a standard of living adequate for their health and well-being and their right to food, medical care and the necessary social services, while reaffirming that food and medicine must not be used as a tool for political pressure;

(*h*) Refrain from military, political, economic or any other form of coercion, not in accordance with international law and the Charter, aimed against the political independence or territorial integrity of any State;

(*i*) Recommend proper consideration for the issue of the humanitarian impact of sanctions, in particular on women and children, with a view to minimizing the humanitarian effects of sanctions;

(*j*) Promote greater involvement of women in prevention and resolution of conflicts and, in particular, in activities promoting a culture of peace in post-conflict situations;

(*k*) Promote initiatives in conflict situations such as days of tranquillity to carry out immunization and medicine distribution campaigns, corridors of peace to ensure delivery of humanitarian supplies and sanctuaries of peace to respect the central role of health and medical institutions such as hospitals and clinics;

(*l*) Encourage training in techniques for the understanding, pre-
       vention and resolution of conflict for the concerned staff of the
       United Nations, relevant regional organizations and Member
       States, upon request, where appropriate.

107th plenary meeting
13 September 1999

1. United Nations Educational, Scientific and Cultural Organization, *Records of the General Conference, Twenty-eighth Session, Paris, 25 October–16 November 1995,* vol. 1: Resolutions, resolution 5.4, annexes.

2. A/CONF.157/24 (Part I), chap. III.

3. Resolution 41/128, annex.

4. See A/49/261-E/1994/110/Add.1, annex.

5. *Report of the Fourth World Conference on Women, Beijing, 4–15 September 1995* (United Nations publication, Sales No. E.96.IV.13), chap. I, resolution 1, annex II.

6. A/51/201, appendix I.

Appendix C

United Nations Resolutions and Other Reference Documents on a Culture of Peace

A/RES/62/89   International Decade for a Culture of Peace and Non-Violence for the Children of the World, 2001–2010, Adopted 17 December 2007
www.un.org/Docs/journal/asp/ws.asp?m=A/RES/62/89

A/RES/61/45   same as above, Adopted 4 December 2006
www.un.org/Docs/journal/asp/ws.asp?m=A/RES/61/45

A/RES/59/143   same as above, Adopted 15 December 2004
www.un.org/Docs/journal/asp/ws.asp?m=A/RES/59/143

A/RES/58/11   same as above, Adopted 10 November 2003
www.un.org/Docs/journal/asp/ws.asp?m=A/RES/58/11

A/RES/57/6   same as above, Adopted 4 November 2002
www.un.org/Docs/journal/asp/ws.asp?m=A/RES/57/6

A/RES/56/5   same as above – start here, Adopted 5 November 2001
www.un.org/Docs/journal/asp/ws.asp?m=A/RES/56/5

A/RES/55/47   same as above, Adopted 29 November 2000
www.un.org/Docs/journal/asp/ws.asp?m=A/RES/55/47

A/RES/53/25   same as above, Adopted 10 November 1998
www.un.org/Docs/journal/asp/ws.asp?m=A/RES/53/25

A/RES/52/13   Culture of Peace, Adopted 20 November 1997
www.un.org/Docs/journal/asp/ws.asp?m=A/RES/52/13

E/1997/47   International Year for the Culture of Peace, 2000, Adopted 22 July 1997
ap.ohchr.org/documents/E/ECOSOC/resolutions/
E-RES-1997-47.doc

OTHER REPORTS

A/62/97   International Decade for a Culture of Peace and Non-Violence for the Children of the World (2001–2010), Note by the Secretary-General, Issued 28 June 2007
www.un.org/Docs/journal/asp/ws.asp?m=A/62/97

A/61/175   Culture of Peace, Notes by the Secretary-General, Issued 24 July 2006
www.un.org/Docs/journal/asp/ws.asp?m=A/61/175

A/60/279   Midterm global review of the International Decade for a Culture of Peace and Non-Violence for the Children of the World, 2001-2010, Issued 19 August 2005
www.un.org/Docs/journal/asp/ws.asp?m=A/60/279

A/59/223   International Decade for a Culture of Peace and Non-Violence for the Children of the World (2001–2010), Note by the Secretary-General, Issued 10 August 2004
www.un.org/Docs/journal/asp/ws.asp?m=A/59/223

A/58/182   International Decade for a Culture of Peace and Non-Violence for the Children of the World (2001–2010), Note by the Secretary-General, Issued 24 July 2003
www.un.org/Docs/journal/asp/ws.asp?m=A/58/182

A/57/186   International Decade for a Culture of Peace and Non-Violence for the Children of the World, Implementation of General Assembly resolution 56/5, Note by the Secretary-General, Issued 2 July 2002
www.un.org/Docs/journal/asp/ws.asp?m=A/57/186

A/56/349   International Decade for a Culture of Peace and Non-Violence for the Children of the World, 2001–2010, Report of the Secretary-General, Issued 13 September 2001
www.un.org/Docs/journal/asp/ws.asp?m=A/56/349

A/55/377   International Decade for a Culture of Peace and Non-Violence for the Children of the World, 2001–2010, Report of the Secretary-General, Issued 12 September 2000
www.un.org/Docs/journal/asp/ws.asp?m=A/55/377

OTHER REFERENCE DOCUMENTS

World Report on the Culture of Peace

Civil Society report at midpoint of the Culture of Peace Decade,
   Issued 2005
   decade-culture-of-peace.org/report/wrcpx.pdf

Appendix D
About the Culture of Peace Resource Centers

The SGI-USA is involved in non-sectarian, public awareness activities to promote the values of peace, culture and education and works with other civil-society and non-governmental groups to develop youth programs, traveling exhibits, cultural events and symposia.

For more information, go to www.sgi-usa.net/aboutsgi/cultureofpeace/.

Santa Monica Culture of Peace Resource Center
SGI Plaza
606 Wilshire Boulevard, Santa Monica, CA 90401

Chicago Culture of Peace Resource Center
SGI-USA Chicago Culture Center
1455 South Wabash Avenue, Chicago, IL 60605

New York Culture of Peace Resource Center
SGI-USA New York Culture Center
7 East 15th Street, New York, NY 10003

Honolulu Culture of Peace Resource Center
SGI-USA Hawaii Culture Center
2729 Pali Highway, Honolulu, HI 96817

Washington D.C. Culture of Peace Resource Center
SGI-USA Washington D.C. Buddhist Culture Center
3417 Massachusetts Avenue, Washington, D.C. 20007

Index